THE
DEFINITIVE
GUIDE
TO
GOVERNMENT
CONTRACTS

Everything You Need to Apply for and Win Federal
and GSA Schedule Contracts

MALCOLM PARVEY & DEBORAH ALSTON

CAREER
PRESS

Pompton Plains, N.J.

THE DEFINITIVE GUIDE TO GOVERNMENT CONTRACTS

EDITED AND TYPESET BY KARA KUMPEL

Cover design by Toprotype

Printed in the U.S.A.

To order this title, please call toll-free 1-800-CAREER-1 (NJ and Canada: 201-848-0310) to order using VISA or MasterCard, or for further information on books from Career Press.

The Career Press, Inc., 220 West Parkway, Unit 12

Pompton Plains, NJ 07444

www.careerpress.com

Library of Congress Cataloging-in-Publication Data

Parvey, Malcolm.

The definitive guide to government contracts : everything you need to apply for and win federal and GSA schedule contracts / by Malcolm Parvey and Deborah Alston.

p. cm. -- (Winning government contracts)

Includes bibliographical references and index.

ISBN 978-1-60163-111-4 – ISBN 978-1-60163-739-0 (ebook) 1. Public contracts--United States--Handbooks, manuals, etc. 2. Government purchasing--United States--Handbooks, manuals, etc. I. Alston, Deborah. II. Title. III. Series.

HD3861.U6P35 2010
346.7302'3--dc22

2010008888

Contents

Foreword

By Richard Greene, PDCA CEO

This book is designed to give you, as a PDCA member, the advantage you need to do business with the government. Malcolm Parvey and Deborah Alston are experts in this field. With more than 30 years working in this marketplace, these two have helped many small businesses successfully navigate the procedures to bid and win government contract work.

Included in this guide is knowledge about how the federal government makes pur chases, advice on where to find sales opportunities, how design a bid with the best chance to win the contract, and how best to craft the final contract.

As you read this well-written manual about working with the government, pay close attention to the 25 Biggest Misconceptions About Federal Contracting found in the intro-duction; there you will find all the reasons you should be bidding on the vast amount of government work available to small business owners. You'll quickly come to understand that this is a niche area that might help you grow your business.

Woven throughout the 10 chapters of this book is a myriad of tools available to un-derstand the government contracting process and many tips you can use to complete the required paperwork to get you those government contracts.

The authors have provided a simple, easy to use guide to government contracting that any beginner can understand. You will enjoy reaping the benefits of their advice.

Best wishes to you in the learning process you are about to start. There is almost $100 billion in federal contracts available to small business. You deserve a piece of that pie!

A Word From the Authors

First, some facts:

In Fiscal Year 2008, small businesses received more than **$93 billion** in federal prime contracts, according to the Small Business Administration—an increase of $10 billion over the previous year!

Federal regulations state that if any government agency is going to make a purchase estimated to be $100,000 or less, it *must* be set aside for small businesses. Furthermore, federal agencies must set up contracting goals—for example, that 23 percent of all government purchases should be from small businesses. Federal agencies have a statutory obligation to reach out to small businesses and to purchase from them whenever possible.

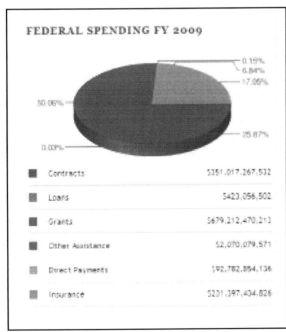

FEDERAL SPENDING FY 2009

■ Contracts	$351,017,267,532
■ Loans	$423,056,502
■ Grants	$679,212,470,213
■ Other Assistance	$2,070,079,571
■ Direct Payments	$92,782,854,136
■ Insurance	$231,397,434,626

(From the USAspending.gov Website.)

As independent sales and marketing consultants with more than 30 years of experience in this marketplace, we have worked closely with many small businesses, helping them to secure federal government contracts.

Our clients come from many different types of small businesses—manufacturers, distributors, service companies, and more. We work closely with them to find appropriate **sales** opportunities, help them fully understand the **requirements**, find any available **drawings** or specifications, find any available **procurement history**, help them to complete the **bid package**, and then **submit** the offer in their name. We also **track** the results so that the clients can see who submitted offers, who was awarded the contract, and what was the awarded price.

In addition, we also work with the client to secure a General Services Administration Federal Supply Schedule contract—commonly referred to as a **GSA contract**. This can take several months of information-gathering and paperwork before the proposal is ready to be submitted, and we are there every step of the way—including the final negotiation phase with GSA prior to the award.

After the award we can also upload the contract details to the GSA online ordering site and prepare the Federal Supply Schedule Catalog—both requirements of the contract award.

In 2008 we wrote a highly successful book, *Winning Government Contracts*, which showed a step-by-step procedure to finding, understanding, and submitting government competitive bids up to $100,000.

Now in this new **definitive guide to government contracts**, much of the information has been extensively updated, and several new chapters have been added.

We are excited to include details on the **GSA contract** proposal, which we only briefly mentioned in our first book. We take you step by step through the GSA contract proposal, from initial research into understanding the contract requirements and finding the correct schedule for your business, to a page-by-page approach to completing all the required paperwork. Finally we show you how to upload your contract details to GSA's online site and prepare your Schedule Contract price list.

Don't Panic! Please don't be daunted by the amount of information in this book! As a "definitive guide" it necessarily includes much information that may not be relevant to your circumstances or requirements. Feel free to cherry-pick from all the information here! We hope that this book will become your guide as you pursue federal contracts, and that you will find yourself turning to it over and over again for clarification and advice.

Most importantly, this guide attempts to explain government contracting to the beginner. It is written in simple language, without using government jargon where it was at all possible. Here are some more key points:

- If you are a complete beginner in federal contracting and don't know where to begin—this book is for you!
- If you have made a few tentative steps, but you don't know how to proceed—this book is for you!
- If you have had some initial success in federal procurement, and you would like to think about securing a GSA contract—this book is for you!
- Even if you already have your GSA contract and feel confident about your company's future in federal contracting—this book could *still* be for you!

If you would like more information about our services, visit us at *www.sell2gov.com*.

Introduction:

The 25 Biggest Misconceptions About Federal Contracting

1. I am too small to do business with the federal government.

The federal government's goal is to set aside 23 percent of its purchases specifically for small businesses. Each agency must do its very best to meet that goal. The bottom line is: If you can supply the product in the volume and time frame required, you are not too small. There are many daily sales opportunities for $10,000 or less.

2. I don't have time to learn about this.

How much time do you currently spend on your most favored customers? Remember, the federal government is the biggest customer in the entire world! This *one* customer can give you more business than all of your commercial customers combined! This book will take you step by step through the entire process of gaining government contracts—from finding the sales opportunities, through putting in a bid, and following through after you are awarded. Much of the paperwork is exactly the same from bid to bid, so once you have prepared a few offers you will feel much more confident; once you are familiar with the format of a particular agency's site, you will find that you can submit many electronic bids in as little as six minutes!

3. You need contacts in the federal government to win an award.

No! You just need to know where the sales opportunities are. The federal government issues more than 10,000 different sales opportunities every day, and many are issued and awarded automatically by computer.

4. I can't make a profit in this marketplace.

You will never know whether or not you are competitive in this marketplace unless you get involved! Using this book you will be able to find out what the government is paying for an item right now, *before* you put in your bid! Also remember that the purchase may be set aside exclusively for small, woman-owned, minority-owned, veteran-owned, or disadvantaged businesses—this book will show you how to identify whether you qualify for these set-asides. Another factor to remember is that often the contract will be awarded using what is known as Best Value Purchasing rather than simply on price alone—if you can offer a better delivery time, or a better warranty than your competitors, you *will* be awarded the contract, even if your price is somewhat higher!

5. I tried this before, but it didn't work out.

A lot has changed in the last few years; what used to take 10 days to complete now—thanks to the Internet—takes only 10 minutes! The e-government initiative has made it much simpler to find bids and submit offers, particularly for purchases under $100,000—known as the Simplified Acquisition Threshold.

6. My small business can't handle multi-million-dollar contracts.

Many smaller bid opportunities are out there for you—you just need to know how to find them, and this book shows you where they are! There are an estimated 10,000 government sales opportunities each day, across all agencies, and 95 percent of them are estimated to be $100,000 or less.

7. I don't understand the jargon.

This book explains each government term in simple, easy-to-understand language that does not assume any previous knowledge in this area.

8. I don't know where to begin.

The first step will be to register your company at the Central Contractor Registration site. You must be registered at this site in order to receive an award. In Chapter 1 of this book we take you through the registration process. We also explain the other important business codes and numbers you will need in order to begin.

9. I am a small service company—there's no market for me.

Are you a small landscaping company? The government contracts for lawn-mowing and grounds maintenance. Are you a staffing agency? The government contracts out much of its administrative work to civilian contractors. Are you a small building company? There are many opportunities for you out there—you just need to know where to find them! Are you a small marketing/public relations firm? A video production firm? An on-line distance-learning company? A computer programming firm? We have had experience helping *all* these types of service companies, and this book can help your company too.

10. The government takes too long to pay.

The federal government is required by regulation to pay small businesses in 30 days; you just need to understand its invoicing system. Many awards are paid via Electronic Funds Transfer, and new systems such as Wide Area Workflow allow you to keep track of your invoice as it travels through the system until you are paid. This book shows you how to get started using these systems.

11. I don't have a GSA contract, so I can't submit competitive bids.

The *only* requirement for you to be awarded a government contract (and to get paid) is to be registered in the Central Contractors Registration (CCR) site. GSA contracts are just one of the many tools the government uses to make purchases, and we discuss the advantages of getting your GSA contract number in this book. But you do *not* need one in order to begin. If you find out that you are competitive and you can win awards, then a GSA contract will be another tool for you.

12. There is too much competition in this marketplace.

Fewer than 2 percent of registered U.S. companies actively seek out this market, which could mean that fewer than 2 percent of your competitors actively seek out this market. This book will show you how to do some research to find out who your competitors are in this market.

13. I sell products that are made outside of the United States.

The Buy American Act places certain restrictions on foreign products, but there are exceptions to this regulation. For example, if at least 51 percent of the cost of producing the finished item is incurred in the United States, Mexico, or Canada it is *not* considered an imported item. Use this book to find out more.

14. There are too many rules and regulations.

Federal agencies are strongly encouraged to make use of accepted commercial standards whenever possible, so this need not be an obstacle.

15. There isn't anyone to go to for direction.

Take advantage of local organizations that can help you get started; for example, the Small Business Administration (SBA), or the local Procurement Technical Assistance Centers (PTAC). Information on how to locate your nearest office is listed in Chapter 1 of this book.

16. I need Drawings and Specifications for my products.

This book will show you step by step where to go and how to download drawings and specifications immediately from the Internet.

17. I am a dealer; I won't be able to sell to the government.

If you are a dealer, you can still sell your products to the government—this book shows you how.

18. I'll just hand this one over to Bob (or Barbara!).

Don't try to give the responsibility for this to someone who already has too much to do, because it won't get done! Assign someone in the company to research this thoroughly so that you give it a fair shot. It doesn't need to be one of your executive staff, but someone in the company should read this book to find out who your competition is, do some research into the market, put in some bids, and follow up on them. If one agency doesn't buy your products or services, look elsewhere. This is the *only* way to really tell if this market is right for your company. You will never know until you try!

19. I'll just skim over the details; there's too much to read.

As with any other sales opportunity you must understand the terms and conditions of the contract before you put in your offer. Everything is there in black and white, and a few moments of checking out the details could save you a lot of time later on. If you have a question on a bid there is always a point of contact on the very first page to answer all and any questions.

20. I need professional training; it will cost too much, and take too much time.

Look at this book as a training manual. Everything you need to know in order to win contracts is in this book. Additionally, many free training seminars are available at your local Small Business Administration (SBA) office, or the local Procurement Technical Assistance Center (PTAC). Also, a number of free online government training resources can help you to master any of the systems you need to understand. For example, the new Wide Area Work Flow (WAWF) system, which tracks products and services from delivery to invoicing and payment, has a free online training session to help you navigate it, as well as a practice site where you can fill out dummy invoices to understand how the system works. Remember that government officers are always willing to help you with any problems—you just have to ask!

21. The agency will never return my calls.

The agency's contracting officer really is there to help you! Send an e-mail to the point of contact listed in the solicitation and you will get a reply from someone—these people really are professional, highly trained, courteous, and patient.

22. I already do business with a federal agency.

Just because you have done business with the United States Postal Service or the Air Force or the Secret Service does not mean you know how to do business with other agencies. Every agency does business differently, but they are all required to use the same basic regulations—in the commercial marketplace you know that every sale is different, even though you are selling the same product or service, and you must tailor your approach accordingly. In a similar way each agency is different because they all have a different mission.

23. I don't need to keep records.

Wrong! The government never throws away records, and neither should you! Keep a record of every sales opportunity you are involved with. If you speak to someone on the phone, send an e-mail to follow up. When you win a contract, keep every record for a minimum of three years after the contract has expired. For example, if you are awarded a GSA contract, the agency has the right to audit your contract up to three years after the contract has expired!

24. My record with one agency won't help me get business with another agency.

You think that being a good vendor only counts with the particular purchasing agent with whom you did business? The government keeps a report card in a central location for each vendor, so that other purchasing agents can see how well they performed on previous contracts. Your good record counts!

25. I'll look at this next week—or next month...

The opportunities for your small business *are* out there! Don't wait for some vague time in the future when you think you will be able to find the time. Find the time **today** and **get started now!**

How to Use This Book

Many different federal government agencies exist, with different responsibilities and mandates, but they *all* need to purchase goods and services. Many agencies use their own Websites to advertise sales opportunities, and in many instances you may submit an offer electronically through the site.

It would be almost impossible to cover every agency's site individually, because there are so many of them, so we have chosen several important sites to look at in detail. Once you are familiar with the way these specific sites advertise their sales opportunities and accept your offers, you will feel confident enough to find your way around most other federal agency sites.

In **Chapter 1** you will find an overview of how the federal government purchases the products and services it needs, an explanation of how the Small Business Administration determines size standards, and a comprehensive list of the business codes and numbers you will need to obtain in order to begin selling to the federal government—plus exactly where to go to get them, and why they are important.

In **Chapter 2** we look in detail at the Federal Business Opportunities Website, or FedBizOpps. This is the central site where most agencies *must* post their sales opportunities if they are estimated to be valued at more than $25,000. The initial notice of such an opportunity is posted in FedBizOpps, and it will contain information on where to find the details of the bid, often via a link or a Web address to the specific agency's site.

Chapter 3 looks closely at the Department of Defense's Website, known as the Defense Internet Bid Board System (DIBBS). The sales opportunities at this site can be for as little as $50, and can reach to as high as several million dollars. (Sales opportunities in DIBBS that are valued at over $25,000 will *also* be posted in FedBizOpps.)

Chapter 4 takes a look at some of the many other government sites you may wish to search, including the Army Single Face to Industry site, Navy Contracting, and others.

In many instances you will be able to submit your bids electronically, which is covered in Chapter 3. Even though other sites may have their specific electronic bid processes, once you have seen exactly how the system works at DIBBS, you will be able to use that knowledge (if you wish) to bid electronically at other agency sites in the future. However, at other times the bid package must be filled in and mailed or faxed in a hard copy, or paper format.

In **Chapter 5** we take you step by step through this process, so that once you have read this chapter you will be more familiar with the way it works.

In **Chapter 6** we look at some additional information that may be required if you are a company that provides a Service.

Chapter 7 looks at what happens once you have been awarded the contract. We discuss packaging, shipping, acceptance, and invoicing procedures.

Chapter 8 discusses the General Service Administration's (GSA) Federal Supply Schedule contract. We explain how the GSA's schedule program works, how to do some initial research to find out who your competitors are in this marketplace, and help you to determine which is the correct schedule for you.

Chapter 9 takes you by the hand through all the information-gathering and administrative paperwork you will need to complete your Schedule proposal, so that you can confidently submit the best possible offer.

Chapter 10 discusses your requirements, once you have been awarded a GSA contract, including uploading to GSA's online site known as GSA *Advantage!*, tracking sales and paying the appropriate fees, and creating your Federal Supply Schedule catalog for submission to GSA.

Finally, in the **Appendix** you will find several useful worksheets and tables of information for you to reference.

A Note on Link Information in This Book

Throughout this book, you will come across many links to Websites. Some links are to government sites, and others are organization sites or commercial sites. These links allow you to follow up on information, or to find more detailed information on a particular topic that may be of interest to you.

Every effort has been made to keep the link information in this book current, but we are aware that any links we provide can quickly become obsolete.

As an extra service to our readers, and to ensure that this book remains as up-to-date as possible, we will be providing updated link information on our company Website, *www. sell2gov.com*.

All links in the book are followed by a number in parenthesis. If you find, upon sitting down at your computer, that one of the listed links has changed, simply go to our Website, where you will find an **Updates** page where you can search for recently updated links.

We also welcome your input! If you find that a link has changed, please let us know via the Contact Us section of the Website—we will do everything we can to ensure that these links remain a valuable source of information.

A Word on Some Necessary Evils

This book is intended as a working manual, something you can refer to regularly as you begin to search the various agency sites for sales opportunities. For that reason there are occasions in the book where information is repeated from one chapter to another, rather than simply referring you to a particular section of the book—that way all the information is right where you need it.

Chapter 1

Introduction to Federal Government Sales

Overview

Are You a Small Business?

In this introductory chapter we begin by examining exactly how the government determines whether you are considered a small business, and how you can find out whether you are eligible to be considered as a small business.

Resources

This is followed by information on the many organizations that can give you advice and assistance on doing business with the federal government, such as the Small Business Administration and the government's Procurement Technical Assistance Centers.

How the Federal Government Buys What It Needs

The next section of this chapter gives you a brief overview of exactly how the federal government buys the things it needs, and explains such terms as *Invitation for Bid*, *Request for Proposal*, *Request for Quote*, and *Best Value Purchasing*. We briefly examine the many government Consolidated Purchase programs that are available, such as Multi-Agency Contracts (MACs), Government-Wide Acquisition Contracts (GWACs) and General Services Administration (GSA) Schedule contracts. In addition, we look at the increasing use of the "reverse auction" mechanism for bids, as well as the use of government Purchase Cards (credit cards).

Important Codes and Numbers

Then we turn to the important business codes and numbers you will need to obtain in order to begin selling to the federal government. Each code is explained in plain language—including why it is important to know these numbers, where you can find them, and so on. We take you step by step through each number and explain clearly where to go to obtain each one. In addition, we take you step by step through the Central Contractors Registration (CCR) site, and the new Online Representations and Certifications Applications (ORCA) site, where you must register your company in order to do business with the federal government.

Are You a Small Business? Determining Size Standards

If you wish to take advantage of the various programs that are set aside for small businesses, you must first determine if you are eligible.

A small business is one that:

- Is organized for profit.
- Has a place of business in the United States.
- Pays taxes, and uses American products, labor, and materials.
- Does not exceed the size standard for its industry.

The Small Business Administration uses the North American Industrial Classification System (NAICS) to determine types of industries and their size standards. We discuss NAICS codes later in this chapter. Size standards are usually stated in terms of either the number of employees in a company or the company's average annual receipts. For a **Products** company the size standard is determined by the number of employees (including both full- and part-time). For a **Service** company the size standard is determined by the annual average receipts.

In the chart that follows, a business in one of the following industry groups is considered to be a small business if its size is not greater than the following:

Construction	• General building and heavy construction contractors: $33.5 million. • Special trade construction contractors: $14 million. • Land subdivision: $7 million. • Dredging: $20 million.
Manufacturing	• About 75 percent of the manufacturing industries: 500 employees. • A small number of industries: 1,500 employees. • The balance: either 750 or 1,000 employees.
Retail Trade	• Most retail trade industries: $7 million. • A few (such as grocery stores, department stores, motor vehicle dealers, and electrical appliance dealers), have higher size standards, but none above $35.5 million.

Services	• Most common: $7 million. • Computer programming, data processing, and systems design: $25 million. • Engineering and architectural services and a few other industries have different size standards. • The highest annual-receipts size standard in any service industry: $35.5 million. • R&D and environmental remediation service industries state size standards as number of employees.
Wholesale Trade	• For small-business federal contracts: 100 employees. • You must deliver the product of a small domestic manufacturer (unless this is waived by the SBA for a particular class of product). • For procurements less than $25,000 you may deliver the goods of any domestic manufacturer.
Other Industries	Divisions include agriculture; transportation, communications, electric, gas, and sanitary services; and finance, insurance, and real estate. Because of wide variation in the structure of industries in these divisions, there is no common pattern of size standards.

Size standards are updated regularly. The SBA's tables include any changes and modifications made since January 1 of the most recent year.

You may wish to research size standards in more detail on the Small Business Administrations' Website: *www.sba.gov/size.* (1)

Resources for Small Businesses

Many places can offer you assistance:
- Small Business Administration: *www.sba.gov* (2)
- Women-Biz: *www.womenbiz.gov* (3)
- SBA Office of Women Business Ownership: *www.sba.gov* (2) At the "SBA Programs" drop-down list on the home page, select "Women's Business."
- SBA Subcontracting Network: *www.sba.gov/subnet* (4)
- Procurement Technical Assistance Centers (PTAC): *www.dla.mil/db/procurem. htm.* (5) Administered by the Department of Defense, these centers offer local, low-cost assistance to companies wishing to market their products and services to federal, state, and local governments.

- Agency Procurement Forecasts: *www.acqnet.gov/comp/procurement_forecasts/index.html* (6)
- GSA Directories: *www.gsa.gov/sbu* (7)

Another great source of contact information can be found at the GSA Offices of Small Business Utilization. On the left-hand side of the home page, click on "GSA Publications." There are nine Regional Procurement Directories available here, with a great deal of useful contact information. For example, the New England Directory contains lists of all the regional small business offices, technical assistance offices, local Procurement Technical Assistance Centers (PTACS), government procurement offices, chambers of commerce, regional federal buildings, and much more. **These directories can be a great marketing source even if you do not yet have a GSA contract award!**

How the Federal Government Buys What It Needs

In 1994 the government enacted the Federal Acquisition Streamlining Act, which simplified the way in which government purchases under $100,000 are made. Specifically, **all federal purchases more than $3,000 but less than $100,000 may be set aside exclusively for small businesses.**

Micro-Purchases

Government purchases of $3,000 or less are classified as "micro-purchases" and can be made without obtaining competitive quotes. These purchases can be made using a Government Purchase Card, which is a government-issued credit card (Visa, MasterCard, or American Express). Micro-purchases are no longer reserved exclusively for small businesses.

Invitation For Bid (IFB)—Sealed Bid

When a government agency has a clear and complete picture of its needs, it will issue an Invitation For Bid (IFB). The IFB contains an exact description of the product or service; instructions for preparing a bid; the conditions for purchase, packaging, delivery, shipping, and payment; contract clauses to be included; and the deadline for submitting bids. On the stated Bid Opening Date and Time, each sealed bid is opened in public at the purchasing office.

Request For Proposal (RFP)—Negotiated Bid

When the value of the contract exceeds $100,000 and the product or service is considered to be highly technical in nature, the government may issue a Request For Proposal (RFP). In this case the agency will describe the product or service that it needs, and solicit proposals from prospective contractors on how they intend to carry out that request, and at what price. Proposals in response to an RFP can be subject to negotiation after they have been submitted.

Request For Quotation (RFQ)

Sometimes the government is simply looking at the possibility of acquiring a product or service. In this case, it will issue a Request For Quotation (RFQ).

Request For Information (RFI), Sources Sought, and Market Research

At times an agency wants to find out whether a commercial solution to its needs exists, and it will issue either a Request For Information (RFI) or a Market Research or Sources Sought notice. In these cases the agency will describe the product or service for which it is looking, and will ask that you submit a capability statement. The agency usually gives specific details of the information it is looking for, and the maximum number of pages it will accept. There is no guarantee that the agency will subsequently issue any solicitation. Often the agency would just like to know if certain categories of businesses are capable of providing the product or service—a disabled veteran–owned business for example, or a woman-owned or minority-owned business. In this case, any subsequent solicitation *may* be set aside for that category of business. We will discuss the various set-aside programs in more detail later in the book.

> ### ~Once Upon a Time~
> A small service company found an opportunity in FedBizOpps that seemed the perfect fit, but didn't realize that the notice was a Request for Information/Market Research posting. The government agency was under no obligation to follow up with a solicitation for the work.
> It might well be a good thing to respond to a Market Research request—but understand there may not be a contract at the end of it.

Indefinite Delivery, Indefinite Quantity Contract (IDIQ)

In this type of contract the agency will award a long-term contract (often a base year with three or four option years), but with no specific quantity or delivery dates. The solicitation document will usually give an estimated quantity, and sometimes a guaranteed minimum. Purchase orders will be issued as needed during the life of the contract.

Best Value Purchasing

One of the most significant things to be aware of in the government contracting arena is the importance of what is known as "Best Value" purchasing, in which, rather than making an award based solely on price, the agency may consider other factors when determining its needs. For example, a higher-priced offer may have a better warranty, a faster delivery date, or a larger range of accessories or options. Many service contracts are awarded based on several criteria, including technical capability, managerial approach, and past performance, in addition to price.

If the purchase is going to be awarded under the "Best Value" criteria, it will be clearly stated in the solicitation document. The weight of the various factors will also be laid out. Technical knowledge may be significantly more important than price in some cases, wheras at other times a fast delivery may be the key requirement.

Consolidated Purchasing Programs

Many agencies have common purchasing needs—carpeting, furniture, office supplies, maintenance, or perishable foods, for example. In many cases the government can save money by centralizing the purchasing of these types of products or services. There are various types of purchasing vehicles like this.

Blanket Purchase Agreement (BPA)

A Blanket Purchase Agreement is used when a single agency has a recurring requirement, for example for office supplies. The BPA is often a multi-year contract that allows the agency to purchase these items as needed throughout the life of the contract—often a five-year term consisting of a base year with up to four option years. At the end of the term of the BPA the agency may reissue the requirement, allowing other companies to compete with the incumbent contractor. An agency may set up a BPA with more than one supplier or may decide to award the BPA to a single company. Generally BPAs are issued by a single agency, but the General Services Administration (GSA) also has some BPA contracts that can be used by many different agencies—more on this later!

Multi-Agency Contract (MAC), Multiple Award Schedule (MAS), and Government-Wide Acquisition Contract (GWAC)

A single government contracting office will establish pricing and terms of business with many different companies, and then allow authorized agencies to purchase from this pre-negotiated contract. Many different contractors are issued "approved" status to supply specific products and services. Federal buyers can issue Requests for Quotation to three or more of these approved companies, knowing that the agency has already negotiated the best possible pricing and terms. One of the best-known, largest, and most important of these is the General Services Administration's Federal Supply Schedule Program, more commonly known as a **GSA Contract**. Later in the book we take a comprehensive look at this program—we explain exactly how the program works, look carefully at the advantages and possible downsides to your company, and help you to decide if you wish to submit a proposal. If you decide to go ahead, we will take you step by step through the paperwork and submission process. We also explain your responsibilities after the contract is awarded, and show you how to maintain the contract throughout its lifetime (which can be up to 20 years!). Once you are awarded a contract, your products and services, pricing and terms are posted to a Website known as GSA *Advantage!*, where many different agency buyers can view your contract.

The terms *GWAC* and *MAC* are sometimes used interchangeably, but more properly the term *GWAC* is used specifically for information technology (IT) contracts, of which there are several, including 8(a) STARS (set aside for small 8(a) disadvantaged IT businesses), Alliant and Alliant SB (for small IT businesses), Commits NexGen, Millennia and Millennia Lite, VETS, and more.

Government Credit Card Purchases

In Fiscal Year (FY) 2007 alone, federal charge card transactions totaled more than $27 billion. According to the General Accounting Office (GAO), there are 720,000 federal government employees with credit cards. Their credit limits vary from $20,000 to $1,000,000 per year, depending on their position within the agency. The following are some rules regarding government credit cards.

- For purchases under $250, there is no requirement to obtain a competitive price. These purchases can be made with any business, either inside or outside the government marketplace.
- For purchases ranging from $251 to $3,000, the credit-card holder must attempt to secure a minimum of three competitive verbal quotes from approved vendors.
- **In the event of a FEMA-declared emergency, this credit limit can be increased to up to $15,000 per purchase order.**

Online Reverse Auctions—FedBid (*www.FedBid.com*) (8)

The services of this commercial company are now being used extensively by federal agencies for relatively simple, small purchases under the Simplified Acquisition Threshold of $100,000. The site works as a "reverse auction"—think of it like eBay, only backwards!

Federal buyers specify exactly what they need, and can set purchase parameters—for example, they may request bids only from small, woman-owned, or veteran-owned businesses, or they may prefer or require participants to be GSA contract holders. The buyers describe exactly the items they wish to purchase and the quantity required, list any special instructions (requiring new items only, for example), and specify shipping and delivery details.

A specific time period for bids is issued, and during this time period you may submit a series of price quotes, which descend in price, using a simple two-page online form.

Requests are issued and contracts awarded very quickly at this site, so you will need your pricing ready to go if you wish to participate! Delivery is often 30 days from the date of award.

This type of reverse auction is becoming popular for agencies when the items they wish to purchase are Commercial Off-The-Shelf (COTS) items, with specific requirements for a particular manufacturer and part number, and price is the major factor in determining an award.

We will look more closely at this exciting new opportunity later in the book.

Getting Started—Important Business Codes and Numbers

To begin selling to the federal government, you must first register your business at certain government sites, and in order to do this you will need to know several important business codes or numbers. These numbers and codes are a requirement. You may already have some of them, which are all easy to get from the appropriate agency. These are the codes we'll explain here:

- Data Universal Numbering System (Dun & Bradstreet)—DUNS
- Tax Identification Number—TIN
- Commercial & Government Entity Code—CAGE
- North American Industrial Classification Codes—NAICS
- Standard Industrial Classification Code—SIC
- Federal Supply Classification Codes—FSC
- Product Service Codes—PSC

Once you have armed yourself with all these codes and numbers, you will be ready to register your company at the Central Contractors Registration site (CCR) and at the Online Representations and Certifications site (ORCA).

The Data Universal Numbering System—DUNS (*http://fedgov.dnb.com/webform*) (9)

There is no cost to obtain a DUNS number, which is required for all companies wishing to do business with the federal government. The number is specific to each location for your business—that is, you will need a separate number for each physical location. You will also need a separate number for each legal division within your company, even if they are at the same physical address.

A DUNS number shows the company's legal business name, the physical and mailing addresses, any other related "doing business as" names; the names of the company principal officers, financial and payment details, industry type, socio-economic status, and so on.

DUNS +4: This number can be used if you have more than one CCR record at the same physical location. For example, you could have two separate CCR records if you have two different businesses, located at the same address, with payment details going to two separate bank accounts.

Tax Identification Number—TINS (*www.IRS.gov*) (10)

This number allows federal agencies to certify the type of organization submitting an offer (Incorporated, Sole Proprietor, and so on).

Your TIN is a nine-digit number that can be from one of two sources:

1. Your Employer Identification Number (EIN) assigned by the IRS. Go to the IRS Website, and apply for an EIN at the Online Services section.

2. Alternatively, if you are registering as a Sole Proprietor, you may use your Social Security number, assigned by the Social Security Administration (SSA).

IMPORTANT! Your TIN and the taxpayer name you provide when you register at the Central Contractors Registration (CCR) site must match *exactly* the TIN and Taxpayer Name used in federal tax matters. Even a small discrepancy will cause you problems—for example if you list yourself as "The John Smith Company" at one site and "J. Smith & Co" at the other! Also be aware that all tax ID numbers will be validated by the Internal Revenue Service (IRS). You will not be allowed to have an active CCR registration without a validated TIN. The TIN-matching process is a joint effort between the General Services Administration (GSA), Department of Defense (DOD), and the IRS to improve the quality of data in government acquisition systems.

A newly assigned EIN cannot be validated in CCR right away. When you apply for an EIN (whether over the phone, online, by fax, or by mail) it may take between two and five weeks before it becomes active, even if you receive your number immediately. You must wait until you receive the official notice (CP-575) from the IRS confirming that your EIN is active and valid for use before you can register at CCR.

Commercial And Government Entity (CAGE) Codes (*www.dlis.dla.mil/cage_welcome.asp*) (11)

The Commercial And Government Entity (CAGE) code is a five-character identifier that is used extensively within the federal government. This code is unique to your company, and it *must* appear on every contract and invoice. It is made up of letters and numbers (for example: A123B). This code is used to identify your company for payment purposes.

You must have a separate CAGE code for each physical location and separate division at the same physical location. Each separate CCR registration must have its own CAGE code. If you are a U.S. company and you do not have a CAGE code, then one will be assigned to you when you register at CCR.

You may find out another company's CAGE code by searching at the Business Identification Number Cross-Reference System (BINCS), at *www.bpn.gov/bincs*. (12)

North American Industrial Classification System (NAICS) (*www.naics.com*) (13)

Various agencies use NAICS codes for statistical analysis. NAICS codes are used to identify the standards for a Small Business Set-Aside. You must supply at least one when you register at CCR. You can add or change NAICS codes at any time.

There are 20 broad sectors, which are further subdivided for more accuracy.

Code	NAICS Sectors
11	Agriculture, Forestry, Fishing, and Hunting
21	Mining
22	Utilities
23	Construction
31-33	Manufacturing
42	Wholesale Trade
44-45	Retail Trade
48-49	Transportation and Warehousing
51	Information
52	Finance and Insurance
53	Real Estate, and Rental and Leasing
54	Professional, Scientific, and Technical Services
55	Management of Companies and Enterprises
56	Administrative, Support, Waste Management, and Remediation Services
61	Education Services
62	Health Care and Social Assistance

71	Arts, Entertainment, and Recreation
72	Accommodation and Food Services
81	Other Services (except Public Administration)
92	Public Administration

You will need to find the code that is most appropriate for your business. You may search at the site using a keyword, or you may browse through the complete list to find your code. If you know your Standard Industrial Classification (SIC) code there is a tool to cross reference them to the NAICS code. If you are having trouble locating the correct code, the association can also help you.

NAICS categories do not distinguish between small and large business, or between for-profit and non-profit. The Small Business Administration (SBA) developed size standards for each NAICS category.

Whereas the Census Bureau assigns only one NAICS code for each business, based on its primary activity (generally the one that generates the most revenue), some agencies assign more than one NAICS code. The Central Contractors Registration (CCR) requires at least one NAICS code, but will accept up to five or 10 codes.

Important! You are not prevented from bidding on any procurement with an NAICS code that you have not listed in your record.

Standard Industrial Classification (SIC) Codes (*www.osha.gov/pls/imis/sicsearch.html*) (14)

When you register at CCR you will be asked to list all the classification codes that apply to your products and services. Be sure to list as many as apply. SIC codes can be four or eight digits, all numeric. You must supply at least one valid SIC code for your registration to be complete.

Federal Supply Classification Codes (FSC) (*www.dlis.dla.mil/H2*) (15)

Federal Supply Classification (FSC) codes are used to classify products. Product codes are number codes, from 10 through 99. For example:

26   Tires and Tubes
39   Material Handling Equipment
65   Medical Equipment and Supplies
T   Printing Services

Each code is further subdivided, in order to give an exact description of the item. For example, product code "84" is used for Clothing. And again this is subdivided:

8430   Men's Footwear

8450   Children's Clothing

8475   Specialized Flight Clothing

The Federal Classification Guide, known as the H2 Handbook, lists product codes, from 1 to 99, along with a brief description of each. The Defense Logistics Information Service (DLIS) has the handbook available on a CD-rom, or you can search the site. Alternatively, you may wish to download the H2 Manual at *www.fs.fed.us/fire/partners/fepp/h2book.pdf*. (16)

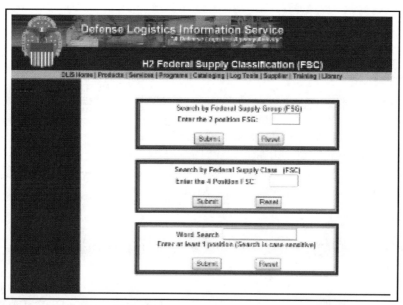

Product Service Codes (PSC)

Product Service Codes (PSC) are used to classify services. Service codes are letter codes, from A to Z. For example, service code "S" is used for Utilities & Housekeeping Services. This code is then further subdivided:

S201   Custodial-Janitorial

S208   Landscaping Services

S209   Laundry and Dry Cleaning Services

PSC Codes for Services can be found at *www.fpds-ng.com/downloads/psc_ data_10242006.xls*. (17) In the Appendix of this book you will find a list of the broad categories for both the products and services codes, to help you get started.

Registering at the Central Contractor Registration (CCR) Site (*www.ccr.gov*) (18)

All vendors must register at this site in order to be awarded government contracts. To do so you must provide basic information about your company, which is used to confirm your company status, and also allows future payments to be made via electronic funds transfers. The information you provide will be shared with authorized federal government offices.

This site has been redesigned since our first book came out in 2008, but the basic information needed to register is the same.

Click on the Contractors link near the top of the screen to download a user guide, or to look at the step-by-step screenshots provided to help you with the registration process. The FAQ section may also help you understand the registration process.

Before you begin, be sure you have these key pieces of information, in addition to your DUNS and TIN.

- Your company's **average annual receipts** throughout the last three fiscal years.
- Your company's **average number of employees** throughout the last 12 months, both full- and part-time.
- **Electronic Funds Transfer** (EFT) information for payment of invoices. (This is not required for non-U.S. registrants.) This includes your bank's ABA routing number; your company's account number and type, or Lockbox Number; an Automated Clearing House Point of Contact in your company; as well as points of contact for both remittance and accounts receivable.

Remember that this information will be used to pay your invoices, so make sure the details are correct!

Information-Gathering—Before You Begin

The following table lists all the information you will need to register at CCR, as well as what it is generally and/or how to find it.

DUNS and/or DUNS+4	Dun & Bradstreet Number.
CAGE	Commercial And Government Entity code.
TIN	Tax Identification Number.
Legal business name	
"Doing Business As" name	If applicable.

28   THE DEFINITIVE GUIDE TO GOVERNMENT CONTRACTS

Division name and number	If applicable.
Registration URL	
Physical address—street, city, state, zip, country	Taken directly from your D&B registration. If it is incorrect you will need to go to D&B and make the necessary changes.
Mailing address	If you cannot receive mail at the physical address, you may enter a mailing address here, including a post office box if necessary.
Business start date	
Fiscal year end date	
Average number of employees—by location (optional) and worldwide (mandatory)	Average number of employees for each pay period over the latest 12 months. Include employees of any parent, affiliate, or branches. Must be updated annually.
Average annual receipts—by location (optional) and worldwide (mandatory)	Total income (or gross income for a sole proprietor) plus cost of goods sold—as per your IRS tax returns. Receipts are averaged over the latest three completed fiscal years, rounded to the nearest whole number. (Do not use decimals, dollar signs, or commas.) Must be updated annually.
Company security level and highest employee security level	If applicable.
Information opt-out	As of July 2008, you may choose to "opt out" of public display of your record. Be aware that this may result in fewer business opportunities, and that if you are considering subcontracts you will not be visible to prime contractors.
Type of relationship with the U.S. federal government	• Grants—for federal government assistance awards. • Contracts—for federal government contracts. • Both contracts and grants.

Type of organization	• Federal, State, Local, Tribal, or Foreign Government entity/agency. • Business or organization.
Business or organization	Check <u>all</u> that apply. You must choose at least one. If you are a small, emerging, 8(a), or HUB Zone business, this information will be automatically inserted here from the SBA.
Type of organization	• Corporate Entity, Not Tax Exempt. • Corporate Entity, Tax Exempt. • State or Country of Incorporation. • Partnership or Limited Liability Partnership. • Sole Proprietorship (name/phone # of the owner). • International Organization. • Limited Liability Company. • Subchapter S Corporation. • Foreign Owned and Located. • Small Agricultural Cooperative. • For Profit Organization. • Non Profit Organization. • Other Not for Profit Organization.
Socio-economic categories	Business size and SBA programs are validated by SBA, and are no longer self-certified. Small Business status will be listed using the information you gave in the preceding sections. These categories include Small, Disadvantaged, Veteran, Service-Disabled Veteran, Woman or Minority-Owned (Asian-Pacific, Subcontinent Asian, Black, Hispanic, or Native American).
Nature of business	• Architecture and Engineering. • Construction Firm. • Manufacturer of Goods. • Research and Development. • Service Provider.

Native American entities	Alaskan native, American Indian, Indian tribe, native Hawaiian, or tribally owned.
NAICS code	At least one.
SIC codes	At least one.
PCS codes	For services.
FSC codes	For products.
Electronic Funds Transfer	Bank name will be automatically filled in when you provide the ABA routing number, which must be for Electronic funds transfer (EFT), *not* wire transfer. Account number, type, and lockbox number needed.
Automated clearing house	Contact information for the *bank's* coordinator.
Remittance information	Contact information for *your* accounts receivable person.
Credit card information	Do you accept credit cards for payment?
CCR Primary and Alternate Points of Contact (POC)	List the name of the person that acknowledges that the information provided in the registration is current, accurate, and complete. CCR primary and alternate contacts are the *only* people authorized to share information with CCR Helpdesk personnel. Must be updated annually.
Government business POC	The person responsible for marketing and sales with the federal government. Must be updated annually.
Electronic business POC	The person responsible for authorizing access to federal government electronic business systems such as Electronic Document Access and Wide Area Workflow. Must be updated annually.

Marketing Partner ID Number (MPIN)	Create your own MPIN password (nine characters, including one letter and one number, with no spaces or special characters). This information will be shared with other authorized applications, such as ORCA.
Previous business name	If applicable.
Past Performance POC	The person responsible for administering federal government past performance reports and response efforts.
Corporate POC	Any person who is able to address general questions about your business—CEO, office manager, and so on.
Electronic Data Interchange (EDI) POC	If you wish to use EDI. More on this later!
Disaster Response	If you wish to do business with agencies such as the Federal Emergency Management Agency (FEMA) in the event of a natural disaster. Additional information on FEMA disasters may be found at *www.fema.gov/hazard/index.shtm*.
Bonding levels	For certain types of service contracts and for construction. If your industry does not normally require bonding, leave the section blank.
Geographic area served	The State, County, or Metropolitan Statistical Area where you provide or deliver products or services. Used to identify contractors who can deliver emergency supplies/services in a FEMA-declared disaster area.
ORCA	Online Representation & Certification Application. Allow 48 hours after your CCR registration before you complete registration at the ORCA site. (We discuss this later in this chapter.)

If you cannot complete the registration in a single session, you may save the partial data and resume the process at another time. To do this, click "Save/Validate Data" and make a note of the temporary code you are given. This code, along with your DUNS number, will allow you to pick up the registration where you left off, when you return to it at a later date. You can easily see which information is incomplete by viewing the "Show Errors" section of the screen.

Your CCR registration will take one to two business days to clear the TIN Match process. As we mentioned earlier in the chapter, a newly assigned EIN cannot be validated in CCR right away, even if you receive your number immediately. You must wait until you receive the official notice (CP-575) from the IRS confirming that your EIN is active and valid for use before you can register at CCR, which could take anywhere from two to five weeks.

Your registration must be updated at least every 12 months, and more frequently if necessary.

Updating Your CCR records

In December 2009, CCR changed the way existing users accessed their files in order to make changes to their records. Until that date the system issued users a Trading Partners Identification Number (TPIN). This has now been replaced with a user-defined password system. You will set up a username and password that allows you access to your information to make any modifications you need. Any active registrations that have not been converted to this system by the end of 2009 will have to contact the service desk for assistance, either by phone or online (check the Website for details). Expired registrations that have not been converted to this new system will be deleted.

Registering at the Online Representations and Certifications (ORCA) Site (*http://orca.bpn.gov*) (19)

Until recently, each and every bid you submitted to the federal government had to be accompanied by a document called Representations and Certifications. This document allowed you to self-certify the size of your company, whether it was eligible for any set-aside programs, and so on. In 2005 the government initiated the ORCA program, which allows you to certify your company profile electronically, where you will be required to renew your registration annually. You may update your company's information at any time.

To log in to this program, you will need your Dun & Bradstreet (DUNS) number and the Marketing Partners Identification Number (MPIN) that you created when you registered at the Central Contractors Registration (CCR) site. The following are the steps to register.

- You will be asked to certify that you have read and understand certain regulations that apply to government contracting, such as fair labor practices laws, non-discrimination laws, equal opportunity laws, and so on. The links to the left take you directly to the specific federal regulation that applies.

- You will further certify that you have not been de-barred or suspended, and that no money was used to influence government employees.

- There are also provisions concerning veterans' employment and reporting requirements, and many others. **You should take the time to read and understand each provision before you proceed**.

- In the next section, much of the information will have already been filled in for you—the ORCA program takes the information you provided when you registered at the CCR site and transfers that information here; for example, your Tax Identification Number (TIN), the type of organization, and size of your company. If you find that any of this information is incorrect, you will need to return to CCR and update your records there, before returning to the ORCA registration. Allow about 24 hours for the updates in CCR to show up on the ORCA site.

- Just like CCR, you will be able to save a partially completed record and return to it at a later date.

- Once you have submitted your ORCA application, you will be able to save a copy for your own records.

A Checklist for You

As you can see, there are many important codes that you will need to keep safe in order to do business with the federal government. The following brief overview helps you to keep track of all this information.

Government Code	Description
SBA size standards	Determine size standards for eligibility as a Small Business.
DUNS number	Company identification number.
TIN	Tax Identification Number.
CCR registration	Registration mandatory for all government contracting.
CCR login password	Created by you, and replaces the TPIN.

MPIN	Created by you during CCR registration.
CAGE code	Assigned by CCR if your company does not already have one.
NAICS codes	Industrial Classification Codes—general business type.
FSC codes	Product codes—identify specific items you can supply.
SIC codes	Service codes—identify specific services you can supply.
ORCA registration	Online Representations and Certifications site.

Help!

If you have any questions about this chapter, we would be happy to try to help you. Go to our Website, *www.sell2gov.com*, and at the Contact tab you can send us an e-mail with your questions. Please put "Definitive Guide" in the subject line.

Chapter 2

Searching the Federal Business Opportunities Website

Overview

In this chapter we take you step by step though the Federal Business Opportunities website, otherwise known as **FedBizOpps**, which is the single government point of entry for federal government procurement opportunities over $25,000. At this site you can search, monitor, and retrieve opportunities solicited by the entire federal contracting community.

Searching

In this chapter we take you step by step through this important procurement site. We show you how to search for business opportunities, and fully explain the results of the search so you can understand exactly what you see. Each term is explained in plain language, so that you understand exactly what the government is looking for—Synopsis, Solicitation, Pre-Solicitation, Modification, Amendment, Sources Sought, and more. We discuss how to narrow your search so that you find only those opportunities for which you are fully qualified. Once you have found an opportunity that interests you, we explain clearly the different documents that you must examine in detail in order to know the exact terms and conditions of this bid, and the red flags that could determine whether or not you place a bid—Technical Data Packages, Statements of Work, and so on.

Set-Aside Programs

In the next section we discuss the set-aside programs for Small, Small Disadvantaged (8a), Woman-Owned, Veteran-Owned, Minority-Owned, and Hub-Zone businesses. We clearly define each of these set-asides, and give you links where you can get more details on each of these programs.

Other Government Programs

Next we explain some other programs that you may come across when you search this site, and look at how they may affect your ability to place an offer—Sole Source, Qualified Products Lists, Federal Acquisition Regulations (FAR), shipping and packaging requirements, and so on.

The Federal Business Opportunities Website

When an agency is going to make a purchase that is estimated to be $25,000 and higher, then they are required to advertise that information at a Website called **Federal Business Opportunities** or **FedBizOpps** (*www.fbo.gov*). (20)

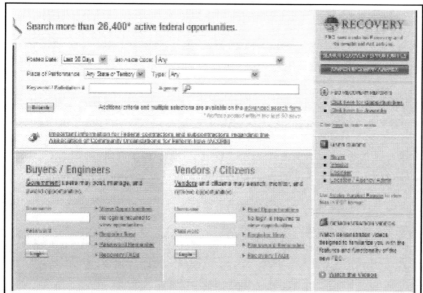

Since our original book was published in 2008, the FedBizOpps site has been extensively updated, with new features and a new layout.

At the top of the page is a simple search option, where you may search for opportunities by the **date** posted, by **set-aside** program, by **place** of performance, by **type** (Solicitations, Sources Sought, and more—these will be explained later in this chapter), by **keywords**, or by **agency**.

This simple search section may seem to be a good place to begin, but unless you are familiar with the site and with the terms that are used, you will be better served by beginning at the **Vendors/Citizens** box further down on the page.

Registration

Although you do not have to register in order to view opportunities, you will find that once you begin to search you may not be able to access details of the requirements (Technical Data Packages, Statements of Work, and so on) unless you are registered. Because registration takes very little time, it is easier to do this right at the beginning.

Begin the registration process by entering your Dun & Bradstreet (DUNS) number. (We discussed how to get this number in the previous chapter.) Again, although this is an optional step, unless you list your DUNS number you will be unable to view certain documents. Enter your company information, create your username and password, and log in.

Once you are at the My FBO page, you can begin to search the site for opportunities. Rather than beginning at the Find Opportunities tab, which would seem the obvious choice, instead click on **Search and Create Saved Searches**, which takes you to the Advanced Searches tab.

Setting Your Search Parameters

Posted Date: Options here range from two to 365 days.

Place of Performance: If you wish to limit your search to certain geographical areas.

Documents to Search: Solicitations are usually archived 30 days after the bid.

Opening Date: Awards are usually archived 30 days after the Award Date. Click on the Active button here, unless you are searching specifically for an older notice.

At this point leave these search parameters blank, make sure "Active" documents is chosen, and scroll further down the page....

Set-Aside Codes

If you wish to limit your searches to any of the set-aside categories that you qualify for, you can do so here. You can choose to search for all opportunities that are available to you, or limit your search—to only the partial or total Women-Owned Small Business Set-Asides, for example. The most common category here would be Small Business Set-Aside, which represents approximately 20 percent of all sales opportunities available on a daily basis. A more detailed description of the Set-Aside program is given later in this chapter. For the moment, leave this section blank.

Procurement Types

A **Pre-Solicitation** notice lets you know that the agency plans to issue a **Solicitation** in the near future, and often will give an estimated date for the release of the solicitation package. A **Synopsis** is a brief description of the items that will be in the solicitation document. Sometimes agencies issue a pre-solicitation synopsis, followed by the official solicitation document; at other times these are issued simultaneously as a **Combined Synopsis/ Solicitation** document.

Agencies sometimes issue notices that are known as **Sources Sought, Market Research**, or **Request for Information (RFI)**. The agency is asking for some preliminary information in order to determine the type of contract document it may post. For example, the agency may wish to know if there are any small, veteran-owned businesses capable of supplying a particular product or performing a service. At other times the agency may know of only one company that can provide this product or service, and is gathering information to see if any other companies respond. The agency will usually ask for a **Capability Statement** from interested companies. The notice will spell out exactly the sort of information the agency is looking for, and will often list a maximum number of pages and so on. Bear in mind that if you submit a capability statement, the agency is under no obligation to subsequently issue a solicitation.

The term **Modification** is used to notify changes to synopses, whereas the term **Amendment** is used when there are changes to solicitation packages. Both amendments and modifications can change specifications, due dates for offers, or could even cancel the request completely. If you put in an offer, always check the Website for any modifications or amendments, as they could significantly alter the details of the bid. It is your responsibility to check for any modifications or amendments, and you *must* include all of them as part of your offer. Failure to acknowledge receipt of any amendment/modification may mean that your offer is rejected.

The government occasionally conducts **Sales of Surplus Property**—items that are surplus to their requirements. **Special Notices** cover many different aspects of federal procurement, including upcoming trade shows, sponsorship opportunities, industry days, and so on. **Foreign Government Standards** notices could be relevant if you are planning to ship an item overseas.

If you wish to find out the details of a bid once it has been **awarded**, click the **Award Notice** button.

Justification & Approval (J&A) documents are required whenever an agency plans to award a contract on a **Sole Source** basis. A sole-source solicitation is used when the agency is only aware of a single company that is qualified to supply that product or service. However, if you believe that you can also supply this item, you may respond to the agency and submit a proposal. Specific criteria the agency must use to justify the sole-source contract are all detailed in the appropriate Federal Acquisition Regulation (FAR). We discuss Sole Source Programs, and the Federal Acquisition Regulations, later in this chapter. Justifications must be in writing, and the Contracting Officer must certify the accuracy of the justifications, and obtain the necessary approvals before proceeding.

For the moment, you may wish to begin by choosing Pre-Solicitation, Combined Synopsis/Solicitation, Modification/Amendment, Special Notice, and Sources Sought.

Narrow by Specific Agencies

Here you may limit your search to specific agencies, if you know that your product or service will only be purchased by certain agencies. If you click this option, a drop-down box will allow you to select those agencies. For now, choose to search by All Agencies.

The 2009 American Recovery and Reinvestment Act—ARRA

This new option allows you to search only those opportunities that are funded by the American Recovery and Reinvestment Act of 2009. Unless you wish to specifically include *or* exclude any of these opportunities, click on Ignore for this option.

On October 2, 2009, the Small Business Administration reported that almost 26 percent of all federal stimulus contracting dollars was awarded to small businesses—more than $4 billion! By the end of September 2009 the Department of Defense (DOD) had awarded over $2 billion in Recovery Act contracts, and 58 percent went to small businesses—many DOD contracts were for construction or facility maintenance projects.

Keywords, FSC Codes, NAICS Codes

These options allow you to search by Keywords, by North American Industrial Classification (NAICS) codes, or by Federal Supply (FSC) codes. Remember that you are *not* restricted to submitting offers on only the NAICS codes that you listed when you registered at the Central Contractor Registration (CCR) Website. Searching for appropriate sales opportunities should really be a combination of all these options, especially in the beginning. Many times you will come across opportunities "hidden" in areas that you don't expect, under codes you would not have initially chosen, or with keywords you might not think of. Try all three methods and see where the opportunities lie.

Keyword Searches

This option supports keyword searches and Boolean search strings using *and*, *or*, and parentheses. Search too broadly and you will be wading through solicitations that are not relevant; search too narrowly and you may miss some great opportunities! The Tips button at the side of the Keyword box has some good explanations to help you get started—but beware of getting too complicated in your keyword searches; a simple approach is best, especially to begin with.

Search by Classification Codes. In the previous chapter we discussed North American Industrial Classification (NAICS) codes, as well as Product and Services Classification codes (FSC and PSC) ranging from 10 to 99 for products and from A to Z for services. Click on all the categories that apply. **Always search for FSC Code 99 (Miscellaneous)—you can often find opportunities hidden here!**

Justification and Approval. We discussed these earlier in this chapter. If you wish to limit your searches to any of the J&A notices you may do so here.

Search by Date Range. Click here to bring up a calendar to narrow your search parameters. My suggestion to begin would be to search by Posted Date Range, going back perhaps one month.

A Word About Searches

Remember that searching for the right opportunities can often be as much an art as a science! Even though we have been using this site to search for opportunities for our clients for many years, it still takes some trial and error to come up with the right combination.

~Once Upon a Time~

An event-planning company began searching for opportunities under FSC Code R (Professional Services),
but also found opportunities in codes S (Housekeeping),
U (Training), W, and X (Lease of Facilities and Equipment).

There were even opportunities posted where they didn't expect; for example, in code Q (Medical Services), where there was a posting for a medical conference. Another time the company found a conference listed under code 69 (Training Aids).

More opportunities were found by using the keywords Audio/Video, Tent, and Marquee, such as when an agency wanted to rent equipment for a specific event.

Automating the Search Process

The new **Saved Searches** feature allows you to create automated searches that are sent directly to your e-mail address as often as you wish. Use this feature only *after* you have tried all the searching options we have already mentioned, to set up several automatic searches.

At the top of the Advanced Searches page, click on the **Search Agents** tab.

At the **Search Agent Label** option you will need to name this particular search. This allows you to set up and name several different automatic search agents—one using keywords, another using FSC, codes and a third using NAICS codes, for example. Each search can be set up using different parameters; you will soon gain a good overall picture of which search strategies work the best for you.

Once you have selected the search parameters, click on the **Save and Schedule Search Agent** tab, and click **Yes** to set up a schedule for your searches (for example, One Day), then click **Save**.

Each search you set up will be run as often as you wish, and the results will be sent to your e-mail inbox. You can edit search parameters or cancel the searches at any time.

Electronic Bidding Option

You may see a new option in FedBizOpps that allows for Electronic Bidding. We discuss this in more detail in the next chapter of the book, at the Department of Defense's Internet Bid Board System (DIBBS), but there are several other sites where electronic bidding is becoming the way forward, such as the Army Single Face to Industry site (ASFI), the Dept. of the Interior Website (known as IDEAS-EC), the FedBid online reverse auction site, and many others (see Chapter 4 for a more detailed description of these sites).

Understanding the Results of Your Searches

Here is an example of the results screen:

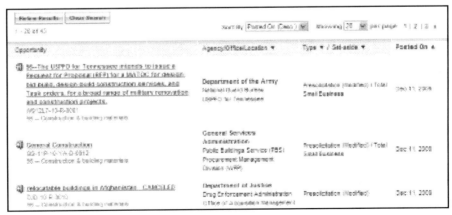

You can see that for the particular search parameters I set, there are 43 total opportunities, listed on three pages. Here you can see each opportunity, the classification code, the purchasing agency, the type of notice, and the posted date. If you see an opportunity that seems interesting, click on the title link. Let's look at some of the information you may see posted, and understand how it affects your ability to submit a bid.

Here's the top of the notice page, giving details of the general title and the purchasing agency:

As you can see, the tabs across the top also allow you to view any technical packages that may have been posted, as well as an **Interested Vendors List** tab, which shows you any businesses that have indicated an interest in this solicitation, and could be a great way for you to find competitors or possible subcontracting opportunities. However, because you are not required to be listed here in order to submit an offer, the list is not comprehensive. If you wish to add your company to this list, there is an option for that here, which could lead to possible subcontracting opportunities for your company.

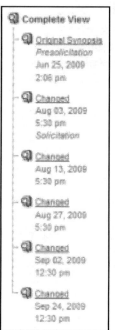

Amendments and Changes

At the left side of the page you can see that a pre-solicitation notice was issued on June 25, followed by the solicitation document on August 3. Amendments were issued on August 13 and 27, September 2, and September 24.

As we mentioned earlier, you *must* include any amendments with your submission. Failure to acknowledge them could result in your offer being rejected. It is important to keep track of these changes, as they can often substantially change the terms of the solicitation, or even cancel the solicitation altogether.

Later in this chapter we will discuss several of the terms you might come across in the narrative portion of the solicitation document that may need clarification. If in doubt contact the Contracting Officer listed as the Point of Contact for the solicitation. They are always available to answer any questions you may have.

For now, let's continue to take a look at the search page, to understand the information that can be found there.

To the right of the page you will find links to the various documents that have been issued—the solicitation document as well as various amendments.

Remember that FedBizOpps is the central Website for opportunities over $25,000 for *all* federal agencies. This means that once you click on any of these links you will be directed to the specific agency site for details.

In this particular case the agency involved was part of the U.S. Navy, and so the documents were posted on the Navy site, Navy Electronic Contracting Online (NECO).

Remember that any opportunity estimated to be over $25,000 will be posted *both* at the agency site *and* at FedBizOpps—but you may also wish to search the agency sites directly for smaller opportunities. (Later in the book we will show you how to search directly at some of these other sites.)

In the General Information section on the right-hand side, take particular notice of the **Response Date**. Be sure to submit your response on time!

It is also important to be aware of the *time* for responses as well as the date. Unless otherwise specified, the due date for receipt of offers will be Close of Business (COB) in the *agency's time zone*, on the date specified. Sometimes, however, the actual time for submissions is different—in this particular case the response time was listed on the NECO site as 3 p.m.—at other times it could be as early as before noon of that day.

Commonly Used Contract Terms

You may come across many different terms as you read and try to understand the solicitation package. I have listed some of the most common terms here, but if you find any others, your first step would be to contact the Contracting Officer, who will be able to help you.

It is in the descriptive section of the solicitation document that you will find the details of exactly what the agency is looking for. For a product, the section is often referred to as the Procurement Item Description (PID). For a service there will be a section called the Statement of Work (SOW), Performance Work Statement (PWS), or Statement of Objective (SOO).

We have separated these terms into the following broad types, for clarity:

- **Contract Type:** Some of the terms that describe how the contract is structured.
- **Product Description:** Terms you may see in the descriptive section of the solicitation.
- **Drawings, Specification, and Standards:** Where to find Technical Data Packages.
- **Restricted and Approved Sources:** Products that have more stringent requirements.
- **Quantity Requirements:** Details you need to be aware of.
- **Delivery Requirements.**

Contract Type

Under a **Firm Fixed Price (FFP)** contract the price you quote is fixed, and cannot be adjusted at a later date. **Economic Price Adjustments (EPA)** allow for price increases or decreases throughout the life of the contract. Other contract types may include **cost-plus-fixed-fee; time-and-material, or labor hours.**

Blanket Purchase Agreement (BPA)

This type of agreement is used when an agency has a recurring need for particular items, such as office products. The BPA allows the agency to restock the items as needed, without having to place a new Request for Quote each time. The agency will issue a BPA for a specific period of time, and the items may be purchased without the need for additional competition.

Defense Priority Allocation System (DPAS)

Department of Defense contracts are assigned priority ratings using this system. Orders are rated DX (the highest priority), DO (the next level), or Unrated. Website: *www.bis.doc.gov/dpas*. (21)

Set-Asides

Solicitations may be set aside for certain categories of business. This is discussed in more detail later in the book. If there are no set-aside programs associated with a solicitation, it is called **Unrestricted**.

Product Details

Not all products have **National Stock Numbers (NSN)**; rather, it is a number that uniquely identifies a particular product that is repeatedly purchased or stocked by the federal government. The NSN is a 13-digit number with a specific format: The first four digits correspond to the Federal Supply Class; the next two digits show the country of origin (00 and 01 signify the United States), and the final digits uniquely identify the item. Manufacturers and suppliers *cannot* request that an item be assigned an NSN—it is the federal agency or military service that identifies the need and makes the request. You may also come across the acronym **NIIN** (National Item Identification Number), which is simply the NSN minus the first four digits (in other words, minus the Federal Supply Classification code).

More information can be found in this booklet from the Defense Logistics Agency (DLA): *www.dlis.dla.mil/PDFs/NSN.pdf*. (22)

You may search for an NSN or NIIN at this site: *www.dlis.dla.mil/webflis*. (23) At the home page, click on Public Search.

Drawings, Specifications, and Standards

There is no single place to access all drawings, specifications, and standards issued by all federal agencies.

Standards and Specifications

Sometimes a solicitation will reference commonly used industry standards, such as those published by the Society of Automotive Engineers (SAE) at *www.sae.org* (24), or the American National Standards Institute (ANSI) at *www.ansi.org* (25). You may also be able to find standards at the National Resource for Global Standards at *www.nssn.org* (26)

If a solicitation references certain military or government specifications or standards, the solicitation document should clearly state where you can find them. You should be able to download Department of Defense specifications or standards at its Acquisition Streamlining & Standardization Information Systems (ASSIST) database here: *https://assist.daps.dla.mil*. **(27)** At the Quick Search tab you can search by document number or title, or by Federal Supply Classification Code (FSC).

Some agencies maintain their own standards. If you cannot find the standard referenced in the solicitation document, you should e-mail the Contracting Officer for information.

Drawings

At the Department of Defense Internet Bid Board System (**DIBBS**), drawings can be accessed via the cFolders system. If technical documents are available you will see the icon listed. (We discuss the DIBBS Website in more detail in the next chapter.)

| 23 | 5360-00-014-3403 SPRING, HELICAL, TORS | Tech Docs SPMS14-09-T-0772 Q MORE | | 0020524322 QTY: 78 | 11/13/2008 | 11/27/2008 |

Click on this icon and you will get to the Defense Logistics Agency's cFolders site, where you can download the Technical Data Package (TDP).

Folder Contents			History	List of PR/Procurement Numbers	Download Solicitation
Material Group/Number	Description		Base Document	Download	File Size
5360 000143403	SPRING.HELICAL.TORS		6-50204	000143403	162KB

The **Army Single Face to Industry** (AFSI) Website (discussed in more detail later in the book) lists solicitations from several Army locations, including TACOM (Tank Automotive and Armaments Command). The solicitation details where you can find the Technical Data Package (TDP). In the main body of the solicitation document, immediately following the Contract Line Item Number (CLIN) listing, you will find this clause:

---

5 52.211-4072 TECHNICAL DATA PACKAGE INFORMATION JAN 2005 (TACOM)

The following "X"d item applies to this solicitation:

[ ] There is no Technical Data Package (TDP) included with this solicitation.

[ ] The TDP for this solicitation is on a CD ROM and must be ordered. Ordering instructions can be obtained at Uniform Resource locator (URL): *http://contracting. tacom.army.mil/bidreq.htm*.

[ ] This solicitation contains one or more Web-located TDPs. If multiple Contract Line Item Numbers (CLINs) are listed, each one will have its own URL just under the CLIN listing. The URL will take you to that CLIN's Web-located TDP. To access the TDP, you will have to copy or type the link's URL into your Web browser address bar at the top of the screen. Note: To copy a link from a .pdf file, click on the Text Select Tool, then highlight the URL, copy and paste it into your browser, and hit the enter key.

TDP Link (URL): http://.............

If a TDP is available you will either be able to order it on a CD-ROM or there will be a link to the Technical Data Package. Any link information would be listed at the bottom of the paragraph, and you would need to copy/paste this into your browser. The link would take you to the specific agency site, such as TACOM, for the details of the Technical Data Package.

U.S. Army Tank-automotive and Armaments Command

Warren, Michigan 48397-5000

TECHNICAL DATA PACKAGE DOCUMENT NUMBER	5TK4604	19207
TDP DATE	9/24/2009	
SPECIFICATION		
NATIONAL STOCK NUMBER	- -	
NOMENCLATURE	BATTERY RELOCATION ACCESSORY KIT	

It includes details of the product structure, drawings, quality assurance documents, specifications and standards, and so on.

Another Army site takes you to this page, where you can download any available TDP.

Restricted Drawings

Sometimes Technical Data Packages are listed as Restricted, but you may still be able to access a restricted drawing or TDP, depending on the type of restrictions that have been placed on them.

In this example from the Department of Defense Internet Bid Board (DIBBS) site, you can see that one folder has unlimited access, whereas the others are restricted in some way, and, as it says, "additional access is required."

Folder Contents										Download Solicitation
Document Number	Download	CAGE Code	Document Data Code	Drawing Revision	Number of Sheets	Rights in Data	License Agreement	Distribution Statement	Export Control	Foreign Secure
NAI-1115	NAI-1115	76823	SS	A	0004	U		D	N	N
6-40663	(Add'l Access Required)	76823	DD	B	0001	X	14	B	Y	N
MP-225	(Add'l Access Required)	76823	SS	B	0005	X	14	B	Y	N
6-40663	(Add'l Access Required)	76823	AL	BH	0001	X	14	B	Y	N

In this particular case you can see that the last two columns show that the documents are **Export Controlled**, but are not **Foreign Secure**.

The License Agreement column indicates that **Non-Disclosure License Agreement** #14 is in effect for three of the documents. (Licensing Agreement #14 is for proprietary data from Northrop Grumman.) If you wished to access these drawings, you would need to click on the link, and download and complete the forms that allow you access to these drawings, certifying that you will not copy or disseminate them to other parties, and will destroy them once they are no longer needed. These documents would be faxed to the agency listed at the top of the form, which would then allow you access to the drawings. Other licensing agreements are in effect with Boeing, McDonald Douglas, Caterpillar, Colt, Howitzer, General Electric, Hughes Helicopter, and Lockheed Martin.

The **No Foreign** designation requires you to submit a form that certifies that you are a United States citizen or permanent resident and that you will not distribute or disseminate the package.

Drawings may be **Export Controlled**, and in that case, in order to receive the TDP you must complete form **DD 2345, Militarily Critical Technical Data Agreement**.

TDPs are also given a **Distribution Statement** ranging from A to X:

- A—Unlimited.
- B—Limited to U.S. government agencies.
- C—Limited to U.S. government agencies and their contractors.
- D—Limited to DOD and U.S. DOD contractors only.
- E—Limited to DOD only.
- F—Distribution to be determined by the controlling DOD office.
- X—Limited to U.S. government organizations and private individuals or enterprises with a current DD 2345.

Approved or Restricted Sources

Qualified Lists (QPL/ QML/QSL)

The agency wants to buy a product from a supplier whose product has been commercially tested and certified by an independent laboratory to perform a specific task. If you are interested in determining whether your company is capable of producing a Qualified Products List item, then your first step would be to contact the Contracting Officer, whose contact information appears at the end of the Synopsis.

The Defense Supply Center Columbus (DSCC) has a master index of all the **Qualified Products Lists** (QPL) and **Qualified Manufacturers Lists** (QML), and they are available for download from the DSCC. These items are primarily from Federal Supply Codes 16, 25, 29, 30, 43, 47, 48, 59, 60, 61, 66, and 99. They include Custom Devices (Electronic Microcircuits), Electronic Devices, Hybrid Devices, and Passive Devices. You can find the listing at *www.dscc.dla.mil/programs*. (28)

Qualified Suppliers List for Manufacturers (QSLM) and Distributors (QSLD)

The Defense Supply Center Philadelphia runs a program in which manufacturers and distributors may pre-qualify to supply certain items to the agency. In order to pre-qualify, you must show that your standard controls comply with certain criteria, which ensures that the products conform to specification requirements.

For more information on some of the most common Qualified Supplier Lists, go to the Defense Supply Center Philadelphia site at *www.dscp.dla.mil*. (29). Click on Supply Chain—Construction & Equipment, and then Quality Assurance for a list of various Quality Assurance Provisions.

At the DSCP site you may click on Quality Assurance to find the Qualified Suppliers Lists for Manufacturers & Distributors of items such as bulk metals; Class 2 and 3 Threaded Fasteners; rope, cord, twine, and tape; rivets; O-rings; and quick release pins. At this site you can also view which companies are currently on these lists.

~Once Upon A Time~

Some initial searching in FedBizOpps was all it took for a sheet metal manufacturer to realize that being listed on the Department of Defense's Qualified Supplier List for Bulk Metals was going to be essential for him to compete in the federal marketplace.

Once he was awarded the qualification he found many sales opportunities available to him—definitely worth jumping through the necessary hoops!

Sometimes some hard work at the beginning can really pay off!

Critical Safety Items

These are parts whose failure would cause loss of life, permanent disability or major injury, loss of a system, or significant equipment damage; for example, aircraft or missile parts.

Quality Assurance Provisions (QAP)

At the Defense Supply Center Richmond (DSCR) Website you can use the Site Map to find the link to the QAPs: *www.dscr.dla.mil*. (30)

Approved Sources

Sometimes the agency knows of a number of "approved sources" for the particular manufactured part it wishes to purchase. In the solicitation document you will see the company or companies listed using the five-digit manufacturer's Commercial and Government Entity (CAGE) code followed by the part number. We discussed this code in the previous chapter.

If only the CAGE code is listed rather than the manufacturer name, you can use the Business Identification Number Cross-Reference System (BINCS) at

```
ITEM DESCRIPTION

WEIGHT, WHEEL, 4OZ.

NO DATA IS AVAILABLE.  THE ALTERNATE OFFEROR IS
REQUIRED TO PROVIDE A COMPLETE DATA PACKAGE
INCLUDING DATA FOR THE APPROVED AND ALTERNATE
PART FOR EVALUATION.
D L INDUSTRIES INC                    0A6U7 P/N 83906
```

www.bpn.gov/bincs (31) or the Central Contractor Registration (CCR) Website at *www.ccr.gov* (32) to look up the manufacturers that are listed here. In these cases drawings and specifications will not be available, as they are proprietary to the manufacturer.

This is a great way to find sales opportunities if you are a distributor for manufactured parts! Use the search option to enter the CAGE code of any companies that you can supply. Here is an example from the Department of Defense Internet Bid Board System (DIBBS), looking for spare parts from the Caterpillar Company. For this list we search using the Caterpillar CAGE Code #11083

12	2540-01-564-4439 HANDLE, DOOR, VEHICUL	None	SPM7L2-10-T-D230 Quote		0024806061 QTY: 28
13	2590-00-135-6277 HORN, ELECTRICAL	None	SPM7L2-10-Q-0472 Quote		0024481896 QTY: 4
14	2590-01-177-2347 CAP, FILLER OPENING.	None	SPM7L2-10-T-Q524 Quote		0024869773 QTY: 53

~Once Upon a Time~

A company that was a distributor of manufactured parts from several large international concerns searched using the manufacturer's CAGE codes, and found many "smaller" opportunities to supply these items. The original manufacturer was interested in the larger opportunities, but that still left a lot of room for this small supplier to bid—and win—sales opportunities.

(In this case the company also found many smaller opportunities in the Dept of Defense's online site known as DIBBS, which we will discuss in the following chapter.)

These "smaller" bids can add up to BIG opportunity for your business!

Source Approval

Earlier in this section we described how an agency may be aware of only one or two companies who can supply a particular item—for example if they have purchased these items from them in the past. When the agency issues an RFQ, the contracting officer will only list these manufacturers and their part numbers—even though *you* may make or supply an item that is functionally the same but is not listed as a source of supply, because the agency does not know that you can supply an alternate item.

If you believe that your item is functionally the same as the listed manufacturer's part, then you may wish to submit the item to the agency for it to decide if your item is acceptable for future purchases. Your "alternate" product will be evaluated, and may be included in the next procurement notice.

For noncritical items, you would need to contact the agency directly and ask for the details on where to send your request to have your item evaluated for Source Approval as a functional equivalent item. Once this is complete your item will be listed as an acceptable alternative manufacturer and part number.

Items that are designated as "critical safety" have more stringent requirements. In this case you would need to follow the particular agency's requirements. The Department of Defense's process for evaluation of alternate items is described in the Defense Supply Center Richmond (DSCR) Source Approval Booklet at *www.dscr.dla.mil*. (33)

Other agencies will have their own specific processes for evaluating an alternate item. For example, the Navy Supply Systems Command has a "Navy Inventory Control Point Source Approval brochure," which can be found at the Naval Supply Systems Command Website at *www.navsup.navy.mil*. (34) Type "source approval" into the search option to find information on how to apply to have your item evaluated.

Mandatory Source—Ability One

The Jarvits Wagner O'Day (JWOD) program, recently renamed Ability One, is a mandatory source program that *requires* federal personnel to purchase certain products and services from agencies that employ those who are legally blind or have severe disabilities—that is, from the National Institutes for the Blind (NIB) and the National Institute for the Severely Handicapped (NISH). The program supplies janitorial products; office products, such as pens, binders, and paper goods; disposable cutlery; and medical supplies, such as catheters and masks, as well as janitorial services, warehouse services, recycling, food services, laundry, and grounds maintenance.

If you supply any of these items, you should be aware of what the Ability One program provides. Federal agencies may still be able to purchase items from you, if they are not "essentially the same" as Ability One's products. For example, Ability One could provide a generic cleaning product, but your product may be more specialized, have better environmental qualities, and so on. Determination of "Essentially the Same" is made by Ability One. Alternatively, you may wish to apply to become a distributor of their products. (Website: *www.jwod.com*.) (35)

Preferred Source—The Federal Prison Industries (UNICOR)

Federal Prison Industries (FPI) was set up to provide paid employment to prison inmates, mainly through the manufacture of products for the federal government, under the trade name UNICOR. More than 19,300 inmates are employed in more than 100 FPI factories at 71 prisons. UNICOR has several different product lines, including clothing and textiles, electronic parts, vehicle parts, industrial products, office furniture, and recycling.

In addition, it offers services such as distribution, order fulfillment, assembly and packaging, document conversion, call center support, printing services, and laundry services. At the UNICOR Website you can find a complete listing of products and services. Categories are listed as Mandatory if federal agencies must give priority to UNICOR when it can supply the product, within the desired timeframe, and at a competitive price. Agencies need not purchase from FPI unless it determines that their products or services provide the best value. If FPI does not provide the best value, then the buying agency may purchase from other sources. (Website: *www.unicor.gov*.) (36)

Quantities

Contract Line Item Numbers (CLINS)

You would think that the quantity you see initially in the synopsis listing is self-evident, but that is not necessarily the case! In this example you can see that in the FedBizOpps notice the quantity is listed as 21:

> Proposed procurement for NSN 2520011368717 SHIFTERFORK,VEHICU: Line 0001 Qty:00021

However, once you link to the agency site, in this case the Department of Defense, you can see that the actual quantity requested is 120.

If you click on the link to the solicitation and scroll through the document you will see that Line Item #1 is for a quantity of 21, and Line Item #2 is for an additional quantity of 99.

LINE ITEM 0001			
PURCHASE REQUEST	QUANTITY	UNIT OF ISSUE	UNIT PRICE
001 361 2620	21	EA	

LINE ITEM 0002			
PURCHASE REQUEST	QUANTITY	UNIT OF ISSUE	UNIT PRICE
001 361 2620	99	EA	
PACKAGING DATA			

There are several reasons why this occurs. One of the most common is that **First Article Testing** (FAT) is required to ensure the item is satisfactory before the remainder of the order is shipped. In that case Line Item #1 would be for an initial quantity for quality testing (often just a single item), and Line Item #2 would be for shipment of the remaining quantity at a later date. (In certain cases you will see a notice that FAT has been waived for certain manufacturers and part numbers.)

Another reason for this quantity discrepancy is if the items are going to be **shipped to different locations**. That is the case in our example to the right, where 21 items are to be shipped to Pennsylvania and the remaining 99 items will be shipped to California.

```
                              SHIPPING DATA
PARCEL POST/FREIGHT ADDRESS:
W2S61U
SU TRANSPORTATION OFFICER
DDSP NEW CUMBERLAND FACILITY
2001 MISSION DRIVE DOOR 113 134
NEW CUMBERLAND PA 17070-5001
US
```

On other occasions different line items may be given for **different delivery times**—for example, a specific amount in 30 days, followed by an additional amount at a later date.

```
                              SHIPPING DATA
PARCEL POST ADDRESS:
W62G3T
XU DEF DIST DEPOT SAN JOAQUIN
TRANSPORTATION OFFICER
PO BOX 960001
STOCKTON CA 95296-0130
```

In the case of contracts for more than one year, the solicitation will list each year on a separate line, and you will be able to supply pricing for the initial year and a separate pricing for any option years.

Indefinite Delivery Indefinite Quantity Contract (IDIQ)

In this case the contract will be awarded for a specific time period (often one year with several option years), and the agency will order from the contract as needed. There is no specific quantity given, but sometimes a minimum guaranteed amount, or an estimated annual quantity, is listed.

Option to Increase Quantity

In the solicitation package you will find the percentage of estimated volume the agency has the option to increase, with no price adjustment.

Surge and Sustainment

This is defined as the ability to supply an increase in quantity or a faster delivery time if the agency requires it. A "surge" would be the ability to quickly increase the quantity available if required, and a "sustainment" would be your ability to sustain that increase throughout the contract period.

If Surge and Sustainment is required, the details will be clearly stated in the contract. If a Validation Plan is required, it should clearly define how you intend to meet this requirement—how you will work with your suppliers, how you will arrange for transport and delivery of the items, and so on.

Delivery

Delivery Dates (ARO/ADO/ADC)

These acronyms detail the delivery requirements in terms of the number of days After Receipt of Order, After Delivery of Order, or After Receipt of Contract. Remember, your item must be *delivered* by that date—not shipped!

Activity Address Codes (DODAAC)

The Department of Defense Activity Address Code identifies a specific unit, activity, or organization that has the authority to purchase and/or accept ordered items. There may be separate mailing, shipping, and billing addresses for a unit, so pay careful attention to the section in the solicitation that states these addresses; you may not necessarily be shipping an item to the same address as that of the ordering agency listed on the first page. You may search for a specific DODAAC code at the Wright Patterson Air Force Base site: *https://dodaac.wpafb.af.mil*. (37)

Inspection and Acceptance Points

The agency has the option to inspect the product at the place where it is being manufactured, prior to award. The solicitation will spell out where the items will be inspected and accepted. Until the item has had an official acceptance, your invoice cannot be paid. (**Federal Acquisition Regulations (FAR)** are discussed in detail later in the book.)

Progress Payments

This clause allows the agency to assist a small business before the delivery of the final product or service of the contract. Progress payments are used on fixed-price contracts when the deliverable will take more time and money to produce than the contractor is able to finance with its own money

Evaluation Factors

Whereas price may be a significant factor in the evaluation of offers, the final award decision will be based upon a combination of price, delivery, past performance, socio-economic programs, and other evaluation factors as described in the solicitation document. Federal Acquisition Regulations clearly specify that all offers must be evaluated in accordance with the criteria set out in the solicitation document. For many commercial items, this can simply be a combination of technical aspects, price, and past performance.

Technical Evaluation

A Technical Evaluation for a product could include examination of the product literature and specifications, product samples, technical features, and warranty provisions. For a service contract, this technical evaluation may take into account how well you show an understanding of the service to be performed, your managerial approach, how you intend to keep the project on time and budget, how you deal with problems, and so on. Technical factors help ensure that you fully understand the requirements, and that you are capable of supplying the item. Relevant experience and past performance, a suitable management plan, company resources, and the overall quality of your submission will also be taken into consideration

If a factor other than price determines the basis for the award decision, the solicitation will state the relationship of price to the non-price factors. Other considerations may be, for example, Life Cycle Costs, Energy Conservation and Efficiency Costs, and overall Multi-Year Costs.

Past Performance Evaluation

This will take into account any previous contracts, both federal and commercial, in order to determine how well your company performed—did you deliver a quality product or service? Were you on time and on budget? How well did you resolve any issues that arose? How is your relationship with your customers?...and so on.

Cascade Method of Evaluation

In some cases the solicitation will be issued as a set-aside for a particular type of small business; for example, a business located in a HUB-Zone. However, if there is inadequate competition at this level the contracting officer may decide to use a "cascade method" to award the contract. For example, the first priority for the award might be for HUB-Zone companies, but if there is not adequate competition at this level then the next priority might be for a service-disabled veteran-owned company, and so on. Adequate competition is considered to be at least two qualified offers from companies in any set-aside category.

Automated Evaluation: PACE

The Department of Defense Internet Bid Board System (DIBBS) uses a fully automated evaluation system known as PACE (Procurement Automated Contract Evaluation). We will discuss this system in more detail in the next chapter on electronic bidding at the DIBBS site.

Automated Best Value System (ABVS)

This is a computerized system that collects information on how well a vendor has fulfilled the terms of any previous contracts, and converts that into a numeric score. The contracting officer will use this information as an additional evaluation factor when making Best Value Award decisions. The system looks at your company's performance in fulfilling government contracts during the previous 24 months, and its score is a combination of how well you fulfilled the contract both in terms of the quality of your product or service, and whether you delivered on time. The Delivery Score is affected by any shipments that were not shipped or received in their entirety by the contract delivery date. The Quality Score is affected by any products that do not pass inspection, or any products that were not packaged appropriately. Any discrepancies will be reflected in your ABVS score—even if you replace or repair a defective item, your score will still be affected. If your records reflect negative quality data, they are listed with one of these Discrepancy Codes:

A1–A5	Stored Material Deficiencies
C1 C6	Supplies Damaged or with Expired Shelf-Life
L1–L8	Wood Product Deficiencies
P0–P8	Packaging Deficiencies
Q1–Q7	Product Quality Deficiencies
T1–T6	Technical Data Deficiencies
W0 –W9	Wrong Item/Incomplete Item Shipped
X1–XL	Damaged Material

If you have no performance history, your score will be neutral; that is, you will not be evaluated either favorably or unfavorably.

Website: *www.dscr.dla.mil/proc/abvs/abvs.htm*. (38)

Past Performance Information Retrieval System (PPIRS)

This is the site where government agencies note how well you performed on any awarded contract, and this information is shared among other government agencies. You can have access to your own records, and may comment upon anything in the report, but you do not have access to the records of other contractors.

Website: *www.ppirs.gov*. (39)

Effective July 1, 2009, federal regulations require agencies to post all contractor performance evaluations at this site.

Numbered Notes

These are used like footnotes, to reference certain commonly cited information that appears in various announcements. Some of the most common are:

- Numbered Note 1: The proposed contract is 100 percent set-aside for small businesses.
- Numbered Note 9: Where to obtain military documents or specifications.
- Numbered Note 12: The solicitation is subject to the Trade Agreements act.
- Numbered Note 13: The procurement is restricted to domestic sources only.
- Numbered Note 22: The government will only purchase this item from a single source.

A complete list of these notes can be found at the Dept of Commerce Website: *http://cbdnet.gpo.gov/num-note.html.* (40)

Understanding Amendments and Modifications

Amendments and Modifications are issued at the earliest possible time after a synopsis is issued. As we explained earlier in this chapter, the term *modification* is used to notify changes to a synopsis, whereas the term *amendment* is used when there are changes to solicitation packages. Both amendments and modifications can change specifications or due dates for offers, or could even cancel the request completely. The change can be as minor as a change in the solicitation number, or as major as cancellation of the entire solicitation. Amendments and modifications are also used to extend the bid opening date, or to change the date or time of day that your offer must be received. They may be changes, additions, or cancellations to the original synopsis document. It is your responsibility to monitor the Website for amendments and modifications. Any amendments and modifications that are issued relating to a specific solicitation *must* be submitted along with your offer, or you may not be in compliance, and your offer could be rejected simply because you did not submit them.

If you notice that an amendment or modification has been posted to the FedBizOpps Website, you will be able to click on the **Track Changes** link, which highlights the changes that have been made. This is particularly useful if the descriptive section of the notice is a long one, so that you can quickly tell if the amendment affects your ability to submit an offer.

> **Synopsis:**
> Added Dec 10, 2009 2:34 pm   Modified Dec 14, 2009 10:25 am   Track Changes
> This is a combined synopsis/solicitation for commercial items prepared in accordance with the format in Federal Acquisition Regulations (FAR) Subpart 12.6, as supplemented with additional information included in

The following image is the first section of a formal Amendment document. One thing to notice on the first page (in Block 11) is whether or not the due date for the receipt of offers has been extended.

AMENDMENT OF SOLICITATION/MODIFICATION OF CONTRACT		1. CONTRACT ID CODE	PAGE OF PAGES 1 5
2. AMENDMENT/MODIFICATION NO. 000001	3. EFFECTIVE DATE 11/06/2009	4. REQUISITION/PURCHASE REQ. NO.	5. PROJECT NO. (if applicable) R961962D0
6. ISSUED BY CODE 00600 Social Security Administration Office of Acquisition and Grants 1st Floor - Rear Entrance 7111 Security Boulevard Baltimore MD 21244-1811		7. ADMINISTERED BY (if other than Item 6) CODE OAG SOCIAL SECURITY ADMINISTRATION Office of Acquisition and Grants 1st Floor - Rear Entrance 7111 Security Boulevard Baltimore MD 21244-1811	
8. NAME AND ADDRESS OF CONTRACTOR (No., street, county, State and ZIP Code)		9A. AMENDMENT OF SOLICITATION NO. SSA-RFP-10-1013	
		9B. DATED (SEE ITEM 11) 11/06/2009	
		10A. MODIFICATION OF CONTRACT/ORDER NO.	
CODE	FACILITY CODE	10B. DATED (SEE ITEM 13)	
11. THIS ITEM ONLY APPLIES TO AMENDMENTS OF SOLICITATIONS			
[X] The above numbered solicitation is amended as set forth in Item 14. The hour and date specified for receipt of Offers [X] is extended. [ ] is not extended. Offers must acknowledge receipt of this amendment prior to the hour and date specified in the solicitation or as amended, by one of the following methods: (a) By completing Items 8 and 15, and returning _____ 1 _____ copies of the amendment; (b) By acknowledging receipt of this amendment on each copy of the offer submitted; or (c) By			

Scrolling further down the page, in Block 14, you will find the details of the amendment. Sometimes the details are listed on a second page.

14. DESCRIPTION OF AMENDMENT/MODIFICATION (Organized by UCF section headings, including solicitation/contract subject matter where feasible.)
Disability Case Processing System (DCPS) AMENDMENT ONE (1): The purpose is as follows: 1. To extend the proposal due date from 12:00 p.m., EST on December 7, 2009 to 2:00 p.m., EST on January 5, 2009. 2. Have the past performance questionnaire due date coincide with the RFP closing date. 3. To post a partial list of answers to vendor's questions and clarifications as a result of the RFP posting. (Attachment 1) Continued ...

The Contracting Officer's contact information is also listed so that you can ask questions about this if you need to.

Later into the Amendment document the exact changes that have been made are noted. Some of these changes might be very important to you, so you should make every effort to read and understand them before you make your offer.

Again, notice that it states that all Amendments must be acknowledged. This means that you *must* incorporate these documents into your submission package in order to be considered eligible for an award.

ITEM NO. (A)	SUPPLIES/SERVICES (B)
	4. To post a list of attendees at the Prepreposal Conference. (Attachment 2)

	Attachments: Vendor Q and A's List of Prepreposal Attendees
	All other terms and conditions shall remain the same. -----------------------
	RETURN A SIGNED COPIED OF ALL AMENDMENTS WITH YOUR PROPOSAL TO THE FOLLOWING ADDRESS:
	Social Security Administration Office of Acquisition and Grants Attn: Ida Ryan 7111 Security Blvd., Ste. 100 Baltimore, Maryland 21244. ---------------------------

The Site Visit

SUBJECT: Minutes for Site Visit of Demineralized Water Project, Solicitation, FA4801-05-R-0007

1. The site visit was held at 0830 on 4 January 2006. The contractors met at the Holloman AFB's Visitor Center and caravanned to all visited locations. The following individuals were in attendance:

NAME	ORGANIZATION/COMPANY	TITLE	PHONE
Ms. Sally Roberts	49 CONS/LGCA	Contracting Officer	505-572-7785
Ms. Stephanie Mills	49 CONS/LGCA	Contract Specialist	505-572-3577
Mr. Dale Woosley	49 CES/CEOES	Quality Assurance Person	505-572-3296
Jeff Derryberry	Rayne Water	Service Manager	623-551-5952
Tom Derryberry	Rayne Water	President	623-551-5952
Mr. Andrew Riggs	Quality Water	Manger	505-437-6500
Mr. Miles Beauguard	WHB Environmental, Inc.	Vice President	813-766-7724

2. While at the Visitor's Center, Mr. Woosley went over essential aspects for the requirements of this acquisition. Mr. Woosley presented a map of the base and pointed out the different areas on the base map where services are required. Mr. Woosley stated we would visit multiple buildings in order to view each type of unit required for this project.

In this particular instance, a Site Visit was held to allow potential contractors to fully understand the requirements. An announcement of an impending site visit will be made in the Synopsis or Pre-Solicitation documents. If you are unsure of whether a site visit has been scheduled, you should ask the contracting officer. Sometimes the site visit is mandatory; at other times it is voluntary—but if you choose not to attend a site visit, you may not be able to fully understand the requirements.

Details of the site visit, including a list of attendees, various questions that were raised during the visit, and the agency's answers, will be posted so that anyone can view them. This document could give you valuable information about potential competitors!

The Solicitation Package

Solicitation 01 (Posted on Dec 14, 2005)

Description	Size (Bytes)	File Format
1-1 SF 1449 Solicitation FA4891-05-R-0037	1,012,224	Microsoft Word
1-2 Attachment 1 PWS (Includes App. A - App. E)	167,424	Microsoft Word
1-3 Appendix F Map 1	4,977,664	Microsoft Word
1-4 Appendix F Map 2	4,482,048	Microsoft Word
1-5 Appendix F Map 3	2,098,688	Microsoft Word
1-6 Appendix F Map 4	1,263,104	Microsoft Word
1-7 Appendix F Map 5	3,083,776	Microsoft Word
1-8 Appendix F Map 6	3,264,000	Microsoft Word
1-9 Appendix F Map 7	2,131,968	Microsoft Word
2-1 Appendix F Map 8	832,352	Microsoft Word
2-2 Appendix F Map 9	647,168	Microsoft Word
2-3 Appendix F Map 10	2,277,376	Microsoft Word
2-4 Appendix F Map 11	1,012,736	Microsoft Word
2-5 Appendix F Map 12	625,664	Microsoft Word
2-6 Attachment 2 Wage Determination	74,752	Microsoft Word
2-7 Attachment 3 Past Performance Questionnaire	49,152	Microsoft Word
All Files	25,960,516	Zip Compression

This particular Solicitation is for a Service contract, and there are many documents that need to be read and understood.

- **Standard Form (SF) 1449** is the first page of the Solicitation document, and it must be completed in order to be considered for an award. We discuss this in more detail later in the book.
- Attachment 1 contains the **Performance Work Statement (PWS)**, sometimes referred to as the **Statement of Work (SOW)** or **Statement of Objectives (SOO)**. These documents contain detailed descriptions of the work requirement, as well as details of the delivery timetable, security requirements, estimated work quantities, and detailed costing schedules.
- The following **Appendices** contain maps that are relevant to this particular solicitation.

- Attachment 2 contains the **Wage Determination** document that details exactly the required pay scales for various employees. We discuss Service contracts and their specific requirements in more detail later in the book.
- Attachment 3 contains a **Past Performance Questionnaire**, in which you give reference details of your past customers.

Procurement Preference Goals and the Set-Aside Programs

All federal agencies have procurement goals for contracting with certain categories of small businesses. The Small Business Administration (SBA) is responsible for tracking this program. Procurement preference categories and their percentage goals are:

- Small business (23%).
- Small disadvantaged business (5%).
- Section 8(a) business (5%).
- Woman-owned small business (5%).
- HUB Zone small business (3%).
- Veteran-owned small business (3%).
- Service-disabled veteran-owned small business (3%).

Bear in mind, however, that these are only "goals" the agency tries to achieve through various procurement programs. The official definition of a particular set-aside will be included in the quote that you are offering.

Small Businesses

Eligibility for Small Business status is determined from information provided by the Small Business Administration (SBA). The Small Business Administration uses the North American Industrial Classification System (NAICS) to determine the types of industries and their size standards. One of two criteria is used to define a Small Business: either the average number of full-time employees throughout the last three years, or the average gross sales throughout the last three years. The NAICS codes and Small Business eligibility can both be found at the Small Business Administration Website at *sba.gov/size*. (1)

Small Disadvantaged Businesses and the 8(a) Program

A **Small Disadvantaged Business** is at least 51 percent owned by one or more individuals who are both socially and economically disadvantaged. The company must also have been operational for at least two full years.

A **Socially Disadvantaged Individual** is defined as someone who has been subjected to racial or ethnic prejudice or cultural bias. An Economically Disadvantaged Individual is defined as someone whose abilities to compete in the free enterprise system have been impaired due to diminished capital and credit opportunities.

At one time, in order to be certified as a Small Disadvantaged Business (SDB) you needed certification from the Small Business Administration (SBA). This certification allowed you to benefit from a clause known as the Price Evaluation Adjustment (PEA), which enabled agencies to award contracts to SDBs whose prices were up to 10 percent higher than a non-SDB. However, by Fiscal Year 2007 (FY2007), contract dollars going to SDBs had increased to more than $25 billion, or by more than 6 percent, with very little need for the PEA clause. Therefore, in October 2008 the SBA decided that businesses may self-certify as Small Disadvantaged Businesses.

The **SBA's 8(a) program** is not affected by this change, and you *will* have to go through a certification process in order to be admitted to this program. The 8(a) program offers mentoring, procurement, and financial assistance and training, but it does not guarantee or entitle you to receive federal contracts. The program is divided into: a Developmental stage that lasts for up to four years, and a Transitional stage that lasts for up to five years. As a general rule, to be considered for this program your business must meet the following criteria:

- Socially Disadvantaged: racial or ethnic group members who can show personal business discrimination.
- Economically Disadvantaged: a net worth of $250,000 or less, excluding the value of your residence and business.
- Majority ownership and full-time management operation of the business.
- Meet the SBA's specific size standards.
- In operation for more than two years.
- Sound management experience.
- Offers products or services suited to federal contracts.

Website: *www.sba.gov/8abd.* (41)

An online self-assessment tool can help you to determine if your business meets the 8(a) criteria. It is available at: *training.sba.gov:8000/assessment.* (42)

Minority-Owned and Small Minority-Owned Businesses

A Minority-Owned Business is any business, large or small, that is at least 51 percnet owned and operated by a minority. A Small Minority-Owned Business is a small business that is at least 51 percent owned and operated by a minority

Woman-Owned Businesses

This is a business that is at least 51 percent owned and controlled by a woman, who works in that company on a full-time basis. In the last few years there has been a lot of confusion about woman-owned businesses. Currently there are *no* set-asides specifically for woman-owned businesses, even though they are part of the procurement preference program. An initial SBA study suggested that women-owned businesses were under-represented in only a small number of specific industries. When certain business organizations disagreed with these findings, a revised plan increased the number of under-represented industry categories. The SBA has sent the study back for further review, so that at this point the issue is still not completely resolved.

Although you will *not* see a set-aside category specifically for woman-owned businesses, if you indicate that you are a woman-owned business whenever you can do so (such as when you register your business at the Central Contractors Registration site, when you complete the Online Representations and Certifications Application, and whenever you submit an offer), your status as a woman-owned business will be noted, and your offer *may* be given preference, as the agency tries to achieve its mandatory preference goals.

 In 2009 the Small Business Administration developed an online training course that is specifically geared toward women-owned businesses are interested in federal contracting. The course is available at: *sba.gov/fedcontractingtraining/index.html*. (43)

Historically Under-Utilized Business Zones (HUB-Zones)

This program encourages economic development in Historically Underutilized Business Zones, or HUB-Zones. In order to qualify, a small business must be located in a HUB-Zone, as defined by zip code. The business must be owned and controlled by a US. citizen, and at least 35 percent of its employees must reside in the HUB-Zone area. The company must also maintain a "principal office" in the HUB-Zone. Existing businesses that choose to move to qualified areas are eligible, as long as 35 percent of the employees reside in the HUB-Zone. Employees must live in a primary residence within that area for at least 180 days or be a currently registered voter in that area.

Contracts can be 100 percent set aside for HUB-Zone businesses, or, alternatively, a competitive contract can be awarded to a HUB-Zone business, even if its prices are not the lowest received—this is known as the **Price Evaluation Preference clause**. The HUB-Zone business's offer can be up to 10 percent higher than that of a business not located in a HUB-Zone.

Website: *www.sba.gov/hubzone*. (44)

Veteran-Owned and Service-Disabled Veteran-Owned Businesses

A **Veteran-Owned Business** is a business of any size that is owned and operated by a certified veteran of the armed forces. A Service-Disabled Veteran-Owned Business is one that is owned and operated by a certified disabled veteran of the armed forces.

A **Veteran** is defined by the government as someone who has served in the active military (Army, naval, or air service), and who was discharged other than dishonorably. A

Service-Connected Disability means that the disability was incurred in the line of duty in the active military, naval, or air service. A **Service Disabled Veteran** is a person who served in the active military, naval, or air service, whose disability was incurred or aggravated in the line of duty in that service. A **Service-Disabled Veteran-Owned Small Business Concern** is a small business that must be at least 51 percent directly and unconditionally owned by one or more Service-Disabled Veterans. The management and daily business operations of the business must be controlled by one or more Service-Disabled Veterans. In addition, the Service-Disabled Veteran must hold the highest officer position in the business. At the SBA Website, *www.sba.gov*, (2) use the SBA Programs drop-down box to find information on the Veterans program.

In December 2009 the Veteran Administration issued a final rule that requires VA contracting officers to set-aside procurements between $100,000 and $5 million if they expect two or more eligible veteran-owned or service-disabled veteran-owned small businesses to submit a fair and reasonable offer. VA contracting officers also will be allowed to let sole-source contracts to these firms, for awards from $3,000 to $5 million.

Sole Source

A Sole Source solicitation is used when the government agency is only aware of a single company that is qualified to supply that product or service. However, if you believe that you can also supply this item, you may respond to the agency and submit a proposal. In the Sole Source notice the agency will have to justify why they intend to purchase from only one source. There are various reasons, including:

- **Unusual and Compelling Urgency** (Federal Acquisition Regulation [FAR] 6.302-2). If the agency's need for a particular item or service is urgent, and delay in awarding the contract could result in serious injury, it is permitted to limit the number of sources for soliciting bids. The contracting officer will try to get verbal proposals from as many sources as possible, but a formal solicitation document will not be issued. After the award has been made, the agency will publicize the requirement, so that it can identify other sources for future bidding.

- **Specialized Knowledge or Expertise** (FAR 6.302-3). In which, if a particular contractor has extensive knowledge of a particular area, participated in drawing up standards, or wrote documentation for the agency, then, if the contract were to be awarded to another firm there would be duplication of training cost and other unacceptable delays.

- **International Agreement or Treaty** (FAR 6.302-4). Sole Source may be justified if full and open competition is precluded by the terms of an International Agreement or Treaty. Also, if a purchase will be reimbursed by a foreign country, it may require that those products be obtained from a particular firm. For example, if the agency will be conducting business in another country, you may see solicitation notices such that the contract will only be awarded to a firm from that country.

- **Authorized or Required by Statute** (FAR 6.302-5). Certain laws require the agency to acquire a product or service from a particular source, such as the Federal Prison Industries (UNICOR), the Association for Blind or Severely Disabled (JWOD), the Small Disadvantaged Business Program (8a), or a HUB-Zone.

- **National Security** (FAR 6.302-6). In which the disclosure of the agency's needs might compromise the national security. This justification cannot be used merely because the acquisition is classified, or if access to classified matter will be necessary to submit a proposal or to perform the contract.

- **Public Interest** (FAR 6.302-7). If the agency head determines that it is not in the public interest in the particular acquisition concerned.

Justifications & Approvals (J&A)

Justifications must be in writing, and the contracting officer must certify the accuracy of the justifications and obtain the necessary approvals before proceeding.

Federal Acquisition Regulations (FAR)

Federal Acquisition Regulations apply to all federal contracting, and are used by all federal agencies when they purchase supplies or services. Every solicitation will cite these regulations.

Remember that not all the regulations listed in a solicitation document necessarily pertain to that particular bid. In many cases the complete list of regulations is listed, with any regulations that are relevant to this particular solicitation shown by an X marked next to them. The regulations not marked with an X are not relevant in that particular instance.

At times the regulation is printed out in its entirety, in the section called Clauses Incorporated in Full. At other times the regulations are simply mentioned, in the section called Clauses Incorporated by Reference. Even if a regulation is only referenced, it has the same legal weight as if it was printed in full. It is your responsibility to read and understand these regulations. You will find that many of them refer to standard business practices such as Equal Opportunity, Child Labor Laws, and so on.

The FAR is updated regularly, as necessary. You can download the complete current version of the regulations at the Website: *acquisition.gov/far/index.html*. (45)

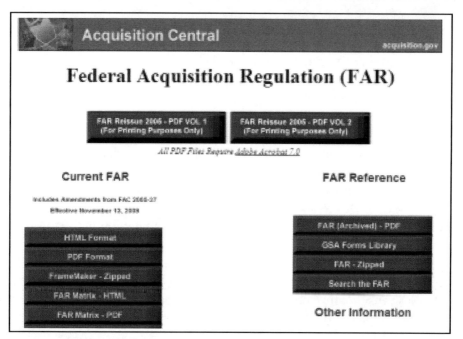

The FAR is divided into 52 subsections, each dealing with a specific aspect of federal acquisition law. Here is a listing of each of the 52 parts of the FAR, with a description of the scope of each section.

- **Part 1: The Federal Acquisition Regulation System.** Basic policies and general information about FAR.

- **Part 2: Definition of Words and Terms.** Definitions of frequently used words and terms found in the FAR.

- **Part 3: Improper Business Practices and Personal Conflicts of Interest.** Avoiding improper business practices and personal conflicts of interest.

- **Part 4: Administrative Matters.** The administrative aspects of contract execution, contractor-submitted paper documents, distribution, reporting, retention, and files.

- **Part 5: Publicizing Contract Actions.** Publicizing contract opportunities and award information.

- **Part 6: Competition Requirements.** Promoting full and open competition in the acquisition process.

- **Part 7: Acquisition Planning.** Developing acquisition plans, determining whether to use commercial or government resources, deciding whether it is more economical to lease equipment rather than purchase, determining whether functions are inherently governmental.

- **Part 8: Required Sources of Supplies and Services.** The acquisition of supplies and services from government supply sources, such as the Federal Prison Industries (UNICOR), the Committee for Purchase From People Who Are Blind or Severely Disabled (JWOD), the General Services Administration (GSA), as well as both Mandatory and Optional Federal Supply Schedules.
- **Part 9: Contractor Qualifications.** Contractor responsibilities; debarment, suspension, and ineligibility; Qualified Products; First Article Testing and Approval; Contractor Team Arrangements.
- **Part 10: Market Research.** Conducting market research to arrive at the most suitable approach to acquiring, distributing, and supporting supplies and services.
- **Part 11: Describing Agency Needs.** Policies and procedures for describing agency needs.
- **Part 12: Acquisition of Commercial Items.** Policies and procedures unique to the acquisition of commercial items. It implements the federal government's preference for the acquisition of commercial items (Federal Acquisition Streamlining Act of 1994) by establishing acquisition policies more closely resembling those of the commercial marketplace and encouraging the acquisition of commercial items and components.
- **Part 13: Simplified Acquisition Procedures.** Acquiring supplies and services when the aggregate amount does not exceed the Simplified Acquisition Threshold. Special authority to acquire commercial items exceeding this threshold but not exceeding $5.5 million ($11 million for certain acquisitions), including options.
- **Part 14: Sealed Bidding.** The basic requirements of contracting for supplies and services by sealed bidding. Includes the information to be included in the solicitation, procedures for the submission of bids, requirements for opening and evaluating bids and awarding contracts, and procedures for two-step sealed bidding.
- **Part 15: Contracting by Negotiation.** The policies and procedures that govern both Competitive and Non-Competitive negotiated acquisitions. A contract awarded using other than sealed bidding procedures is a negotiated contract.
- **Part 16: Types of Contracts.** Describes the types of contracts that may be used in acquisitions. Policies, procedures, and guidance for selecting a contract type appropriate to the circumstances of the acquisition.
- **Part 17: Special Contracting Methods.** Acquiring supplies and services through special contracting methods, including multi-year contracting, options, and leader company contracting.
- **Part 18: Emergency Acquisitions.** Identifies certain flexibilities that may be used to streamline the standard process, in the event of an emergency acquisition.

- **Part 19: Small Business Programs.** Implements sections of the Small Business Act as well as applicable sections of other relevant acts. It covers eligibility, the roles of executive agencies and the SBA, and the various Set-Aside programs (the subcontracting assistance program, the 8(a) program, women-owned small businesses, Price Evaluation Adjustments for small disadvantaged businesses, Price Evaluation Preference for HUB-Zone small businesses, the Small Disadvantaged Business Participation Program, veteran-owned small business concerns, and Sole Source awards to HUB-Zone small business and service-disabled veteran-owned small business concerns).

- **Part 20: Reserved.**

- **Part 21: Reserved.**

- **Part 22: Application of Labor Laws to Government Acquisitions.** General policies regarding contractor labor relations as they pertain to the acquisition process. Policies and procedures for implementing these laws.

- **Part 23: Environment, Energy and Water Efficiency, Renewable Energy Technologies, Occupational Safety, and Drug-Free Workplace.** Ensuring a drug-free workplace, and protecting and improving the quality of the environment via pollution control, efficient energy and water use, renewable energy, acquisition of energy- and water-efficient products and services, acquisition of environmentally preferable products and products that use recovered materials, and requiring contractors to identify hazardous materials.

- **Part 24: Protection of Privacy and Freedom of Information.** The Privacy Act of 1974 and the Freedom of Information Act.

- **Part 25: Foreign Acquisition.** Acquiring foreign supplies, services, and construction materials. The Buy American Act, trade agreements, and other laws and regulations.

- **Part 26: Other Socioeconomic Programs.** The Indian Incentive Program; Disaster or Emergency Assistance Activities; Historically Black Colleges/ Universities and Minority Institutions.

- **Part 27: Patents, Data, and Copyrights.** Policies, procedures, and contract clauses pertaining to patents. Ensuring that agencies develop coverage for Rights in Data and Copyrights.

- **Part 28: Bonds and Insurance.** Obtaining financial protection against losses. Bid guarantees, bonds, alternative payment protections, security for bonds, and insurance.

- **Part 29: Taxes.** Using tax clauses in contracts (including foreign contracts), asserting immunity or exemption from taxes, and obtaining tax refunds. An explanation of federal, state, and local taxes on certain supplies and services, and the applicability of such taxes to the federal government. It is for general information only—it does not present the full scope of tax laws and regulations.

- **Part 30: Cost Accounting Standards Administration.** The policies and procedures for applying the Cost Accounting Standards Board rules and regulations to negotiated contracts and subcontracts. This part does not apply to sealed bid contracts or to any contract with a small business concern.

- **Part 31: Contract Cost Principles and Procedures.** Cost principles and procedures for pricing contracts, subcontracts, and modifications whenever cost analysis is performed. The determination, negotiation, or allowance of costs when required by a contract clause.

- **Part 32: Contract Financing.** Payment methods, including partial payments and progress payments based on percentage or stage of completion; loan guarantees, advance payments, and progress payments based on costs; administration of debts to the government arising out of contracts; contract funding, including the use of contract clauses limiting costs or funds; assignment of claims to aid in private financing; selected payment clauses; financing of purchases of commercial items; performance-based payments and Electronic Funds Transfer (EFT) payments.

- **Part 33: Protests, Disputes, and Appeals.** Policies and procedures for filing protests and for processing contract disputes and appeals.

- **Part 34: Major System Acquisitions.** Policies and procedures for use in acquiring major systems, and the use of an Earned Value Management System in acquisitions designated as major acquisitions. Subpart 34.1 describes the procedures for testing, qualification, and use of industrial resources that have been manufactured or developed with assistance provided under the Defense Production Act, which allows various forms of government assistance to encourage expansion of production capacity and supply of industrial resources essential to national defense.

- **Part 35: Research and Development Contracting.** Policies and procedures of special application to research and development (R&D) contracting.

- **Part 36: Construction and Architect & Engineer Contracts.** Policies and procedures peculiar to contracting for construction and architect-engineer services. It includes requirements for using certain clauses, and standard forms that apply also to contracts for dismantling, demolition, or removal of improvements.

- **Part 37: Service Contracting.** Policies and procedures specific to the acquisition and management of services by contract. This part applies to all contracts and orders for services, regardless of the contract type or kind of service being acquired. This part requires the use of performance-based acquisitions for services to the maximum extent practicable and prescribes policies and procedures for use of performance-based acquisition methods.

- **Part 38: Federal Supply Schedule Contracting.** Policies and procedures for contracting for supplies and services under the Federal Supply Schedule program, which is directed and managed by the General Services Administration. GSA may delegate certain responsibilities to other agencies (for example, GSA has delegated authority to the Department of Veterans Affairs to procure medical supplies under the VA Federal Supply Schedules Program). The Department of Defense's schedule for military items.

- **Part 39: Acquisition of Information Technology.** Policies and procedures for use in acquiring Information Technology, including financial management systems.

- **Part 40: Reserved.**

- **Part 41: Acquisition of Utility Services.** Policies, procedures, and contract format for the acquisition of utility services.

- **Part 42: Contract Administration and Audit Services.** Policies and procedures for assigning and performing contract administration and contract audit services.

- **Part 43: Contract Modifications.** Preparing and processing contract modifications for all types of contracts. This regulation does not apply to orders that do not otherwise change the terms of contracts (for example, delivery orders under indefinite-delivery contracts), or to modifications for extraordinary contractual relief.

- **Part 44: Subcontracting Policies and Procedures.** Policies and procedures for subcontracts; review, evaluation, and approval of contractors' purchase systems.

- **Part 45: Government Property.** Policies and procedures for providing government property to contractors; contractors' use and management of government property; reporting, redistributing, and disposing of contractor inventory.

- **Part 46: Quality Assurance.** Ensuring that supplies and services acquired under government contract conform to the contract's quality and quantity requirements. Included are inspection, acceptance, warranty, and other measures associated with quality requirements.

- **Part 47: Transportation.** Applying transportation and traffic management considerations in the acquisition of supplies, and acquiring transportation or transportation-related services by contract methods other than bills of lading, transportation requests, transportation warrants, and similar transportation forms.

- **Part 48: Value Engineering.** Using and administering value engineering techniques in contracts.

- **Part 49: Termination of Contracts.** Complete or partial termination of contracts for the convenience of the government or for default. Contract clauses relating to termination and excusable delay. Instructions for using termination and settlement forms.

- **Part 50: Extraordinary Contractual Actions.** Entering into, amending, or modifying contracts in order to facilitate the national defense under the extraordinary emergency authority granted by Public Law 85-804 (50 U.S.C. 1431-1434) and Executive Order 10789.

- **Part 51:** Use of Government Sources by Contractors. The use by contractors of government supply sources and interagency fleet management system vehicles and related services.

- **Part 52:** Scope of Part. Using provisions and clauses in solicitations and/or contracts. Sets forth the solicitation provisions and contract clauses prescribed by this regulation, and presents a matrix listing the FAR provisions and clauses applicable to each principal contract type and/or purpose (for example, fixed-price supply and cost-reimbursement research and development).

Some Commonly Listed FAR Regulations

- FAR 52.212-1: Instructions to Offerors—Commercial Items.
- FAR 52.212-2: Evaluation—Commercial Items.
- FAR 52.212-3: Offeror Representations and Certifications—Commercial Items.
- FAR 52.212-4: Contract Terms and Conditions—Commercial Items.
- FAR 52.212-5: Contract Terms and Conditions Required to Implement Statutes or Executive Orders—Commercial Items.
- FAR 52.29-6: Notice of Total Small Business Set-Aside.
- FAR 52.222-3: Convict Labor.
- FAR 52.222-19: Child Labor—Cooperation With Authorities and Remedies.
- FAR 52.222-21: Prohibition of Segregated Facilities.
- FAR 52.222-26: Equal Opportunity.
- FAR 52.222-35: Equal Opportunity for Special Disabled Veterans, Veterans of the Vietnam Era, and Other Eligible Veterans.
- FAR 52.222-36: Affirmative Action for Workers With Disabilities.
- FAR 52.222-37: Employment Reports on Special Disabled Veterans, Veterans of the Vietnam Era, and Other Eligible Veterans.
- FAR 52.225-13: Restrictions on Certain Foreign Purchases.
- FAR 52.232-36: Payment by Third Party (May 1999)—An Award Can Only Be Made to Contractors Registered in Central Contractor Registration.
- DFARS 252.204-7004 Alt A: Central Contractor Registration.
- DFARS 252.212-7001: Contract Terms and Conditions Required to Implement Statutes or Executive Orders Applicable to Defense Acquisitions of Commercial Items.
- DFARS 252.225-7036: Buy American Act—Free Trade Agreements—Balance of Payments Program.

FAR-Site

In addition to the FAR, each agency can issue its own supplements. For example, the Department of Defense's Supplemental Regulations are known as the DFARS; the Army's regulations are known as AFARS; and so on. At the FAR-Site Website—***http://farsite.hill.af.mil*** (46)—you can view all these supplemental regulations. Use the FARSearch tab at the top of the page to search for a particular regulation by keyword, by title, or by regulation number. The following are some relevant federal regulations acronyms and which group uses them.

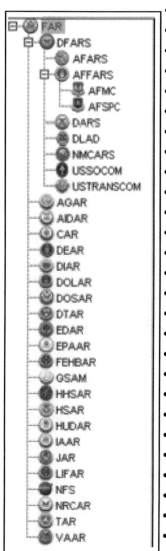

- DFARS—Dept. of Defense Supplements
- AFARS—Army FAR Supplements
- AFFARS—Air Force FAR Supplements
- AFMC—Air Force Material Command
- AFSPC—Air Force Space Command
- DARS—Defense Information Systems Agency
- DLAD—Defense Logistics Acquisition Directive
- NMCARS—Navy Marine Corp Acquisition Regulation
- USSOCOM—U.S. Special Operations Command
- USTRANSCOM—U.S. Transportation Command
- AGAR—Dept. of Agriculture
- AIDAR—Agency for International Development
- CAR—Dept. of Commerce
- DEAR—Dept. of Energy
- DIAR—Dept. of Interior
- DOLAR—Dept. of Labor
- DOSAR—Dept. of State
- DTAR—Dept. of Treasury
- EDAR—Dept. of Education
- EPAAR—Environmental Protection Agency
- FEHBAR—Office of Personnel Management
- GSAM—General Services Administration
- HHSAR—Dept. of Health and Human Services
- HSAR—Dept. of Homeland Security
- HUDAR—Dept. of Housing Development
- IAAR—U.S. Broadcasting Board of Governors
- JAR—Dept. of Justice

- LIFAR—Office of Personnel Management
- NFS—National Aeronautics and Space Agency (NASA)
- NRCAR—Nuclear Regulatory Commission
- TAR—Dept. of Transportation
- VAAR—Veterans Affairs

The Contracting Officer

The contracting officer is always listed in the solicitation as the government's point of contact, including a name, phone and fax number, and e-mail address. This individual is your best friend! You can ask contracting officers anything about a solicitation. It is their function to assist you in any area of it. They will have the answers to your questions, or they will tell you where to go to acquire the information. These are highly trained, professional, courteous, knowledgeable, hardworking individuals, and should be treated accordingly. The Procurement Contracting Officer (PCO) may be assisted by an Administrative Contracting Officer (ACO).

Additional Resources

Back on the FedBizOpps homepage, you can find links to other relevant contracting sites, as well as a User Guide and demonstration video to help you become more familiar with the site.

- **Frequently Asked Questions** (FAQ) and the new **Federal Service Desk** can help you with many questions about how to use the FedBizOpps site. The Federal Service Desk was added to the site in June 2009.
- The **Recovery.gov** Website is the government's official Website providing information about the 2009 American Recovery Act (ARRA). More information can be found at *www.whitehouse.gov/Recovery*. (47)
- For details of the reporting requirements go to: *www.FederalReporting.gov*. (48)
- The **Business Partner Network** Website gives you access to several key databases across Federal Agencies: *www.bpn.gov*. (49)
- The **Central Contractor Registration** (CCR) and **Online Reps & Cert Application** (ORCA) Websites were discussed in detail in Chapter One.
- The **Federal Agency Business Forecasts** site allows you access to individual agency sites, where you may search for forecasts of future procurements: *acquisition.gov/comp/procurement_forecasts/index.html*. (50)
- At the **Federal Assets Sales** site you can buy new, seized, and surplus government merchandise. Items may be available via online auction, at a fixed price, or via public auction, sealed bid, or contact with a real estate agent. *www.usa.gov*. (51)

- The **Federal Grants** site has information on more than 1,000 grant programs, with access to approximately $400 billion in annual awards. By registering once on this site, your organization can apply for grants from 26 different Federal agencies. *www.grants.gov*. (52)
- **USA.Gov** is the U.S. government's official site, which is a wonderful source of information about federal government contracting, online information, and resources: *www.usa.gov*. (51)
- The **Minority Business Development Agency**, a part of the U.S. Department of Commerce, was created specifically to foster the establishment and growth of minority-owned businesses in America. *www.mbda.gov*. (53)
- The **Small Business Administration's SUB-Net** Website allows you to search for subcontracting opportunities. *www.sba.gov/subnet*. (54)
- At the **Integrated Acquisition Environment** (IAE) site you can learn more about regulations, systems, resources, opportunities, and training. *www.acquisition.gov*. (55)

Other Programs

Section 508

The **Section 508** regulation requires that government agencies purchase electronic and information technology goods and services that are accessible by persons with disabilities. A Product Accessibility Template allows you to describe how your particular product or service complies with this regulation. More information on Section 508 is available at: *www.section508.gov*. **(56)**

Hurricane and Disaster Response Contracting

During times of natural disasters, many products and services are needed for relief, cleanup, and restoration. If you supply products or services that may be needed to support this effort, and you wish to be considered as a potential source of supply, you should send an e-mail to **Katrinasupport@gsa.gov**. The contracting officers working with FEMA during the hurricane relief efforts are using the General Service Administration's e-library, GSA Advantage, and GSA e-Buy to find the products and services they need to support Hurricane Katrina relief and restoration efforts.

A Word on Acronyms and Definitions

Federal agencies LOVE using acronyms or abbreviations, which can sometimes be quite confusing! For further clarification you may wish to use these Websites. If in doubt, ask the contracting officer! **A longer list of commonly used acronyms can be found in the Appendix of this book.**

- **Defense Acquisition University:** *www.dau.mil*. (57) At this site, click on the Publications tab—there is a DoD Information Technology Acronyms link on that page. Also, under General Publications there is a link to download the latest Defense Acquisition Acronyms and Terms.

- **Defense Supply Center Columbus Acronyms.** Search for DoD acronyms at this site: *www.dscc.dla.mil/search/acronym*. (58)

- **Navy Electronic Contracting Online (NECO).** At the very bottom of the NECO home page, *www.neco.navy.mil*, (59) is a link to commonly used abbreviations.

- **AcronymFinder.** Commercial site: *www.acronymfinder.com*. (60)

- **Census Bureau Acronyms.** Frequently used acronyms at this site: *www.census.gov/procur/www/acronyms.html*. (61)

- **DOD Dictionary of Military Terms.** Search for military terms and acronyms here: *www.dtic.mil/doctrine/dod_dictionary*. (62)

- **Environmental Protection Agency.** The Glossary of Contracting-Related Terms can be found here: *www.epa.gov/oam/glossary.htm*. (63)

Help!

If you have any questions about this chapter, we would be happy to try to help you. Go to our Website, *www.sell2gov.com*, and at the Contact tab you can send us an e-mail with your questions. Please put "Definitive Guide" in the subject line.

Chapter 3

Electronic Quoting: The Defense Logistics Agency's Internet Bid Board System (DIBBS) Website

In this chapter we will take a close look at the **Defense Logistics Agency's Internet Bid Board System**, also known as **DIBBS**. At this site, you will be able to search for sales opportunities and submit your quotes electronically. This site contains many smaller sales opportunities, and is a great way for you to get your feet wet with federal contracting. Though many of these sales opportunities are for small amounts, together they can add up to a big opportunity for your company!

Many of these sales opportunities are listed and awarded electronically, so that once you have completed a few of these bids, you will find that much of the work is repeated from bid to bid.

This chapter takes you step by step through searching the site, finding sales opportunities, and submitting your quote online. We discuss the **Procurement Automated Contract Evaluation (PACE)** program, **Approved** part numbers, the **Master Solicitation** document, and the **Automated Best Value System (ABVS).**

This chapter also discusses the **cFolders** system, which allows you access to technical data such as drawings and specifications, as well as the **Quality Shelf Life** program and the Defense Logistics Agency's commitment to **environmental** or **"green" purchasing programs**.

Remember that not every sales opportunity requires you to know about all of these programs, but you may come across some of them as you begin to search this site.

In this chapter we also show you where you can find information on the **purchasing history** of an item—giving you valuable information about the company that supplied the item in the past and its unit delivered price, *before* you submit your offer! Next we take you step by step through the **online quoting system** so that you can feel confident in submitting your offer electronically. Finally, we show you how to track a solicitation, from when you first submit your offer until the final award is posted.

The Department of Defense Internet Bid Board System—DIBBS
Website: *www.dibbs.bsm.dla.mil*. (64)

Vendor Registration

You may search for opportunities at this site without registering, and may decide not to in the beginning, but if you wish to submit quotes electronically you will need to register and receive a login account and password. From the home page, click the Vendor Registration link to begin the registration process. At the registration page you will also have the option to receive notification of solicitations for specific Federal Supply Codes (FSCs), National Stock Numbers (NSNs), or Approved Manufacturers that you select in your profile.

Searching the Site

At the **Solicitations** Tab you may wish to begin by searching for **Requests for Quote** (RFQ), which are opportunities for less than the Simplified Acquisition Threshold ($100,000), which are available for secure online electronic quoting. Later on you may also choose to search for larger **Requests for Proposals** (RFP) and **Invitations for Bids** (IFB) from this tab, once you become more familiar with the site.

Remember that any solicitations estimated to be more than $25,000 will *also* be posted at the Federal Business Opportunities (FedBizOpps) Website.

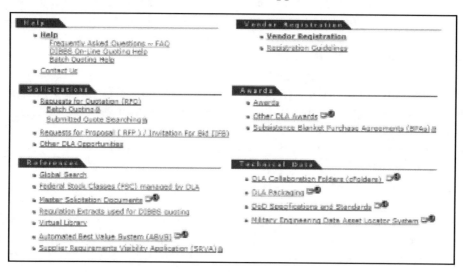

Click on the **Requests for Quotation** (RFQ) link to begin searching.

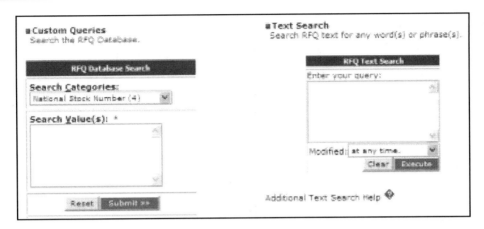

You may wish to begin your search using the **Database Search** box on the left. The drop-down **Search Categories** button allows you various search options:

- Search by **National Stock Number** (NSN) if you have a particular item with a designated NSN.
- Search by **Federal Supply Code** (FSC) to find all the opportunities under a particular general category; for example, 7210: Household Furnishings.

13	1730-00-087-4504 BLANKET, HEAT, DRAG CH	Tech Docs	SPM8RC-10-Q-0101	Q quote		0022431937 QTY: 1
14	2995-00-719-4529 BLANKET, VALVE	None	SPM4A7-09-Q-8317	Q quote		0023422447 QTY: 4
15	3439-01-217-4873 BLANKET, WELDING	None	SPM8E3-08-T-4748	Q quote		0019901920 QTY: 4
16	4210-01-324-2734 BLANKET, FIRE	None	SPM8RH-10-Q-0118	Q quote		0023898807 QTY: 170
17	4820-01-052-5319 BLANKET, INSULATION-	None	SPM7M2-10-T-0785	Q quote		0024840567 QTY: 12
18	6532-01-333-0695 BLANKET, BURNRELIEF	None	SPM3DS-10-T-A260	Q quote		0024099864 QTY: 2

Search by **Solicitation** or **Purchase Request** number if you are looking for a particular document.

Search by **Nomenclature** if you wish to see *all* solicitations with a particular word in the main description section; for example, "blanket." Use the * symbol to widen your search. Notice how choosing this option lists many different types of blankets in various FSC categories—a Heat Blanket Valve for aircraft engines (FSC 1730); a Welding Blanket (FSC 3439); a Fire Blanket (FSC 4210); and a Burn Relief blanket (FSC 6532).

Search by **Approved CAGE** code or **Approved Part Number** if you are a distributor or supplier of items from larger manufacturers. For example, perhaps you are a distributor for Motorola radios and accessories—then use the BINCS Website (*www.bpn.gov/bincs* [31]) to find the appropriate CAGE code and search.

6140-01-568-4830 BATTERY, STORAGE Mil-Spec	Tech Docs "Spec/Stnd Only"	SPM7LA-10-T-0736 Q		0024882409 QTY: 88
6140-01-568-4830 BATTERY, STORAGE Mil-Spec	Tech Docs "Spec/Stnd Only"	SPM7LA-10-T-0619 Q		0024751726 QTY: 200
6515-01-508-9632 HOLSTER, PORTABLE RADI	None	SPM2D1-09-Q-0224 Q		0019913054 QTY: 12
6515-01-508-9632 HOLSTER, PORTABLE RADI	None	SPM2D1-09-Q-0224 Q		0021592087 QTY: 12

You may use the **Text Search** option to search for any instances of a particular word or phrase either in the main description or in the body of the text. This can be useful if you wish to widen your search parameters, but can also come up with a lot of irrelevant options! In addition, the results of this search are listed only by the solicitation number, so you have to open and scroll through each one to see if it is relevant.

~Once Upon a Time~

A client sold truck parts, and he searched the DIBBS site for CAGE codes of the various companies he could supply. In the first year he did $500,000 in sales to the Dept. of Defense; in the second year he did $1 million; in the third year he did $2 million.

He did it by assigning one individual to do nothing but electronic bidding. This person submitted about 25 bids a day and was awarded about 28 percent of them.

By the second year buyers called the client's company to place orders because it had a good report card.

You may also wish to **Narrow Your Search** by the following categories.

- If you choose to see only **Items With Bid Sets** this will eliminate those opportunities for which no drawings or specifications are listed—that is, for items for which the agency is looking for a particular manufacturer or has restricted the bidding to only certain pre-approved manufacturers.
- **Fast Award** bids have an estimated value of $2,500 or less, and they may be awarded *before* the return date on any automated solicitation. Because of this, you

should submit your quote as soon as possible, rather than waiting until the due date.

- You may limit your search to only those solicitation documents that are **set aside** for Small Businesses, Businesses located in a HUB-Zone, Service Disabled Veteran-Owned Small Businesses, or a combination of all set-asides.

- Auto-IDPOs are Indefinite Delivery, Indefinite Quantity (IDIQ) awards that are estimated to be valued at below the simplified acquisition thresh-old ($100,000). Auto-IDPO uses pricing logic and other automated filters to make fully auto-mated IDPO awards. These awards do not specify an exact quantity of supplies other than a minimum quantity. Auto-IDPOs are awarded with a base year and usually one option year.

- Click on the RFP/IFB Database option to search for Requests for Proposals and Invitations for Bids, which are large purchases with an estimated value of $100,000 or greater. Remember that these op-portunities will *also* be posted at the Federal Business Opportunities (FedBizOpps) Website, because they are estimated to be greater than $25,000.

- Clicking on the **Other DLA Opportunities** option simply takes you back either to the RFQ quot-ing section for opportunities up to $100,000, or to RFP/IFB oppor-tunities over $100,000.

Understanding the Solicitation Numbering System

It may not be absolutely necessary to understand the way solicitations are numbered, but knowing how the system works can give you some insights into the process.

Most importantly, the first four digits of a Defense Logistics Agency solicitation number is a site identifier:

SPM1   Defense Supply Center, Philadelphia—Clothing and Textiles

SPM2   Defense Supply Center, Philadelphia—Medical

SPM3   Defense Supply Center, Philadelphia—Subsistence

SPM4   Defense Supply Center, Richmond

SPM5   Defense Supply Center, Philadelphia

SPM7   Defense Supply Center, Columbus

SPM8   Defense Supply Center, Philadelphia—Construction and Equipment

This is followed by the last two digits of the fiscal year in which the solicitation number was assigned.

A "T" or "U" in the ninth position of a solicitation number indicates that the RFQ was generated by an automated system. Once inventory of a particular item reaches a predetermined minimum level, the agency's computer will automatically generate a purchase request. These are eligible for award under the automated Procurement Automated Contract Evaluation (PACE) system. An "R" in the ninth position indicates either a Request for Proposal or an Invitation for Bid (RFP/IFB).

How Solicitations Are Awarded

Automated Awards (PACE)

The Procurement Automated Contract Evaluation or PACE program is an automated system that evaluates bids and makes an award electronically.

If you have received an automated award, you will find this notice in the solicitation document:

```
THIS BUY IS A CANDIDATE FOR AUTOMATED AWARD.  ALL QUOTES MUST BE
SUBMITTED VIA THE DLA INTERNET BID BOARD SYSTEM (DIBBS) AT
https://www.dibbs.bsm.dla.mil.

MICRO-PURCHASE QUOTES MAY BE AWARDED PRIOR TO RETURN DATE
UNLESS THIS SOLICITATION HAS BEEN DESIGNATED FOR AUCTIONING.


DFARS 252.225-7001, BUY AMERICAN ACT--BALANCE OF PAYMENTS
PROGRAM, APPLIES TO ALL QUOTES ABOVE THE MICRO-PURCHASE
THRESHOLD.

DESTINATION INSPECTION REQUIRED - FAR 52.246-1 APPLIES.

THIS BUY IS NOT FAST PAY

NO VARIATION IN QUANTITY ALLOWED
```

The program uses pricing and other automated filters to make fully automated awards valued at $100,000 or less. Everything is done electronically: The solicitation is issued, offers are evaluated, and contracts are awarded. PACE only considers "qualified quotes" for award. Qualified quotes are in exact compliance with the requirement stated in the solicitation, and must be submitted via the DLA Internet Bid Board System. PACE evaluates all qualified quotes on the basis of price alone and does not consider quantity price breaks. In the event of a tie between qualified quotes, the award will be based on the following order of precedence:

- First: A domestic end-product offer over a non-qualifying-country end-product offer.
- Second: A small business offer over a large business offer.
- Third: An offer with the shortest delivery.
- Fourth: The first quote submitted.

Manual Awards

If the solicitation initially stated that it was a candidate for PACE evaluation but now PACE is unable to make price-reasonableness or contractor-responsibility determinations, then the quote will be evaluated and awarded manually. In this case the contracting officer may consider quantity price breaks offered without further solicitation or discussion. If the requirement is evaluated manually, then price, delivery, and past performance will be considered.

Automated Indefinite Delivery Purchase Order (IDPO) Awards

This is a part of the Defense Logistics Agency's e-Commerce system that creates Indefinite Delivery Indefinite Quantity (IDIQ) awards below the simplified acquisition threshold ($100,000). Auto-IDPO uses pricing logic and other automated filters to make fully-automated and buyer assisted automated IDPO awards. These awards do not specify a firm quantity of supplies other than a minimum quantity. Auto-IDPOs are awarded with a Base Year and one option year. You *must* submit your quote via DIBBS. Quotes received by mail, fax, or e-mail will not be considered for award.

Bid Types

Bids Without Exception are quotes that submit pricing and delivery for all quantity ranges, destinations, and option years, and are in *exact compliance* with the solicitation requirements. That is, they offer the exact product, the quote is valid for a minimum of 90 days, and they comply with the terms listed on the solicitation for packaging, FOB point, source inspection, and allowable quantity variance.

Alternate Bids offer an item other than the exact approved item cited in the procurement item description (PID).

Bids With Exception are quotes that do not submit pricing and delivery for all quantity ranges, destinations, and option years as solicited, or quotes that take exception to solicitation requirements for minimum-quote valid days, packaging, FOB point, source inspection, and quantity variance allowed. These types of bid are considered "bids with exception" and will *not* be considered for automated award.

Approved and Alternate Part Number Bids come into play if the solicitation lists an approved manufacturer—you must provide that manufacturer's Commercial and Government Entity (CAGE) code and part number. But if you wish to supply your own part and be recognized as an approved source, you will have to submit your bid as an Alternate Offer/Bid. For solicitations that are eligible for award under the PACE automated system, alternate offers will not be considered for award, but they may be submitted for acceptance for future procurements. For Indefinite Delivery Purchase Orders, you may bid an Alternate Product, and you must submit all technical data to the buyer.

The References Tab

Global Search

This link allows you to search for a specific solicitation number, NSN number, or purchase number, if you are not sure whether it is located in the RFQ, RFP, or Awards database.

> **References**
> - Global Search
> - Federal Stock Classes (FSC) managed by DLA
> - Master Solicitation Documents
> - Regulation Extracts used for DIBBS quoting
> - Virtual Library
> - Automated Best Value System (ABVS)
> - Supplier Requirements Visibility Application (SRVA)

FSC Classes Managed By DLA

This link gives you a complete listing of all the FSC codes that are managed by the Defense Logistics Agency (DLA).

Master Solicitation Document

You will need to download this very important document, which gives exact details of the regulations that apply to the contract, terms and conditions, and so on. This document is used for Request for Quotes (RFQs) and Purchase Orders for automated Business System Modernization (BSM) acquisitions valued up to $100,000 for each of the Defense Supply Centers (Columbus, Philadelphia, and Richmond). You will need to read the document carefully in order to understand the solicitation, evaluation, and award process. Each provision is provided in full text in Part I of this Master Solicitation.

The Master Solicitation document is updated from time to time to reflect changes to regulations or acquisition policies. Do not assume, once you have downloaded a copy, that it will remain effective. Updates are identified by a date and revision number, and changes are highlighted in each revision.

Part I contains important information about this document, the Internet Bid Board System, and the Procurement Automated Contract Evaluation (PACE) system.

Part II contains information about Indefinite Delivery Purchase Order (IDPO) contracts, which do not specify a firm quantity of supplies other than a minimum quantity. In these cases delivery orders will be issued during the period of the contract.

Part III contains the clauses, provisions, or notices that apply to automated solicitations and orders. Web links are provided to the Federal Acquisition Regulations (FAR) as well as to the Defense Federal Acquisition Supplement (DFARS) and others. Each center's clause list is also provided. If clauses, provisions, or notices are incorporated by reference, and the full text is not provided, they still have the same force and effect as if they were given in full.

Regulation Extracts Used in DIBBS Quoting

This link contains a list of the Federal Acquisition Regulations (FAR) and the Dept. of Defense Supplemental Regulations (DFARS) that apply.

Virtual Library

Links to regulations, supplements, and more.

Automated Best Value System (ABVS)

This is a computerized system that collects information on how well a vendor has fulfilled the terms of any previous contracts, and converts that into a numeric score. The contracting officer will use this information as an additional evaluation factor when making Best Value Award decisions. Your ABVS score is a combination of both delivery and quality evaluation. If you have no performance history your score will be neutral—that is, neither favorable nor unfavorable. We also discussed ABVS scores in Chapter 2.

Supplier Requirements Visibility Application (SRVA)

This link contains information on the agency's future anticipated requirements. You will need to log in with your user ID and password to access the information, which is refreshed every month. Although these are not binding requirements, they can give you a great deal of valuable information about upcoming opportunities—up to 24 months ahead! You may choose to search by a number of criteria, including NSN or FSC code.

Technical Data

Collaboration Folders (cFolders)—Drawings and Technical Documents

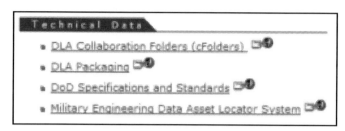

4710-00-001-3670 TUBEASSEMBLY, VENT	None	SPM4A5-09-T-D887 𝒬 ssts		0023484083 QTY: 2
4710-00-010-4038 TUBE, HYDRAULIC BUFFER	Tech Docs	SPM7M4-10-Q-0147 𝒬 ssts		0022775748 QTY: 56
4710-00-010-4038 TUBE, HYDRAULIC BUFFER	Tech Docs	SPM7M4-10-Q-0147 𝒬 ssts		0023383764 QTY: 56
4710-00-011-0848 TUBEASSEMBLY, METAL	None	SPM7M4-10-T-C337 𝒬 ssts		00246362l0 QTY: 4

When you search for opportunities you may notice a **Tech Docs** icon, which will link to the cFolders site, where you may download drawings, specifications, military standards, or any other technical documents that are available for this solicitation.

Restricted Drawings

Sometimes drawings and Technical Data Packages have restrictions on who may view them or how they may be distributed. This was discussed in Chapter 2.

Viewing Drawings

Drawings can be in several different formats, and you may find that you will need to download specific viewer software in order to view these drawings. You are probably familiar with Adobe Acrobat and Microsoft Word, Excel, and PowerPoint, but you may be less familiar with other viewing software.

You can, at the Army Single Face to Industry site (ASFI), go to the Acquisition Tool Set—Web Browser Plugins link to download several different viewers, including the **MaxReader** (for .max, .cal, and .svd file formats) as well as the **ImageR** viewer (.c4 file format).

Here is a typical drawing list in the cFolders file.

Folder Contents									Download Solicitation		
Document Number	Download	CAGE Code	Document Data Code	Drawing Revision	Number of Sheets	Rights in Data	License Agreement	Distribution Statement	Export Control	Foreign Secure
☐ 12369004	12369004	19207	DD	G	0001	U		A	N	N
☐ 11618937	11618937	19204	PS	A	0001	U		C	N	N
☐ 11618937	11618937	19200	DD	C	0001	U		C	N	N

As you can see, in this particular folder there are three documents in all. Each of these documents contains only a single page, but in other cases they could contain several pages each. The table shows Commercial and Government Entity (CAGE) codes and document types (DD refers to Drawings; QS is used for Quality Assurance Provisions; PS refers to Packaging instructions, and so on). The Revision numbers are also listed. You can also see that in this case the documents are not Export Controlled, or Foreign Secure, and that no Non-Disclosure License Agreements are in effect.

We also discussed finding Drawings and Technical Data Packages in Chapter 2.

Still can't find what you are looking for?

If the drawings you are looking for do not seem to be available, you might begin by checking whether the solicitation is a Request for Proposal (RFP) or a Long Term Contract. (You can tell this by looking for an "R" in the ninth position of the solicitation number.)

The Defense Supply Centers in Columbus (DSCC) and Philadelphia (DSCP) will supply the information on a CD by e-mail request:

- DSCC: **CDDWGS@dscc.dla.mil**.
- DSCP: **dscpdrawings@dla.mil**.

DLA Packaging

We discuss packaging in more detail in Chapter 7, "Fulfilling the Terms of your Contract."

DOD Specifications and Standards

The Acquisition Streamlining and Standardization Information System (ASSIST) allows you access to DOD-wide standardization documents: ***https://assist.daps.dla.mil***. (27)

Military Engineering Data Asset Locator System (MEDALS)

This program is the Dept. of Defense's central locator system for engineering drawings. The system can quickly determine the location of engineering drawings or documents, and is restricted to DOD staff.

The Quality Shelf Life Program

Certain items that can deteriorate over time need special handling. The Defense Logistics Agency's Quality Shelf Life Program controls those items in order to ensure that when they are purchased they are within appropriate shelf-life dates.

Typical shelf-life items include food, medicines, batteries, paints, sealants, adhesives, film, tires, chemicals, packaged petroleum products, hoses/belts, mission-critical o-rings, and Nuclear/Biological/Chemical equipment and clothing.

The term *shelf life* refers to the total period of time that an item may remain in the wholesale and retail storage system, and still remain usable. Time is calculated beginning with the date of manufacture, cure, assembly, or (for subsistence items) pack. If an item is controlled by this program it will be assigned a specific shelf-life code, with shelf-life ranging from one month (Code A) to 20 years (Code Z).Type I items have a definite non-extendible period of shelf life, ending with an expiration date. Type II items have an assigned shelf life that may be extended after inspection or testing. It will be given an inspection or testing date.

The Dept. of Defense and the FDA (Food and Drug Administration) also has a program specifically for medical material, drugs, and biologicals, called the **Shelf-Life Extension Program (SLEP)**. This program aims to defer drug replacement costs for date-sensitive medical material by extending their useful life beyond the manufacturer's original expiration date. All testing for extensions is done at FDA test facilities.

Website: *www.shelflife.hq.dla.mil*. (65)

Environmental "Green" Purchasing Programs

The Defense Logistics Agency's Green Procurement Program

This program encourages the purchase of products that have a lesser or reduced effect on human health and the environment, compared to other similar products. The DLA then assigns Environmental Attribute Codes (EACs) to these items.

These programs mainly come under the authority of the Environmental Protection Agency, the Dept. of Energy, and the Dept. of Agriculture (for bio-based products).

Energy Conservation

In March 2009 the Dept. of Energy issued a final rule that requires federal agencies to purchase energy-compliant products (Energy Star products), subject to certain exclusions and exceptions. The new regulation applies to products and equipment purchased through any type of procurement, whether they are purchased directly (for example, from commercial sources), or indirectly (such as when items are purchased as part of construction, renovation, or services contracts). This regulation also applies to purchases via government credit cards. An exception may be made if the agency finds that an Energy Star product is not cost-effective or that no product is available that meets the agency's requirements. Exceptions are also made for combat or combat-related missions. The regulations cover approximately 60 categories, including Lighting, Commercial and Industrial Equipment, Food Service Equipment, Office Equipment, Home Electronics, Appliances, Residential Equipment, Plumbing, and Construction Products. Federal agencies are also required to procure devices that use no more than one watt of energy in the standby power consuming mode. See the Energy Star Website at *www.energystar.gov*. (66)

Recovered Materials

The Environmental Protection Agency (EPA) issues a list of products designated as Environmentally Preferable, including products containing a certain percentage of recovered or recycled materials. This is known as the EPA's Comprehensive Procurement Guidelines (CPG). Federal agencies must buy products containing recovered materials if they spend more than $10,000 a year on that item. Exceptions can be made if the cost is unreasonable, if there is not enough competition in the marketplace, if the items cannot be delivered in a reasonable time, or if the items do not meet the agency's specifications. The agency is responsible for implementing the program, and for obtaining certification of the recovered-materials content of an item. The EPA's list of designated products are grouped into eight separate product categories, including Construction, Landscaping, Office, Paper, Park and Recreation, and Transportation and Vehicle Products.

Website: *www.epa.gov/cpg/products.htm*. (67)

Water Efficiency

The EPA's WaterSense program qualifies water-efficient products and services. This program covers such products as bathroom fixtures and landscape irrigation

Website: *www.epa.gov/watersense*. (68)

Energy Efficiency and Renewable Energy

This program is run by the Dept. of Energy's Federal Energy Management Program (FEMP) and includes programs aimed at reducing building and facility energy use, creating sustainable buildings, instituting advanced metering and measurement programs, increasing water and data center efficiency, reducing petroleum use, increasing use of alternative fuels, and instituting fleet management programs. In addition, the **Laboratories for the 21st Century** program aims to reduce federal laboratory energy use.

Website: *www1.eere.energy.gov/femp*. (69)

Bio-Based Products

The U.S. Dept. of Agriculture (USDA) is responsible for creating a bio-based product list for federal use. Again, federal agencies are required to give preference to these items. Programs include the Building for Environmental and Economic Sustainability tool (BEES). The Bio-Preferred catalog includes construction and road maintenance products, furniture and furnishings, housewares and cleaning supplies, industrial supplies, landscaping and agriculture, office supplies, and personal care and toiletries.

Website: *www.catalog.biopreferred.gov*. (70)

Important Websites

- Defense Logistics Agency's Green Procurement Plan: **www.dla.mil/dss/dss-e/gpp.pdf (71)** and **www.dla.mil/J-4/cric/GreenProcurement.asp**. (72)
- Environmental Technologies Opportunities Portal (ETOP): *www.epa.gov/etop*. (73)
- The General Services Administration also has a **Go Green Initiative** covering environmentally friendly products and services, construction of green buildings, and more. (We discuss the General Services Administration in more detail later in the book.): *www.gsa.gov/Portal/gsa/ep/home.do?tabId=11*. (74)

Some Programs and Regulations Concerning Green Procurement

- **Public Law 107-171** set up the Dept. of Agriculture's bio-based product program, which provides recommendations for agencies when they purchase these items.
- The EPA's **Comprehensive Procurement Guidelines** (CPG) lists items that are— or can be—made with recovered materials.
- The **EPA Policy Act** covers topics such as energy and water conservation, alternative energy, reducing the use of fossil fuels, and sustainable building design. It also includes the procurement requirements for energy-efficient products and the increased use of cement/concrete with recovered mineral content.
- **Federal Acquisition Regulations** (FAR) 23.2, 23.4, and 23.7 describe the policies and procedures for acquiring energy- and water-efficient products and services, and products that use renewable energy technology.
- **Executive Order #13423** concerns vehicles, petroleum conservation, alternative fuels, energy efficiency, renewable power, sustainable building, water conservation, toxic

chemicals, and electronics management, as well as solid waste diversion, waste prevention, and recycling programs.

- **Executive Order #13221** concerns energy-efficient standby power devices, and requires federal agencies to purchase products that use no more than one watt in their standby power-consuming mode. The Dept. of Energy has developed a list of products that meet this requirement.

- **Recovered Materials Advisory Notices** from the EPA guide agencies who are purchasing energy-efficient items. These notices are for guidance only. Their recommended recycled-content ranges are based on current commercially available recycled-content products, and may change as marketplace conditions change.

- **The Federal Green Construction Guide** helps federal building project managers meet mandatory requirements and recommendations.

- The Dept. of Defense **E-Mall** allows agencies to easily purchase "green" items and uses a number of green icons to indicate them on their site.

- The DOD also has a **Green Procurement Report** to track environmentally friendly purchases at *www.dlis.dla.mil/erlsgpr*.

- The Dept. of Agriculture's **Bio-Preferred Program** has information on how to submit products to be considered for the program, as well as instructions on how to purchase bio-based products.

- The **Energy Star** program, a joint program of the Environmental Protection Agency and the Dept. of Energy, encourages the purchase of energy-efficient products.

- The Dept. of Energy's **Federal Energy Management Program (FEMP)** aims to reduce both costs and environment impact by advancing energy efficiency and water conservation, promoting renewable energy, and improving utility management decisions at federal sites.

- **The Electronic Product Environmental Assessment Tool (EPEAT)** helps buyers to evaluate, compare, and select desktop computers, notebooks, and monitors based on their environmental attributes. The tool also provides performance criteria for the design of products.

- Certain European regulations may also apply if you plan to ship items overseas.

- The **Regulation, Evaluation, Authorization of Chemicals (REACH)** regulation standardizes regulation of chemical substances in the European Union. The Dept. of Defense wishes its suppliers to be able to adapt to these requirements, and encourages you to evaluate whether or not your products may be regulated under REACH. Website: *http://ec.europa.eu/environment/chemicals*. (75)

- The **RoHS Directive** stands for "the restriction of the use of certain hazardous substances in electrical and electronic equipment." This directive bans the placing on the EU market of new electrical and electronic equipment containing more than agreed levels of lead, cadmium, mercury, and other chemicals. Website: *http:// www.rohs.gov.uk*. (76)

Procurement History

In many cases the solicitation document will also contain information on past procurement. That is, which companies have supplied this item in the past, and their unit delivered price. This is valuable information for you to have *before* you submit your offer!

Here is an example of procurement history embedded on the second page of the solicitation document:

PROCUREMENT HISTORY FOR NSN: 56600014959581					
TYPE	CAGE	CONTRACT NUMBER	QUANTITY	UNIT COST	AWD DATE
DVD	0VYY9	SPMSE608M2258	000200	131.00000	06/12/08
DVD	0VYY9	SPMSE608M2021	000244	131.00000	06/12/08
DVD	55722	SPMSE608M2138	000255	139.56000	06/10/08
DVD	55722	SPMSE608M2018	000088	135.70000	04/23/08
DVD	55722	SPMSE607M1893	000460	139.10000	10/01/07
TYPE	CAGE	CONTRACT NUMBER	QUANTITY	UNIT COST	AWD DATE
STK	0VYY9	SPMSE609V0049	000252	130.52000	10/09/08
STK	55722	SPMSE608M2580	000504	132.48000	07/22/08
STK	7E553	SP057006M4689	000150	126.74000	02/15/06
STK	7E553	SP057005M7018	000100	136.81000	06/30/05

The item is identified by its National Stock Number (NSN).

In the first column you will either see the letters STK, indicating a Stock Buy, or DVD, indicating a Direct Vendor Buy

The second column shows you the company that supplied the item, using its Commercial and Government Entity (CAGE) code. Use the Business Identification Website (*www.bpn.gov/bincs* [31]) to identify the company. Remember that if a company has more than one location or division, it will have separate CAGE codes for each.

The third column lists the exact contract number that was awarded. If you wish, you may enter that number in the Awards tab on the DIBBS home page and view the complete contract.

Column Four shows you the quantity that was ordered.

Column Five gives you the Unit Delivered Price.

Column Six lists the date the contract was awarded.

At other times this same information can be found on the final page of the solicitation document, in a slightly different format

Quoting in DIBBS

You must be registered and logged into DIBBS in order to submit quotes on RFQ solicitations.

Once you have found a solicitation for which you would like to quote, find your Solicitation via the RFQ Search and then click on the Quote icon displayed next to the solicitation number.

Once you have completed the form, make doubly sure that the information is accurate, and then click on Submit. You will receive a message that your submission was successful. You may want to print a copy of this page for your records.

i **Tip:** Instead of printing out only the "Bid Successful" screen, you may prefer to print out each page of your offer *before* you go on to the next screen. This way you will have a clear copy of exactly what was submitted for your records.

You may **review** your submitted quote any time until the requirement is either awarded or cancelled, and you will be able to **revise** your quote if you wish. You may **withdraw** a quote by submitting a revised quote and choosing No-Bid under the drop-down menu for Bid Type. Make sure to click the Submit button again, and make sure you receive the message that your new submission was successful.

Late Quotes. The solicitation return date/time is not a firm closing date on RFQs, except for auctions. Quotes received after the return date/time will continue to run through the automated award process until the award process has begun. (Remember that solicitations with the Fast Bid icon may be awarded before the posted due date.) Once the award process has begun (on the closing date), late quotes will only be considered if the contracting officer determines that it is in the best interests of the government and that accepting the late quote would not unduly delay the award.

Auctions. Be aware that if you see a gavel icon on the RFQ search results or on the Web quote form, then the requirement is an auction candidate. By submitting a quote on an auction solicitation you agree that your quoted price, and other price-related factors, may be publicly displayed. Bidders remain anonymous. If you wish to view open auctions you must be logged in to the secure portion of DIBBS.

Step by Step Through Your Online Quote in DIBBS

This section takes you step by step through the Defense Internet Bid Board System's (DIBBS) online quoting system, and shows you exactly how to complete the form and submit your offer.

Solicitation #	Enter the Solicitation number here.
Login CAGE	Enter the CAGE code of the user who is registered in DIBBS.

Quoting for CAGE	You may register yourself as an authorized representative who can submit bids on behalf of another company. If this is the case, enter the CAGE code of the company who will receive the award. Otherwise leave this section blank.
Buyer Code	Enter the buyer code here.
Bid Type	**Bid Without Exception:** Your quote is in exact compliance with the solicitation requirements. **Bid With Exception:** There are exceptions to the solicitation requirements. For example, exceptions to packaging requirements or to FOB point, quoting *destination* inspection when the solicitation requires *origin* inspection, exceptions to the solicited quantity, quoting a quantity variance when not allowed by the solicitation, or seeking exceptions to the quantity variance that *is* allowed by a solicitation. **Alternate Bid:** This indicates that a substitute product is being offered, or that there are other variations from the item description. **No Bid:** This indicates that you do not wish to bid. For example, if you wish to withdraw a previous bid before the due date for offers has passed, you may use this option to do so. Quoting a zero quantity for all line items will force a bid type of "No Bid."
Discount Terms	Select from pick list of the six most common discount terms.
Vendor Quote #	This is an optional fill-in for your reference only.
Quote Valid For	State the number of days that your quote will remain valid.
Meets Packaging and RFID Requirements	The *only* acceptable tags are EPC Class 1 passive RFID tags that meet the EPC global Class 1 Generation 2 specification. Class 0 and Class 1 Generation 1 tags are no longer accepted. You must affix passive RFID tags, at the case and palletized unit load packaging levels. For more information, read the complete DFARS clause here: *https://dibbs2.bsm.dla.mil/Downloads/Docs/DFAR/dfars_252_211-7006.html*.

Federal Supply Schedule (FSS), Basic Ordering Agreement (BOA), Blanket Purchase Agreement (BPA)	If you have a Federal Supply Schedule contract number (also known as a GSA contract), a Basic Ordering Agreement (BOA), or a Blanket Purchase Agreement (BPA) Number, you must enter it here, along with the expiration date.
Free on Board (FOB) Point	Also sometimes known as Freight on Board. **FOB Origin:** The agency is responsible for freight charges. **FOB Destination:** You are responsible for freight charges.
Govt. Inspection Point	For Origin Inspection, supply the CAGE code where you want the government to inspect the supplies—either at your facility (enter your CAGE code), or at the manufacturer's plant (enter their CAGE code). **Packaging CAGE code:** If you want inspection at your facility or plant, use your CAGE code. If it is at a packaging house, use its CAGE code.
SPI Process Proposed	The Single Process Initiative (SPI) is a DOD program in which you may propose an alternate management or manufacturing process in lieu of a specific military or federal specification or standard. If you have a process that has already been approved under this program, you would enter that number here. For details see DFARS 252.211-7005.
Price and Delivery Data Area	
Price and Delivery (Non-Indefinite Delivery Contract)	Enter your price, and your delivery, in number of days ADO (After Date of Order).
Minimum Order Quantity	Enter your Minimum order quantity here.
Quantity Variance	Enter any variation in the quantity that you propose, compared to the quantity requested in the solicitation document. In the solicitation document you will find a section where an allowable percentage of variance is listed.

Quantity Available for Immediate Shipment	Is there a quantity available for immediate shipment? If so, enter the quantity, price, and number of delivery days.
Price-Break Ranges	Enter price break ranges and unit prices here.
Pricing and Delivery	Enter quantities and pricing for specific quantities. For example, you may wish to quote one price for a quantity range from 1 to 10 and another price on a quantity from 11 to 50. Enter the prices and ranges here.
Indefinite Delivery Purchase Order Alternate Price-Break Ranges	An Indefinite Delivery Purchase Order does not specify a firm quantity, only a minimum quantity. Delivery Orders will be issued during the term of the contract. You must submit prices and delivery times for all the quantity ranges, geographical zones, and option years that have been solicited.
Quantity Variance	Enter any variation in the quantity that you propose, compared to the quantity requested in the solicitation document. In the solicitation document you will find a section where an allowable percentage of variance is listed.
Product Offered Representations Data Area	
Supplies Offered	Are the items offered: • In accordance with the cited specifications, standards, or drawings? • Based on a different revision of these specifications, standards, and drawings? • Based on changes to the cited specifications, standards, or drawings? • Based on other technical data? Is there an error in the item description?

Part Number Offered	When an approved manufacturing source or sources is specified you may elect to offer an Exact Product, an Alternate Product, or a Reverse-Engineered Product.
	An Exact Product means it is the identical product described by the approved manufacturer's CAGE and part number. It is manufactured by, under the direction of, or under agreement with the specified manufacturer.
	Any other product is considered an Alternate Product, even if it is manufactured in accordance with the drawings and/or specifications of the approved manufacturer.
	If you are offering an Alternate Product, enter the CAGE and part number offered.
Qualification Requirements	If an item is listed on the Qualified Products List, enter the manufacturer's CAGE, the Source's CAGE (if known), the Item Name, Service ID, and Test Document Number.
	For more details see FAR 52.209-1.
Manufacturer or Dealer	State whether you are the Manufacturer, Dealer, Qualified Supplier List Manufacturer, or Qualified Supplier List Dealer.
Higher-Level Quality	If a higher-level quality standard/system is required you must select the standard/system that applies. If you select "other equivalent system" you must enter a description. See (FAR 46.202-4).
Material Requirements	Identify whether the item offered is used, reconditioned, remanufactured, or new/unused government surplus.
Hazardous Material Identification and Material Safety Data	If these documents are required, you must list them here. See DFARS 252.223-7001.

Buy American Act—Balance of Payments Program Certification	Is the item being offered: • A Domestic End Product? • A Qualifying Country End Product? (Choose from the list.) • A Non-Qualifying Country End Product? (List the country.)
Buy American Act—North American Free Trade Agreement Implementation Act—Balance of Payments Program Certification	Is the item being offered: • A Domestic End Product? • A Qualifying Country End Product? • A Free Trade Agreement Country End Product? • An Other Foreign End Product?
Duty Free Entry Requested	Select "yes" if duty-free entry is requested. • Are the foreign supplies now in the United States? • Has the duty been paid? • What amount is included in the offer to cover such duty?
Certification Regarding Knowledge of Child Labor for Listed End Products	Are you providing an end product that may have been mined, produced, or manufactured by forced or indentured child labor? This list currently includes items from Burma and Pakistan, including bamboo, beans, bricks, chilies, corn, pineapples, rice, rubber, shrimp, sugarcane, and teak. The Dept. of Labor's current list of these products and corresponding countries is at *www.dol.gov/ILAB/regs/eo13126/main.htm*.
Contractor Representations Data Area	
Taxpayer Identification Number (TIN)	Enter your Taxpayer Identification Number, and choose the Organization Type.

Small Business and Other Business Type Representation	Are you: • A Small Business? • A JWOD Participating Nonprofit Agency? • A Historically Black College/University or other Minority Institution? • An Educational Institution? • An Intragovernmental Institution? • A Large Business? • If you are a Small Business, are you: • A Small Disadvantaged Business? • A Woman-Owned Small Business? • A Veteran-Owned or Service-Disabled Veteran-Owned Small Business? • A business located in a HUB-Zone?
Affirmative Action Compliance	Select from a list of representations regarding affirmative action programs. See FAR 52.222-25 and FAR 52.212-3(d)(3).
Previous Contracts and Compliance Reports	Select from a list of representations regarding previous contracts and compliance reports. See FAR 52.222-22 and FAR 52.212-3(d)(3).
Alternate Disputes Resolution	Do you agree to use alternate dispute resolution? See DLAD 52.233-9001.
Remarks	You may add remarks here, except for bids that are eligible for Automated (PACE) awards. PACE awards are identified by a "T" or a "U" in the ninth position of the solicitation number.

Batch Quoting

If you are able to find multiple opportunities in DIBBS for which you wish to submit bids, you may wish to look at this option. Batch Quoting is a faster way for you to submit multiple RFQ quotes. You prepare your quotes using a preset comma-delineated format, up to 75 lines in one file. Once you have them all ready, you can then upload all the quotes to DIBBS at one time.

All the same information you enter each time you complete an online quote is in the batch quote file, in the exact same order, separated by commas. Because much of the information you must enter whenever you submit an electronic quote is the same each time (company name, CAGE code, and so on), this method of quoting is very useful if you find you are able to place many smaller bids.

For example, instead of entering "contract number," "solicitation type" (F for Fast Award; P for PACE), "set aside" (Y, N), "Return by Date," and so on, the document would look something like this:

"SPM70004T0092", "P", "N", "N", "02/17/2004"...

Any blank entries, where information does not apply are shown as "", "", "",....

Here's a section of a batch file example that shows Purchase Request #—NSN—Unit of Issue—Quantity—Unit Price—Delivery Time:

"0000008027", "4820012016903", "EA", "14", "1.27", "89"

You can download the Batch File Format at *www.dibbs.bsm.dla.mil/Refs/help/BatchFileFormat.htm*, (77) and you may look at a sample file at *www.dibbs.bsm.dla.mil/Refs/help/bqSample.zip*. (78) If you prefer, you may use a Microsoft Access 2000 table to format your batch quotes (more instruction on this method of submitting quotes is also available at: *www.dibbs.bsm.dla.mil/Refs/help/BatchQuoteFileImportExportDirections.pdf* (79)).

Awards

Once an award has been made, you may access it from the Home Page link (refer to page 78 of this chapter). You can search for a specific award by NSN, nomenclature, manufacturer (using the CAGE code), part number, and so on.

Contract #	Delivery Order #	Awardee CAGE	Award Date	Total Contract Price	NSN/ Nomenclature	PR # or Req # / Solicitation	Award Posted
SPM4A029M1769		35X01	5/13/2009	See Award	6685015352975 THERMOSTAT,FLOW CON	0021389647	5/15/2009
SPM4A029M1772		35X01	5/13/2009	See Award	6685015352975 THERMOSTAT,FLOW CON	0021879990	5/14/2009
SPM4A029M1356		35X01	5/11/2009	See Award	6685015352975 THERMOSTAT,FLOW CON	0022240676	5/12/2009
SPM4A029M1280		35X01	5/11/2009	See Award	6685015352975 THERMOSTAT,FLOW CON	0022156970	5/12/2009

This is very useful information for future research, even if you do not win the contract yourself. As you can see, you can find out who won the contract, and the total contract price.

Sometimes the company that was awarded the contract did not necessarily offer the lowest price: If the award was made using the PACE automated program, then a bid that did not conform exactly to the stated requirements would not be considered, even if it was the lowest bid. Perhaps the company did not bid on the exact product, or did not conform to packaging or marking requirements.

Icons Used in DIBBS

Icon	Description
Q quote	Click on this icon to submit a quote.
✓	Quote Submitted
⚠	Revise Quote.
	The requirements changed since you quoted. A new quote is required.
	There is a Submitted Quote
	There is a bidset available for the NSN
	Specifications or Standards are available
Mil-Spec	The NSN has an associated Military Specification.
QPL	The NSN has an associated Qualified Products List.
	There are Technical Documents available for the NSN
	Solicitation may not include all pertinent data
✈	This is a Fast Award candidate. Quotes $2500 or less may be awarded prior to the solicitation return date
	There is an RFQ document available
	Automated Indefinite Delivery Purchase Order
SB	Small Business Set-Aside.
HUBZone	HUB-Zone Set-Aside
sdvosb	Service Disabled Veteran-Owned Small Business Set-Aside
Combined	Combined Set-Aside.

Help!

If you have any questions about this chapter, we would be happy to try to help you. Go to our Website, *www.sell2gov.com*, and at the Contact tab you can send us an e-mail with your questions. Please put "Definitive Guide" in the subject line.

Chapter 4

Additional Procurement Sites

In the previous chapters we looked closely at two important Websites—Federal Business Opportunities (**FedBizOpps**), the central site for sales opportunities over $25,000 for most agencies; and the Department of Defense's electronic bidding site (for products only) known as the Dept. of Defense Internet Bid Board System (**DIBBS**).

Of course there are many other agency sites where you may find sales opportunities, and we will take a look at some of these alternate sites here. Some agency sites simply direct you to FedBizOpps for postings, but others have procurement opportunities at their sites that you may wish to explore.

We will look at:

- Army Single Face to Industry (ASFI)
- FedBid® Online Reverse Auctions
- Navy Electronic Commerce Online (NECO)
- Veterans Administration (VA)
- Dept. of Energy (DoE)
- Dept. of Interior Electronic Site—IDEAS-EC
- United States Postal Service (USPS)
- Federal Prison Industries (UNICOR) and the Federal Bureau of Prisons
- U.S. Patent Office
- Government Printing Office

Remember that any solicitations estimated to be valued at $25,000 or more will *also* be posted at FedBizOpps, in addition to the agency's own site.

When you search at FedBizOpps for opportunities, you may find yourself directed to one of these sites, in order to view details of a solicitation.

Army Single Face to Industry (ASFI)

Website: *https://acquisition.army.mil/asfi*. (80)

Searching the Site

At this site you will need to search separately for both Contracting Opportunities and Combined Synopsis/Solicitations.

The Quick Search option allows you to search only for opportunities that are posted or due today, or for a specific solicitation number.

Further down the page you may choose to search for opportunities from a specific agency office, or via a text search for a specific word or phrase.

Alternatively, you may search by North American Industrial Classification (NAICS) or Federal Supply Classification (FSC) codes. We discussed these codes in Chapter 1.

Your search results will show you the solicitation number, the buyer's e-mail address and telephone number, a brief description of the requirement, and the closing date for submission of offers. Sometimes the NAICS code is also indicated. Notice also that the notation "-0001" at the end of the solicitation number indicates an amendment ("-0002" would indicate a second amendment, and so on).

The "(E)" at the end of the solicitation number indicates that this link will take you outside of the Army Single Face to Industry Website, to another agency site. An "(R)" indicates a link to a restricted site.

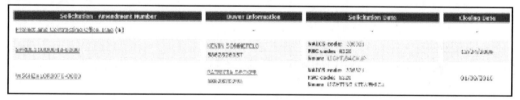

Once you have found an opportunity that is of interest, click on the Solicitation link to view more details.

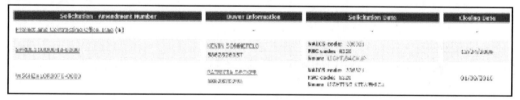

At the bottom of this page are links to more details. These links can take different forms:

Sometimes there is a link to an attachment that contains the solicitation documents.

| Solicitation View |
| Government Buyer Options | Attachments |

| Return to Contracting Opportunities Search |

Sometimes the solicitation details are found at another agency site. Click on that link (shown at the bottom of the last image on the previous page) in order to view the document.

At other times the details you need can be found at the bottom of the screen under CLINs, or Contract Line Item Numbers.

| Clins | Clin Message Clauses | Message Clauses |
| Shipping Detail for ALL CLINS |
| Solicitation View |
| Government Buyer Options | Attachments |

At times the buyer has uploaded to details directly to the site.

Solicitation Attachments: *(If you feel there are missing attachments, please contact the contract specialist listed above.)*

Government User Uploaded Solicitation Files

Description	File Size	Upload Date
BUILDING TRANSCEIVER (.doc)	213 KB	12/14/2009

Message Clauses reference specific Defense Federal Acquisition Regulations Supplements (DFARS).

Reference Type	Reference Number	Reference Date	Reference Text
Defense Federal Acquisition Regulations (DFAR)	252.204-7000	12/01/1991	N
Defense Federal Acquisition Regulations (DFAR)	252.204-7003	04/01/1992	N
Defense Federal Acquisition Regulations (DFAR)	252.204-7004 Alt A	11/01/2003	N
Defense Federal Acquisition Regulations (DFAR)	252.211-7003	06/01/2005	N
Defense Federal Acquisition Regulations (DFAR)	252.212-7000	06/01/2005	N
Defense Federal Acquisition Regulations (DFAR)	252.212-7001 (Dev)	11/01/2006	N
Defense Federal Acquisition Regulations (DFAR)	252.225-7000	06/01/2005	Y
Defense Federal Acquisition Regulations (DFAR)	252.225-7001	06/01/2005	Y
Defense Federal Acquisition Regulations (DFAR)	252.225-7002	04/01/2003	N

Shipping details show the shipping terms and the delivery address for each line item.

Here you can see that line item #1 will be shipped FOB Destination; that is, shipping charges are the responsibility of the seller, and the items will be inspected at the destination point. The delivery date is listed, along with the specific shipping address, known as a DODAAC—the Department of Defense Activity Address Code is a six-position code that identifies a particular unit or organization that can requisition and receive material.

Vendor Notification Service

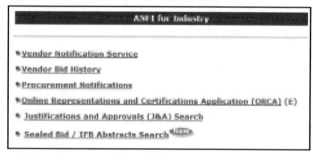

This service lets you receive an e mail notification whenever a solicitation or amendment is posted with a specific NAICS or FSC code that you have listed. This does *not* register you to receive a solicitation package, or put you on a bidders list.

You will need to register for this service using your Commercial and Industrial Entity (CAGE) code and your Marketing Partners Identification Number (MPIN) that you created when you registered at the Central Contractors Registration site (CCR). (See Chapter 1 for more details of the CCR registration process, and the MPIN and CAGE numbers.)

If you elect to receive notices by NAICS code, you must have listed those codes when you registered at CCR. If you wish to see NAICS codes that are not listed in your CCR registration, then you will need to update the CCR information to include these codes.

Remember that when a solicitation is released, you can still submit an offer even if the NAICS code listed is not one that you have listed in your CCR information. However, for this particular notification service, the system uses only the NAICS codes in your CCR listing to send you e-mails. You may edit or unsubscribe to this service at any time.

Submitting Bids at the ASFI Site

Bids for many solicitations listed in ASFI can be submitted via the **Bid Response System** (BRS). The notice posted to the site will indicate this with a Start Offer/Bid icon at the bottom of the screen.

You will need to enter your **CAGE** code and **MPIN** number for verification, and then you will be required to complete details of company name, address, e-mail address, telephone number, and so on. This information will be cross-referenced with the information in CCR. If there is an error this will need to be corrected before you can go any further.

You may be required to upload specific information as part of your submission. The solicitation document will give you all the details you will need to include in this upload. At other times Contract Line Item Number (CLIN) pricing will take you step by step through the bid questions. These include:

- **Is your offer/bid being submitted without exception?** If you state that your bid is Without Exception this means that you agree to all the terms and conditions set out in the solicitation document: delivery times, packaging requirements, the exact manufacturer and part number listed, and so on. A bid With Exception is one that deviates from these terms, and you will be able to provide more details. Bid exceptions apply to *all* the line items in a solicitation, so if there are multiple line items and you have a different part number or delivery for just one of them, then you should state Bid With Exception, even if the other line items do not deviate.

- **Are items offered available from a GSA Federal Supply Contract?** Again, this question applies to the entire solicitation. See later in this book for details of the GSA contract, and how to submit a proposal.

- **Prompt Payment Discount**. Standard options here are 10, 20, or 30 days, but you may list your applicable discounts if necessary.

- **Price Guarantee Days.** How long will you hold your prices?

- **Comments.** You may enter any comments here that you feel may help the contracting officer or buyer to better evaluate your offer.

- **Pricing.** You will be required to enter a Unit Delivered Price for each line item listed.

- **ORCA.** Remember to also include a copy of your current Online Representations and Certifications application (ORCA). (We discussed the registration process at ORCA in Chapter 1.)

Supporting Documents

You will also be able to upload any other supporting documentation that you wish to include, and you will be able to review the details before you submit your offer. You will receive a confirmation with a Price Quote Number for your records.

Making Changes to Your Offer

If you wish to modify or withdraw an offer after it is submitted, you will *not* be able to do so via this system. You will need to contact the contracting officer, referencing your Price Quote Number, and you will be given details of how to modify or withdraw an offer.

Vendor Bid History

You may view a list of all the bids you have submitted by clicking on the Vendor Bid History link at the ASFI home page. The page shows you the Solicitation Number, Submission Date/Time, Price Quote Number, Vendor Representative, and Contract Specialist for bids successfully submitted in the last 60 days. No pricing information will be displayed.

FedBid Online Reverse Auctions

In Chapter 1 we spoke briefly about this commercial site that is now being used extensively by federal agencies for relatively simple, small purchases under the Simplified Acquisition Threshold of $100,000. The site works as a "reverse auction"—think of it like eBay—only backwards!

Website: ***www.FedBid.com***. (81)

Create an Account

You will need to register at this site in order to view and submit offers. Registration is a fairly simple two-step process. At the home page, click on Seller Sign In and then Create a New Account.

You will first be asked to check if your company is already registered at the site, by looking over an alphabetical list of companies currently registered. If you are not registered, you will need to complete an initial Seller Registration form in which you give company details (name, address, telephone, and so on); a Point of Contact name and e-mail; information such as your CAGE code, DUNS number, and Tax ID number; and your company type (veteran-owned, woman-owned, and so on). Once you have submitted the information, FedBid will cross-reference this with the information in the Central Contractors Registration (CCR) site. FedBid will then send an e-mail to the Point of Contact listed, enabling him or her to set up an account with a user ID and password.

Once you have your user ID and password, use it to access the site and search via the Opportunities tab.

Searching for Opportunities

At the **Opportunities** tab you may search by a specific agency. Searching by **Contract Vehicle** allows you to restrict your search to only open market opportunities, or only for opportunities that require a GSA schedule. You may also search by **Set-Aside** (veteran-owned, Hub-Zone, and so on). The **Search Criteria** option allows you to find an opportunity by the FedBid reference number. If an opportunity has been posted to FedBizOpps, you may search for it using the **FedBizOpps solicitation number**. You may also search by description.

The Opportunities tab is divided into **My Opportunities** and **Marketplace Opportunities** listings: The postings at My Opportunities relate to the specific information that you entered in your company profile, but you may also view all other opportunities via the Marketplace Opportunities tab.

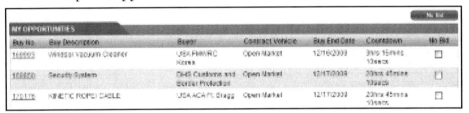

The postings page shows the FedBid reference number, a brief description of the requirement, the purchasing agency, and an indication of whether the item is being purchased via Open Market or GSA Schedules (more on this later). Also listed is the **Buy End Date**—the date when all bidding is closed, as well as a countdown timer showing how long is left before the bid closing. The **No Bid** option allows you to indicate to the buyer that you will not be bidding on this particular request, but that you are still actively looking for appropriate opportunities. If you see an opportunity that interests you, click on the link.

General Buy Information

This section of the posting shows you details of the opportunity—for example, a general description of the item and the Federal Supply Classification (**FSC**) code. Notice that in this case the opportunity has *not* also been posted in **FedBizOpps**, indicating that the estimated value

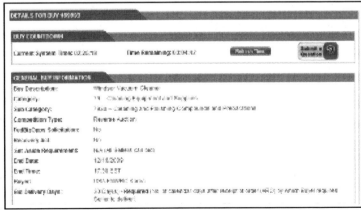

is less than $25,000. There are no **set-asides** in this case. The **buyer** is listed, along with the date and time when bidding will end. Take notice of the **delivery date**, which in this example is 30 days after the receipt of the order (ARO). This is a common time period, but in some cases it can be less—pay attention to this section!

You may submit any questions you have via the **Submit a Question** link at the top of the page. The questions are submitted to the FedBid company, and they are forwarded to the buyer for clarification. However, because the time frame for submissions at this site is often quite short, there may not be enough time for the buyer to reply to your questions before the close of bidding.

Contract Information

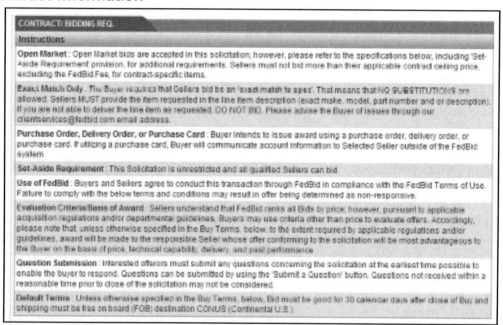

The buyer may indicate **GSA Schedules Preferred** or **GSA Schedules Required**. Alternatively the purchase may be via **Open Market** and the items do not need to be on a GSA schedule contract. (For more information on the GSA schedule contract program, see later chapters in this book.)

The buyer may stipulate an **Exact Match** to the manufacturer, part number, or specifications listed, as is the case in this example. Alternatively the buyer may list **Meet or Exceed** or **Brand Name or Equal**, which would allow you to offer an equivalent or better item.

Other details in this section refer to the way the reverse auction will be conducted, including minimum bid decrements, evaluation criteria, and so on. Notice whether the solicitation has a set-aside (for small, veteran-owned, or HUB-Zone businesses, for example). Also pay attention to the **Default Terms** paragraph, which details how long you must hold your prices, and the shipping terms.

Bid Terms

This section details several standard bidding requirements, such as registration at the Central Contractors Registration (CCR) site, standard Federal Acquisition Regulation (FAR) clauses that apply, and so on.

BID TERMS	
Terms	**Criteria**
Equipment Condition	New Equipment ONLY; NO remanufactured or "gray market" items. All items must be covered by the manufacturer's warranty.
Offer Period	Bid MUST be good for 30 calendar days after close of Buy.
Shipping Condition	Shipping must be free on board (FOB) destination CONUS (Continental U.S.), which means that the seller must deliver the goods on its conveyance at the destination specified by the buyer, and the seller is responsible for the cost of shipping and risk of loss prior to actual delivery at the specified destination.
CCR Requirement	Offeror must be registered in the Central Contractor Registration (CCR) database before an award can be made to them. If the offeror is not registered in the CCR, it may do so through the CCR website at http://www.ccr.gov.
Delivery Requirement	No partial shipments are permitted unless specifically authorized at the time of award.

Solicitation Details

This section shows the delivery address, a detailed line item description, the quantity required, and in many cases one or more attachments that give more detailed information on the requirements.

SHIPPING INFORMATION		
Shipping Address		
French Camp	CA	95231

LINE ITEM(S)			
Item No.	**Description**	**Qty**	**Unit**
001	Windsor Sensor XP12 Upright Vacuum (12" Model)	5	EA
002	Windsor Sensor XP18 Upright Vacuum (18" Model)	5	EA

BUY ATTACHMENT(S)		
No.	**Document Name**	**Document Size**
There are no attachments.		

All-or-None Bidding

If the agency does not state that it is a line item bid, it is an "all-or-nothing" bid. Opportunities at this site are almost always all-or-none. If the solicitation lists several different line items you will *not* be able to submit a partial bid.

Pricing

Requests are issued and contracts are awarded very quickly at this site, so you will need your pricing ready to go if you wish to participate! This site may not be practical for you if you need time to search for a supplier, wait for a reply on price and availability, calculate your pricing, and so forth.

Be Careful!

When you are searching for opportunities at this site, be aware of the number of pages of postings that are available. In the following example you might think at first glance that there are only five pages of results, but look more carefully and you see that in fact there are seven!

 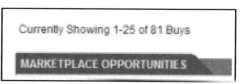

Check the top of the page for the exact number of postings.

Submitting a Bid at the Site

If you wish to submit an offer at this site, you should click on the **Submit Bid** icon at the bottom of the page. This is a fairly simple process as long as you have all the information you need to submit. The idea here is to submit a series of bids that decrease in price until a stated minimum amount. For example, you may begin by submitting a price of $100, to be reduced in $1 increments until the price reaches $75, at which point you will withdraw. Alternatively you may simply submit a single price and leave it at that—which may be a better way to begin.

The buyer can stipulate an **Active Target Price**—that is, a maximum price point that must be under-bid. This may be based on market research, a GSA Schedule catalog price, a previous purchase price, or a funding threshold. Think of it like the reserve price that may be set in a regular auction room.

Once you have submitted your bid the site will indicate whether your offer is in the **Lead** or **Lag** position, but you will not be able to view other competitors' pricing details. Once a Buy has closed, and the contract has been awarded, all those who submitted a bid will be able to see the winning seller's total bid price, but not its identity. Bidding information is not available unless you participated in the auction.

The Lead/Lag ranking at the site is based solely on price. However, if the purchase is being made using Best Value criteria, the buyer may choose to award the contract to a company that is in the Lag position in terms of price, if it can offer a better overall value—for example, better delivery terms or a longer warranty.

Invoicing

There is no cost to register or to submit bids at this site; instead, FedBid adds a small transaction fee to the winning bid. When you submit your pricing, the company adds this fee before it is forwarded to the buyer. If you submit the winning bid you will get an e-mail from the company with the buyer's point-of-contact information. The buyer will then issue a purchase order to you for the item, and the amount will be for your submitted price plus the FedBid transaction fee. FedBid will then invoice you for the fee payment.

For example, let's say you submit a price of $100. FedBid adds its fee (for example, $3), and submits the pricing to the buyer as $103. This is the amount that the buyer sees and that you invoice the buyer. You receive $103 from the agency, and you submit the $3 fee to FedBid as the winning bidder. (Whew!)

ActivityCard®

The company maintains an ActivityCard on each seller, which shows information such as how long a company has been active on the site, how many contracts the company has been awarded, and so on. A **Performance Alert** flags sellers with "materially problematic performance issues." A seller will be able to contact the buyer who issued the alert, and find out whether the problem that caused the alert could impact the award decision. If you are flagged in this way, you will be able to contact the buyer and find out why the alert was posted, and try to resolve the issue.

Navy Electronic Contracting Online (NECO)

Website: *www.neco.navy.mil*. (82)

At this site you may search for synopses, Requests for Proposal (RFPs), and Requests for Quote (RFQs) from more than 300 buying activities.

You may search for opportunities at this site without registering, but you will need to register if you wish to submit an offer. You will need your DUNS number and CAGE code (see Chapter 1 for an explanation of these codes), and once you are registered you will be given a password.

Receiving Daily Notices

You may choose to receive daily e-mail notices alerting you to selected solicitations as they are posted to NECO. You may choose to limit the notices to specific command sites, or to specific Federal Supply Groups (FSG). The Federal Supply Group is the broad 2-digit code, rather than the more specific 4-digit Federal Supply Classification (FSC) code. For example, the two-digit FSG code 71 is used for Furniture, whereas the more specific FSC code 7110 is used for Office Furniture.

Searching for Opportunities at NECO

At the Synopsis Search tab, just as at other sites, you may search for Pre-Solicitations, Modifications, Awards, Sources Sought, and more. You may search by Solicitation Number, Type of Synopsis, Date Range, NAICS Code, Set-Aside Code, Keyword, and Status.

At the Business Opportunities tab you may search for solicitations by Command/Site, Solicitation Number, specified Date Range, Transaction Purpose, FSC, CAGE, and/or Status.

You may see details of each opportunity by clicking on the appropriate link. There may be additional documents as attachments. Solicitations from the Naval Facilities Engineering Command (NAVFAC) may have a Plan Holder List available. There may also be a list of Interested Vendors for you to view, or for you to add your company details. If drawings are available they may either link back to the FedBizOpps site, or to a site called IRPOD (Individual Repair Parts Ordering Data) that houses sensitive technical drawings. A solicitation number in green text with an asterisk after it indicates that a drawing is available. Search using the No Frames option to see a snapshot of available opportunities.

Submitting a Bid at NECO

The process is similar to other sites where electronic bidding is available. Click on the Submit a Bid tab on the home page. Assign your bid a Price Quote Number for your own reference (use the solicitation number, or another internal reference number if you prefer). Indicate your unit delivered price (you may select No Quote for any line item for which you do not wish to bid). Specify how long you will hold your prices, and enter delivery schedules. Download the solicitation from the Business Opportunities tab, complete all the required fields, save the document, and upload it at the Submit a Bid Upload page.

Check the solicitation to be sure which method of submitting a document is acceptable—sometimes you may be able to submit by fax, but at other times faxes will not be accepted.

From the **Home Page** you may also view **Frequently Asked Questions** (FAQs), or submit feedback. The **Associated Links** page supplies references to Clauses, Regulations and Specifications, and links to the Federal Acquisition Regulations site (FAR), the Dept. of Defense Supplemental regulations (DFARS), Navy Supplemental Regulations (NMCARS), and more.

Other tabs list **Classification Codes**, common **Abbreviations and Acronyms**; **Numbered Notes**, and applicable **Clauses**.

The Veterans Administration (VA)

Website: ***www1.va.gov/oamm***. (83)

At the Acquisition and Logistics page, choose the Business tab to find Small Business Opportunities and information on doing business with the VA.

In December 2009 the VA published a final rule that created a set-aside program specifically for Veteran-Owned and Service-Disabled Veteran-Owned Small Businesses (VOSB and SDVOSB). Under this rule, VA contracting officers must set-aside procurements between $100,000 and $5 million if they expect two or more eligible businesses to submit a fair and reasonable offer. VA contracting officers will also be allowed to award sole-source contracts to these firms, for awards from $3,000 to $5 million.

The new ruling also requires the Veterans Administration to give these businesses priority over all other socioeconomic groups, including Hub-Zone and 8(a) small businesses. This is *not* a government-wide ruling, but is specific to the Veterans Administration. The VA awarded 35 percent of its FY2008 contract dollars to small businesses, including 15 percent to VOSBs and 12 percent to SDVOSBs. Prior to this ruling, companies could self-certify as a veteran-owned or service-disabled veteran-owned small business, but now companies must register at the VetBiz Website if they wish to participate: *www.vetbiz.gov*. (84) As of December 2009 there were almost 16,000 veteran-owned small businesses in the database, including about 9,000 service-disabled veteran-owned small businesses.

Veterans Affairs Medical Centers

The VA purchases products and services for its network of medical centers, hospitals, and clinics across the country. These include pharmaceuticals, medical and surgical supplies, perishable subsistence items, facility operation equipment and supplies, maintenance and repair services for medical and scientific equipment, construction, building maintenance and repair, prosthetic and orthopedic aids, and medical gases. Most of the purchases are made via direct delivery through its local acquisition offices.

You can search for a VA facility at this Website: *www2.va.gov/directory*. (85)

Many Veterans Administration contracts are posted to FedBizOpps, and a large number of items are purchased via the General Services Administration's VA schedules. (See the chapters later in the book concerning the GSA contract schedules program.)

The **National Contract Service** is responsible for several different programs, including:

- The Consolidated Mail Outpatient Pharmacy (CMOP).
- The High Tech Medical Equipment program.
- The Medical/Surgical Prime Vendor Distribution program.
- The Pharmaceutical, Subsistence, and Medical/Surgical Standardization program.

In addition, the National Contract Service is responsible for direct-to-patient distribution, I.V. solutions and sets, prescription vials, medical and surgical supplies, dental supplies and equipment, and more.

Website: *www1.va.gov/oamm/oa/nac/ncs*. (86)

The National Contract Service

There are several National Contracts and Blanket Purchase Agreements that are part of the Federal Supply Schedule Program. These programs are open to VA medical centers and related facilities, some State Veterans Homes, the Department of Defense, the Indian Health Service, and the Bureau of Prisons. Most of these solicitations are competitive, best-value procurements. The performance period for these contracts is normally one year with up to four option years.

The High Tech Medical Equipment Program

This program orders medical equipment such as X-ray, CT, MRI, radiation therapy, physiological monitoring, diagnostic ultrasound, and nuclear imaging equipment via several multiple-award contracts with most major equipment manufacturers.

The Medical Surgical Standardization Program

This program covers items such as medical and surgical supplies and equipment, dental supplies, and laboratory, environmental, radiology, and prosthetic devices.

Prime Vendor Distribution Programs

There are three of these—the Pharmaceutical Prime Vendor, the Medical/Surgical Prime Vendor, and the Subsistence Prime Vendor. This program is mandatory for all VA medical centers and consists of six prime vendor contracts. The Medical Centers pay prime vendors a distribution fee plus the product price, which is established using several criteria, including the Federal Supply Schedule Program, the VA National Standardization Program, the Veterans Integrated Service Network, and local contracts.

Website: *www1.va.gov/vastorenac/docs/medsurgmainpage.htm*. (87)

VA Advantage

The VA also operates a VA Advantage site that works much like the GSA Advantage site to allow buyers to purchase products and services from approved vendors. See Chapter 8 for more details.

Website: *www1.va.gov/vastorenac*. (88)

Contract Catalog Search Tool

The National Acquisition Center's **Contract Catalog Search Tool** lets you see which items are available under Federal Supply Service contracts, including cost-per-test, dental, and medical equipment, and wheelchair contracts. You may also search the pharmaceutical catalog and the Medical/Surgical catalog (which includes medical services, equipment and supplies, mobility devices, in-vitro diagnostics and reagents, and X-Ray equipment and supplies).

Website: *www1.va.gov/nac/index.cfm*. (89)

The Department of Energy (DOE)

The department's e-Center has an **Industry Interactive Procurement System (IIPS)** that allows you to browse for opportunities here: *http://e-center.doe.gov*. (90)

At this site, if you click on Browse Opportunities on the left-hand side, and then click on the DOE Acquisitions icon, you will be able to search for opportunities by solicitation number, date, classification code (FSC), and more.

In 2008 and 2009 the agency began the transition process to using a procurement system known as the **Strategic Integrated Procurement Enterprise System (STRIPES)**. This system uses a site called **FedConnect** as a portal between contractors and the STRIPES system, and you will need to be registered at FedConnect if you wish to do business with this agency.

Website: *www.fedconnect.net/FedConnect*. (91)

Department of the Interior

The **Interior Department Electronic Acquisition System (IDEAS)** at this National Business Center site includes opportunities from several agencies, including the bureaus of Indian Affairs, Land Management, Reclamation, Minerals Management; the National Parks Service; the Office of Surface Mining; the Fish and Wildlife Service; and the U.S. Geological Survey.

Website: *http://ideasec.nbc.gov*. (92)

Click on Business Opportunities and then either use the Synopsis/Announcement or the Open Solicitation options to search. Again, you may search by Agency, Federal Supply Classification (FSC), North American Industrial Classification System (NAICS), or by dates.

Once you click on an opportunity, you will find a screen similar to this:

Click on the Associated Documents tab at the top of the page to view more details. There may also be an Attachments tab here.

At the Procurement Forecast tab on the left-hand side of the home page you may search for upcoming opportunities: Click on "Create a Report" and set your parameters to search for a specific bureau, office, NAICS code, estimated value, set-aside (preference program), city, or state.

The United States Postal Service (USPS)

Website: *www.usps.com/suppliers/welcome.htm*. (93)

The U.S. Postal Service (USPS) operates a little differently than other agencies. It is mandated by law to operate like a business, is exempt from many government contracting regulations, and is not covered by the Small Business Act. However, its **Supplier Diversity Program** encourages the agency to do business with small, minority-owned, and woman-owned businesses.

Many opportunities are posted to the **FedBizOpps** Website (See Chapter 2 for information on this site.) Purchases under $10,000 are made at local offices, generally using a credit card, most other USPS purchases are centrally managed through the Supply Management organization's five portfolio teams:

1. **Facilities:** Facility construction, repairs and alterations, facility equipment and signage, facility purchasing facilitation, and utilities.

2. **Supplies:** Computer hardware and software, delivery services equipment, industrial equipment, IT/telecommunications, and vehicle parts, maintenance, purchasing, and leasing.

3. **Services:** Building operational services; cleaning services; commercial printing; contract postal access channels; creative and communication; environmental services; food service operation; maintenance, repair, and overhaul; medical, safety, and security products and services; miscellaneous services; office products and equipment; packaging and containers; professional services; retail products and services; landscaping services; snow removal services; stamp printing; temporary services; total solid waste management; and travel, relocation, and conference services.

4. **Transportation:** Domestic air mail transportation, surface mail transportation, and transportation asset management.

5. **Mail Equipment:** Automation spare parts and repair centers, biohazard detection equipment, field material handling solutions, flats automation equipment, letter and parcel automation equipment, mail transport equipment, mail transport equipment service centers, material handling deployment, and recognition systems technology.

Supplier Registration

If you are interested in doing business with USPS you will need to register at the eSourcing site: *www.usps.com/suppliers/howto/registration.htm*. (94)

Unsolicited Proposals

The USPS has an Unsolicited Proposal Program to consider proposals outside the scope of its regular solicitations. This may include offers of concepts, products, processes, or technology to which your company has a patent, trademark, or other proprietary right. If you wish to submit an unsolicited proposal, you should refer to Postal Service Publication 131, which discusses this program, at *www.usps.com/suppliers/howto/unsolicitedproposals.htm*. (95)

Innovations

The Innovations at USPS program encourages companies to propose new business ideas and new technologies. You may submit your proposal online for evaluation here: *www.usps.com/innovations/welcome.htm*. (96)

Federal Prison Industries (UNICOR) and the Federal Bureau of Prisons

Website: *www.unicor.gov/fpi_contracting*. (97)

UNICOR purchases the raw materials that are used in the Federal Prison Industries factories, located in federal prisons around the country. They produce goods and services for sale to government agencies only. A few facts:

- UNICOR produces goods and services at 109 US factories.
- Almost 62% of purchases came from small and disadvantaged businesses.
- In FY2008 net sales were $854.3 million.

(From: Federal Prison Industries Fact Sheet.)

There are several separate business groups within the Federal Prison Industries, as shown in the following table.

Clothing and Textiles	Clothing for law enforcement, medical, and military personnel, as well as for federal institutions. Also draperies, curtains, mattresses, bedding, linens, towels, and screen-printed textiles.
Electronics	Task lighting systems, wire harness assemblies, circuit boards, electrical components and connectors, and electrical cables.

Fleet Management and Vehicular Components	Remanufactured and refurbished vehicle components, and retrofit services for new vehicles.
Industrial Products	Dormitory and quarters furnishings, industrial racking catwalks, mezzanines and warehouse/office shelving; lockers and storage cabinets, safety and prescription eyewear, fencing, filtration products, awards and promotional gifts, license plates and signs, and custom engraving and printing.
Office Furniture	Office furnishings and accessories, office seating, casegoods and training tables, office systems products, and filing and storage products.
Recycling Activities	Electronic and other recycling.
Services	Distribution and order fulfillment, assembly and packing, document conversion, call-center and help desk support, printing and creative design, and laundry.

You can see an alphabetical listing of these products at:

www.unicor.gov/prodservices/prod_dir_schedule/alphalist.cfm. **(98)**

This listing also indicates whether a particular item is:

- **Competitive:** The Federal Prison Industries will compete for business on the same terms as any private-sector offer.
- **Mandatory:** Federal customers *must* give these procurements to the Federal Prison Industries, as long as the item is available in the required timeframe and at a competitive price.
- **Non-Mandatory:** The Federal Prison Industries has waived the mandatory source requirement for this item.

Remember that UNICOR is interested in purchasing the raw materials for the products made in the prison factories, *not* the finished item. For example, UNICOR will purchase the material and thread required to make clothing, but not the actual finished garment.

The Federal Prison Industry (FPI) regularly posts notices to the FedBizOpps Website, seeking proposals for new products or service arrangements. FPI currently has several business agreements with private sector firms to provide products and services to the federal government, under its **Strategic Business Development Program**. For some business agreements, FPI provides fully equipped and staffed factories, and manufactures products and provides services as turn-key operations for its private-sector partners. For other agreements, FPI simply provides inmate labor and the physical factory space for industrial operations or service.

Website: ***www.unicor.gov/fpi_contracting***. (99)

Federal Prison Industries also publishes an annual sales report, showing sales by industry code (SIC) and Federal Supply Classification (FSC) code. A copy of the latest report is available by request from the agency.

Federal Bureau of Prisons

If you are interested in supplying a specific prison or local correctional institution with your products, you will need to contact the individual institutions directly. Each facility is responsible for buying the necessary supplies, services, and equipment it needs. Solicitations for larger opportunities (more than $25,000) are posted to the FedBizOpps Website, but if you are interested in smaller opportunities then you will need to contact these local institutions directly.

You can search for local institutions at this site: ***www.bop.gov***. (100)

United States Patent Office

Website: ***www.uspto.gov***. (101)

Click on Vendor Information for more details. You must register as an Interested Vendor at this site in order to participate in future procurement opportunities for simplified acquisitions (those estimated to be valued at $100,000 or less). Procurements over $25,000 will still be advertised at the FedBizOpps Website, but you will need to be registered at this Patent Office site in order to submit a quote, and you will have to submit your quote via this new system.

Use the Site Map option to locate the Office of Procurement Web Page, and follow the links to Vendor Self Service.

Subcontracting Opportunities (SUB-Net)

Website: ***www.sba.gov/subnet***. (4)

At the SBA's Subcontracting Opportunities page, called SUB-Net, you can link to each individual state and view a list of companies looking for small business subcontractors. When a large business receives a federal government contract valued at more than $100,000 (or more than $1 million in the case of the construction industry), the company is required to provide a Small Business Subcontracting Plan with its offer. The SBA can help you market your company as a subcontractor to these prime contractors.

Government Printing Office (GPO)

Website: *http://contractorconnect.gpo.gov*. (102)

If you are a small printing business (forms, pamphlets, envelopes, and so on), then this site is for you! The **Quick Quote** online small purchase system lists purchases under $100,000 for which the agency is accepting quotes electronically. You must be registered in order to submit a bid at this site.

Jacket Number	Era	Office Name	Quote Due Date	Date Posted	Product Type	Title	Total Quantity	Ship Delivery Date	Enter Quote
		Agency Marketing Services			Envelopes				Enter Quote
		Agency Publishing Service			Books				Enter Quote
		Agency Publishing Service			Forms				Enter Quote

Click on Jacket Number in the first column to see the specifications. Click on Enter Quote in the last column to submit your bid. You will be able to review your bid before you submit, and a Confirm Quote message will let you know that your bid was received successfully.

Non-Appropriated Funds

Sometimes an agency will pay for an item via non-appropriated funds; that is, using funds that do not come from the agency's regular budget. Where does the money come from?

Well, on all military bases there are many types of services available, similar to those you might find in any small town. For example, a Post Exchange (PX) is similar to a commercial department store: Military personnel and their dependents can shop for items that are not furnished by the government (kitchen appliances, sneakers, jewelry, civilian clothing, and so on). On large military bases these stores can be quite extensive. The PX also publishes a catalog several times a year.

The PX performs a service to military families, and is not required to make a profit. Because it only needs to cover its basic overhead costs, the PX can sell at a lower price than commercial retail outlets. Any profit it makes goes into a general fund that is used to pay for morale-boosting activities, such as a family day at a military base, with free food and entertainment, which may be paid for using non-appropriated funds. Non-appropriated funds may also used for activities for children who attend school on a military base.

There are many other types of services on military bases, such as restaurants, snack bars and cafeterias, commissaries (supermarkets), barber shops and hair salons, movie theaters, and so on. Most—but not all—of these conveniences are operated by commercial companies that have agreed to pay a certain percentage into the fund over and above their operating costs.

The following are two helpful Websites:
- Air Force Non-Appropriated Fund Purchasing Office (AFNAFPO): *www.afnafpo.com*. (103)
- Army-Air Force Exchange System (AAFES): *www.aafes.com*. (104)

Additional Procurement Sites

Many other procurement sites exist that you may wish to search, if you are looking for sales opportunities. Some of them are listed in the following table.

Air Force Small Business	*http://selltoairforce.org* (105)
Air Force—Hanscom	*www.herbb.hanscom.af.mil* (106)
Air Force—Wright Patterson (PIXS)	*https://pixs.wpafb.af.mil* (107)
Agriculture Dept	*www.usda.gov/procurement* (108)
Army Picatinny	*http://procnet.pica.army.mil* (109)
Army Anniston	*www.procnet.anad.army.mil* (110)
Army Warren	*http://contracting.tacom.army.mil* (111)
Army Red River	*www.redriver.army.mil* (112)
Army Rock Island	*https://aais.ria.army.mil* (113)
Army Sierra	*www.procnet.sierra.army.mil* (114)
Army Watervliet	*www.wva.army.mil* (115)
Army RDECom/Natick	*www3.natick.army.mil* (116)
Army CHESS Computer Program	*https://chess.army.mil* (117)
Army Fort Lewis	*www.lewis.army.mil* (118)
Census Bureau	*www.census.gov* (119)
Commerce Department Acquisition	*http://oam.ocs.doc.gov* (120)
Defense Energy Support Center	*www.desc.dla.mil* (121)

Education Department	*www.ed.gov/fund* (122)
Environmental Protection Agency (EPA)	*www.epa.gov* (123)
Federal Aviation Administration (FAA)	*https://faaco.faa.gov* (124)
Housing and Urban Development	*www.hud.gov* (125)
Justice Department (DOJ)	*www.usdoj.gov* (126)
Labor Department (DOL)	*www.dol.gov* (127)
NASA	*http://prod.nais.nasa.gov* (128)
National Guard	*www.nationalguardcontracting.org* (129)
The Federal Acquisition Jump-Station (This very important link provides information on many different acquisition sites.)	*http://prod.nais.nasa.gov/pub/fedproc /home.html* (130)
Where in Federal Contracting? (WIFCON) (The Quick-Kit tab provides a huge amount of information on all aspects of government procurement.)	*www.wifcon.com* (131)

Help!

If you have any questions about this chapter, we would be happy to try to help you. Go to our Website, *www.sell2gov.com*, and at the Contact tab you can send us an e-mail with your questions. Please put "Definitive Guide" in the subject line.

Chapter 5

Step By Step Through a Typical Solicitation Document

In Chapter 3 we discussed the Department of Defense's Internet Bid Board System, known as DIBBS. These bids were for relatively small sales opportunities, up to a maximum of $25,000. But for sales opportunities up to $100,000 you may need to complete a hard copy or paper document. Don't despair; in this chapter we take you page by page through a typical solicitation document, so that you can confidently complete one of these larger bids.

Remember—much of the information you must provide for this offer will be the same for many other bids you might submit in the future. Once you are familiar with these questions, you will realize that most of the work in completing your offer is in understanding exactly what the agency is requesting, and determining your price.

In this chapter we take you step by step through the pages of the document. We point out which sections must be completed, and where to find the exact details of what the government is looking for, as well as delivery details, and terms and conditions. We also discuss the Federal Acquisition Regulations, and Clauses Incorporated by Reference and by Full Text.

Of course each solicitation document will have variations from this example, and you will need to read the package through carefully so that you understand the terms and conditions of your offer before you submit. Once you have finished reading it carefully...read it again!

The Solicitation Numbering System

A solicitation number is made up of several parts. Understanding the numbering system can help you have a clearer picture of what the agency is looking for.
- The first six digits identify the department or agency that is issuing the bid.
- The second two digits identify the fiscal year the bid was issued.

- The single letter following the eight digits identifies the type of solicitation. For example, B for Invitation for Bid; Q for Request for Quote; R for Request for Proposal (a negotiated contract).
- The final four digits identify the particular solicitation. For example:

SPM8ED—10—Q—0021
Buying Office—Fiscal Year—Request for Quote—Solicitation ID Number

Standard Forms

Federal government agencies use several different types of Standard Forms when making purchases. For example:

- **Standard Form 1449** (SF1449): Solicitation/Contract/Order for Commercial Items.
- **Standard Form 18** (SF18): Request for Quotations. This form is used when the agency is looking for information and quotations. It is *not* an offer. If the agency wishes to award a contract as a result of the information in SF18, it will issue an award via another form, usually SF26 Award/Contract.
- **Standard Form 33** (SF33): Solicitation, Offer, and Award. This form is used to both solicit for offers and award a contract. You will complete and sign the document and submit it to the agency. Once it is accepted, the agency will also sign it, which establishes a binding contract.

These are the most commonly used forms, but you may come across others. In most cases the overall requirements will be the same, but there may be slight differences in the layout. (A copy of SF1449, SF18, and the first page of SF33 is included in the Appendix.)

Keep in mind that you will be answering many of the same questions over and over again for each offer you submit. The main difference between each offer is a description of the product or the Statement of Work for the service. Once you are familiar with these questions, you will realize that most of the work in completing your offer is in understanding exactly what the agency is requesting, and determining your price.

You will need to check the solicitation document carefully, to find details on how you may submit your offer—you may have several options available to you, such as e-mail, fax, or regular mail. If you are unsure, contact the contracting officer for clarification.

The Uniform Contract Format

All agencies format their solicitation documents in a specific, consistent way, so that you should be able to find the information you need, even though you may not have seen a particular agency's forms before. This is known as the **Uniform Contract Format**, and it consists of the following:

Section A: Solicitation/Contract Form.

Section B: Supplies or Services and Prices/Costs.

Section C: Description/Specifications/Work Statement.

Section D: Packaging and Marking.

Section E: Inspection and Acceptance.

Section F: Deliveries or Performance.

Section G: Contract Administration Data.

Section H: Special Contract Requirements.

Section I: Contract Clauses.

Section J: List of Attachments.

Section K: Representations, Certifications, and Other Statements of Offerors.

Section L: Instructions, Conditions, and Notices to Offerors.

Section M: Evaluation Factors.

~Once Upon a Time~

A company submitted a proposal *without* taking the time to read through the entire bid package. He had not considered the additional costs he would incur for the specific packaging, marking, and invoicing requirements listed in the solicitation document.

There are only three rules you need to remember
before you submit an offer:

Rule Number One: Read the solicitation package.

Rule Number Two: Get all your questions answered before you submit.

Rule Number Three: Please see Rule Number One.

Section A: Solicitation/Contract Form

On the following page is the typical first page for a Request for Quotations (RFQ) using Standard Form 18.

Is this RFQ a Small Business Set-Aside? How many pages are in this document? (Normally the document will range from eight to 20 pages long.) The following is an explanation of the blocks on this form.

- **Block 1:** The **Request Number**. This is the Solicitation Number, and will always be used as a reference. If you need to speak to the contracting officer concerning this bid, you will quote this number.

- **Block 2:** The **Date Issued**. The date the quote was issued. In many cases the time between the issue date and the offer date is 30 days. But this can vary; for example, if the need is particularly urgent.

- **Block 3:** The **Requisition**/Purchase Request Number is for the agency's records. Sometimes if you call with a question about an RFQ, the contracting officer may ask for this reference number.

- **Block 4:** The **Certificate for National Defense**—for agency use only.

- **Rating:** Department of Defense contracts may be assigned priority ratings using the **Defense Priority Allocation System (DPAS)**. There are two levels of priority—DO and DX. DO-rated orders take preference over unrated orders; DX-rated orders take preference over both DO-rated and unrated orders. In this case the solicitation is unrated. For more information on the DPAS program, go to: *www.ml.afrl. af.mil/dpas/default.html*. (132)

- **Block 5a: Issued By**. This is the name of the **Agency** that issued the quote.

- **Block 5b:** The **Contracting Officer**'s contact information.

- **Block 6: Deliver By**. This is the date by which the product must arrive, or the service must be performed. Be very aware of this date!

- **Block 7: Delivery**. In most instances you will be required to ship **FOB Destination** (Freight On Board Destination, sometimes also referred to as Free On Board). This means that you will pay all the shipping costs and be responsible for loss or damage until the items reach their destination. Alternatively, the term **FOB Origin** indicates that the agency will pay shipping costs.

- **Block 8:** This is where you will enter your **company name and address** as the company submitting the offer.
- **Block 9: Destination**. This is the mailing address where the package will be shipped. Sometimes these details are listed at the end of the solicitation document; particularly if there are multiple shipping addresses.
- **Block 10:** The **due date for submission** of offers. Take particular note of this, including any time that may be listed. If no particular time is specified, you can assume your bid must arrive no later than the close of business on the stated date. Remember that any time listed, including Close of Business time, refers to the *agency's* time zone, not yours!
- **Block 11: The Schedule**. This usually includes the phrase See Schedule, and the details of the requirements will be listed on the following pages.
- **Block 12: Discount For Prompt Payment**. This is where you would give a discount for prompt payment. You are not required to offer a prompt payment discount. Remember that the agency is required by regulation to pay you in 30 days! Unless you wish to offer a discount, you may prefer to add Net 30 days here.
- **Additional Provisions**. If this box is checked there will be additional documents attached that you will need to read and acknowledge. This might include an amendment to the solicitation, or more detailed specifications.
- **Block 13:** The **name and address** of the company that is submitting the quote.
- **Block 14:** The **signature** of the person authorized to sign the quote.
- **Block 15:** The **date** of the signature above.
- **Block 16:** The **printed or typed name** of the signer and his or her telephone number.

Section B—Supplies or Services and Prices

Item No. 0001

This column indicates that this is the first item requested in this bid package. If there was more than one item requested in this solicitation, you would see Line Item 0002 later in the solicitation, followed by the second item details.

SECTION B Supplies or Services and Prices

ITEM NO	SUPPLIES/SERVICES	QUANTITY	UNIT	UNIT PRICE	AMOUNT
0001		3.00	Each		

Power Cables
FFP - Mfg: J & N Avionics, P/N JB8816-100SNJ or equal, 100 ft. LTL braid, 200 amp, 400HZ, single jacket double ended cable assembly, 18 #18's (control), 6 #4's (phase) & 1 #1 for neutral. Molded strain relief behind heads and painted high visibility (yellow).
NSN 6150-03-POW-CABL
MILSTRIP F44LGL31050200
PURCHASE REQUEST NUMBER F44LGL31050200
SIGNAL CODE A

Commodity Line Item Number

You may come across the term **CLIN**, which is an acronym for **Commodity Line Item Number**. There may be only one line item, or there may be several. The agency will use separate line item numbers, not only for requesting different products, but also when they are looking for just one item but need different quantities shipped to different locations, or with different delivery terms. For example, Line Item 0001 may list a quantity of 50 and a delivery to California, whereas Line Item 0002 may be for the same product, but with a quantity of 75, or a requested three-day delivery time, or a delivery to a different location.

Options

In many cases, the purchasing agency will list a certain quantity on Line Item 0001, and then list an option quantity of an additional number of units in Line Item 0002. The agency may choose whether or not to exercise this second option.

Multiple-Year Contracts

If the solicitation is for one year followed by additional option year(s) then each option year will be listed as a separate line item number. In this case the first option year will be listed as either line item 1001 or A001. (This subject is discussed in more detail in Chapter 2.)

Supplies/Services

This section gives you a detailed description of the item they are requesting, including the type of pricing (in this case **FFP**, or Firm Fixed Price), the manufacturer, part number, and product specifications. The term *or equal* means that you are permitted to offer a product that is equal to or better than the specified product. You will need to provide documentation about your equivalent product. MILSTRIP, Purchase Request Number, and Signal Code are for government agency purposes only.

Quantity/Unit/Unit Price/Amount

These columns show you the total quantity requested (in this case three), and the Unit (which is often *each*, but could also be, for example, *dozen*, *gallon*, or *gross*). Be careful here to note the **Unit of Issue**—you don't want to quote for a single bottle if the Unit of Issue (U/I) requested is a 12-bottle case! The next column is where you write in your Unit Price. Remember that your Unit Price is a Unit *Delivered* Price—*always* include freight in your offer. In the final column you would insert the total cost of Line Item 0001.

Section C: Description/Specifications/Statement of Work

Section C of the solicitation document gives you detailed descriptions of what the agency requires. Naturally if you are supplying a relatively straightforward product, there may not be a lot of additional information in this section. However, in a contract for a service, Section C will always include a detailed Statement of Work (SOW); Performance Work Statement (PWS); or Statement of Objectives (SOO). In this case Section C may often be several pages long, and may include such things as Quality Assurance provisions; meeting schedules; qualification requirements for employees; or list the process for making any engineering changes. We discuss Service Contracts in Chapter 6, and go into more detail about their special requirements.

Section D: Packaging and Marking

Commercial Packaging

The federal government uses the term *commercial packaging* to describe any packaging that is developed by the supplier. The American Society for Testing and Material (ASTM) develops and maintains commercial packaging standards that are widely followed and referenced throughout the commercial packaging arena. The Department of Defense has adopted the **ASTM D 3951** (Standard Practice for Commercial Packaging) as its commercial standard. Other commercial standards may also apply, based on the product involved and the agency's particular needs.

Agencies generally prefer to use commercial packaging and performance-based specifications whenever possible—that is, when it is cost effective and will withstand anticipated conditions. Commercial packaging is now used extensively in some areas, such as medical supplies and subsistence. The Defense Logistics Agency has made extensive use of commercial packaging, in up to 90 percent of their transactions overall. The military services have also demonstrated expanded use of commercial packaging.

Military Packaging

This term is used to describe the standard packaging requirements developed by the Department of Defense. This standard is called **MIL-STD-2073-1**. Traditional packaging methods, which would normally serve a commercial customer well, can be unsuitable for the more severe conditions that arise when that same product is shipped to a military customer. In these instances more stringent military packaging requirements may be appropriate.

In this section of the solicitation package you will find the agency's packaging requirements. If possible the agency will specify a performance-based packaging requirement—that is, it will describe the required outcome and provide criteria for measuring and verifying performance, but will not dictate the specific methods to be used to achieve those outcomes. In this case you would propose an appropriate packaging plan, and work with the agency to agree on a mutually acceptable plan of action. (We discuss this in more detail in Chapter 7.)

Section E: Inspection and Acceptance

As we explained earlier, CLINS is an acronym for Commodity Line Item Number. There may be only one line item, or there may be several. The agency will use separate line item numbers, not only for requesting different products, but also when they are looking for just one item but need different quantities shipped to different locations, or with different delivery

terms. This was discussed earlier in this chapter, in Section B (Supplies and Services). In this case the item will be inspected and accepted at the destination point. At other times the agency may wish to inspect the item at its point of manufacture. (We discuss this more detail later in the book, in Chapter 7.)

Section F: Deliveries or Performance

Remember that the delivery date is *not* the shipping date. Your product must *arrive* no later than this stated delivery date. *Never* be late for this date!

As we discussed earlier, FOB Dest means Freight on Board Destination. This means that you will pay the shipping costs, and are responsible for the item until it reaches its destination.

The Ship to Address section tells you the exact shipping address.

Section G: Contract Administration Data

This section discusses payment via **Electronic Funds Transfer (EFT)** and cites the appropriate section of the Federal Acquisition Regulation (FAR). Make sure that the account details on your Central Contractors Registration (CCR) are correct, to ensure you are paid on time. Invoicing requirements, including electronic invoicing via Wide Area Work Flow (WAWF), are discussed in Chapter 7.

Section H: Special Contract Requirements

Section H draws your attention to any special Federal Acquisition Regulations (FAR) that may apply to a particular contract, as you can see in this example. Remember to always take the time to read and understand these regulations before you submit an offer. Naturally our brief explanations are not meant as a substitute for a thorough reading of the regulations!

Section H—Special Contract Requirements

252.203-7002	Display of DOD Hotline Poster Dec/1991
252.204-7000	Disclosure of Information Dec/1991
252.205-7000	Provision of Information to Cooperative Agreement Holders Dec/1991
252.225-7002	Qualifying Country Sources As Subcontractors Apr/2003
252.225-7004	Reporting of Contract Performance outside The United States Jun/2005
252.225-7005	Identification of Expenditures in the United States Jun/2005
252.225-7006	Quarterly Reporting of Actual Contract Performance outside the U.S.
252.225-7013	Duty-Free Entry Jun/2005
252.225-7021	Trade Agreements Feb/2006
252.225-7033	Waiver of United Kingdom Levies Apr/2003
252.225-7043	Antiterrorism/Force Protection Policy for Defense Contractors outside the United States
252.226-7001	Utilization of Indian Organizations, Indian-Owned Economic Enterprises, and Native Hawaiian Small Business Concerns Sep/2004
252.228-7003	Capture and Detention Dec/1991
252.231-7000	Supplemental Cost Principles Dec/1991
252.246-7000	Material Inspection and Receiving Report Mar/2003

252.246-7001	Warranty of Data Dec/1991
252.237-7019	Training for Contractor Personnel Interacting With Detainees Aug/2005
252.217-7026	Identification of Sources of Supply
252.225-7040	Contractor Personnel Supporting a Force Deployed Outside the U.S.
52.204-4005	Required Use of Electronic Contracting

Section I: Contract Clauses—Incorporated by Reference and by Full Text

In every solicitation document there are some Federal Acquisition Regulations that are only referenced, and not printed in full. Even if a regulation is only referenced, it has the same weight as if it was printed in full, so you need to be aware of them all.

Don't be daunted by the long list of regulations that face you! Remember that:

- Many regulations are listed in most or all solicitation documents, which means that, once you have read and understood how the regulation affects your company, you will recognize it in subsequent documents. You will see these same regulations over and over again in each solicitation document.

- Many regulations concern standard business practices that are common to any commercial business, including child labor laws, equal opportunity regulations, and so on.

- In many instances you will see a long list of regulations. You will notice that the regulations that apply are marked with an X in front of them. Those that are not marked do not apply to this particular solicitation.

The Website for the Federal Acquisition Regulations (FAR) is: *http://acquisition.gov/far/index.html*. (45)

Some Commonly Referenced Regulations

In this section we briefly discuss some of the more common clauses you may come across, including:

52.212-1	Instructions to Offerors—Commercial Items
52.212-2	Evaluation Commercial Items
52.212-4	Contract Terms and Conditions—Commercial Items
52.212-5	Contract Terms and Conditions Required To Implement Statutes or Executive Orders—Commercial Items
52.225-1	Buy America Act
52.232-30	Payments by Electronic Funds Transfers

52.222-4   Fair Labor Standards, the Service Contract Act, and Minimum Wage Regulations

52.212-1 Instructions to Offerors—Commercial Items

52.212-1   INSTRUCTIONS TO OFFERORS – COMMERCIAL ITEMS (OCT 2000)

(a) North American Industry Classification System (NAICS) code and small business size standard. The NAICS code and small business size standard for this acquisition appear in Block 10 of the solicitation cover sheet (SF 1449). However, the small business size standard for a concern which submits an offer in its own name, but which proposes to furnish an item which it did not itself manufacture, is 500 employees.

(b) Submission of offers. Submit signed and dated offers to the office specified in this solicitation at or before the exact time specified in this solicitation. Offers may be submitted on the SF 1449, letterhead stationery, or as otherwise specified in the solicitation. As a minimum, offers must show–

(1) The solicitation number;

(2) The time specified in the solicitation for receipt of offers;

(3) The name, address, and telephone number of the offeror;

(4) A technical description of the items being offered in sufficient detail to evaluate compliance with the requirements in the solicitation. This may include product literature, or other documents, if necessary;

(5) Terms of any express warranty;

(6) Price and any discount terms;

(7) "Remit to" address, if different than mailing address;

In this example the Contract Clause has been printed in full. It contains standard information that you must understand in order to be able to fulfill your obligations under this contract. The following is a description of some of the parts of this instruction form:

- **(a)** is a description of the **North American Industrial Classification System (NAICS)** and the size standards for small businesses. We discussed NAICS codes in Chapter 1.
- **(b)** is instruction on **Submission of Offers**. This explains exactly what needs to be submitted with this offer, numbered 1 though 11.
- Note that **number 8** (shown on the following page of this book), **Representations and Certifications**, refers to the Online Representations and Certifications Application (ORCA) that we discussed in Chapter 1.
- Also note **number 9**, Acknowledgment of **Solicitation Amendments**. Always check for any amendments at the agency's Website, where the original solicitation notice was posted, before you submit your offer. It is important to remember that any amendments *must* be acknowledged by your signature and the date, and become part of your offer. Failure to include these amendments with your offer will mean that your offer will not be eligible for consideration.

(8) A completed copy of the representations and certifications at FAR 52.212-3;

(9) Acknowledgment of Solicitation Amendments;

(10) Past performance information, when included as an evaluation factor, to include recent and relevant contracts for the same or similar items and other references (including contract numbers, points of contact with telephone numbers and other relevant information); and

(11) If the offer is not submitted on the SF 1449, include a statement specifying the extent of agreement with all terms, conditions, and provisions included in the solicitation. Offers that fail to furnish required representations or information, or reject the terms and conditions of the solicitation may be excluded from consideration.

(c) Period for acceptance of offers. The offeror agrees to hold the prices in its offer firm for 30 calendar days from the date specified for receipt of offers, unless another time period is specified in an addendum to the solicitation.

- **Number 10, Past Performance Information** is requesting that you also submit information about your recent past customers (Point of Contact Name, Company Address, and Telephone Number). The agency will request information from the companies you list regarding your company's service—Did you deliver on time? Was the company satisfied with the overall product or service? Did any problems get resolved quickly? This will help the agency to evaluate your offer, and ensure that they are dealing with a reputable company with a history of quality and service.

- **(c)** is about the **Period for Acceptance of Offers**. You must honor the price that you have given for a specified number of days from the date for receipt of offers. In this particular case you must hold your prices for 30 days, but this number may vary from one solicitation to another, so it is very important that you check this before you make your offer. In some cases you may be asked to guarantee your prices for as long as 180 days. **(d)** says that if the government requests a **sample** of your product, you must provide one.

- **(e)** You are encouraged to submit **multiple offers** here.

- **(f)** concerns **Late Submissions**, modifications, revisions, and withdrawals of offers. If your offer arrives late, the agency has the option whether or not to consider it. You may modify your offer, revise it, or withdraw it prior to a contract being awarded, even if it arrives after the bid opening date. Section F explains what a late offer is, and exactly how it will be handled. It is always a good idea to follow up to ensure that your offer arrived on time by contacting the contracting officer involved (see Block 5b of the solicitation for details of the contracting officer's name, telephone number, and e-mail address).

- **(g)** is about the **contract award**. In this particular case the contract will be awarded without discussion—in other words, it is *not* a negotiated contract. Remember to always give the government your *best* price!

- **(h)** concerns **multiple awards**. This means that more than one company can be awarded a contract under this solicitation number. At other times only one award will be made.
- **(i)** is the **specifications and standards** section, which tells you where to go to obtain additional documents such as specifications and standards that are cited in the solicitation. This section gives you agency addresses, phone numbers, fax numbers, and Websites in order for you to obtain any additional information pertaining to this quote. We discussed this earlier in the book.
- **Data Universal Numbering System (DUNS) Number:** You are required to have a DUNS number prior to award. This section explains how to acquire a number. (We discussed this in detail in Chapter 1 of the book.)

52.212-2 Evaluation—Commercial Items (Jan 1999)

- **(a): evaluations.** This provision lets you know exactly what criteria the government will use to evaluate your offer, and the method that will be used to award the contract. In many cases, although price will be a factor, it will not necessarily be the only factor or even the determining factor in awarding the contract. Sometimes a company's past performance or technical ability will be more important. At other times, the delivery schedule will be a priority.
- **(b): options.** In many cases the agency will specify a certain quantity of an item, and then specify particular options that it may choose to exercise. For example, the agency may choose to exercise a 100-percent option, doubling the initial quantity requested.
- **(c): award.** Once it has been accepted, the offer is binding.

~Once Upon a Time~

I had a client that manufactured labels. He put in a bid so low that he hardly made any money, but wanted the experience of completing a contract. In the contract the government had the option to double the volume without negotiation. They did. Luckily he broke even and didn't lose any money.

Moral: You are in business to make money, not win government contracts.

52.212-4 Contract Terms and Conditions—Commercial Items

The information in this section explains the terms and conditions of this contract, so that you will have a full understanding of what is required of you from the time you are awarded the contract until you are paid in full. Read through this section so that you fully understand your obligations to the government.

Note particularly the following sections:

- **(f): excusable delays.** Make sure you can honor the terms of the contract before you make an offer. Keep the contracting officer fully informed if you expect unavoidable delays in the completion of this contract.

- **(g): invoices.** Pay particular attention to the format of the invoice you should submit to the government. You do not want any delays in the payment process because you omitted relevant information on your invoice! In more and more cases the agencies are requiring businesses to use certain specific electronic invoicing software, such as Wide Area Work Flow. We discuss this in Chapter 7.

- **(1), (2), (k): Delivery FOB Destination.** When you consider the price you will quote to the government, remember that the terms of delivery must be taken into consideration, as well as any applicable taxes. The price you quote must be net—include all applicable taxes and delivery costs. Unless stated otherwise, all unit prices submitted are for a delivered price.

Remember that FOB means Freight on Board. FOB-Destination means that you are paying the freight to the delivered address—you still own the product until the agency accepts it. FOB-Origin means that the agency owns the product once it leaves your premises. Prices also must include all applicable federal state and local taxes.

52.212-5 Contract Terms and Conditions Required to Implement Statutes or Executive Orders—Commercial Items

You will find these regulations in every solicitation document, but they do not all apply to every solicitation. The contracting officer will note which regulations pertain to a particular quote. Next to each regulation will be a box that the contracting officer will check if that particular regulation applies. If the box is not checked, then that regulation does not apply.

You should familiarize yourself with these regulations, so that you fully understand the terms of the contract. However, many of these regulations will not be relevant to a particular quote, and many regulations will appear each time you bid, so that you will soon become familiar with them.

Notice, for example, the regulations numbered here as 2 through 7 that concern set-asides for small businesses or businesses in a HUB-Zone. (These set-asides were described for you in Chapter 1 of this book.) These do *not* have check marks beside them, so *in this case they do not apply.*

_____ (2) 52.219-3, Notice of HUBZone Small Business Set-Aside (Jan 1999)(U.S.C. 657a).

_____ (3) 52.219-4, Notice of Price Evaluation Preference for HUBZone Small Business Concerns (Jan 1999) (if the offeror elects to waive the preference, it shall so indicate in its offer)(U.S.C. 657a).

_____(4) (i) 52.219-5, Very Small Business Set-Aside (JUNE 2003) (Pub. L. 103-403, section 304, Small Business Reauthorization and Amendments Act of 1994).

_____(ii) Alternate I (MAR 1999) to 52.219-5.

_____(iii) Alternate II to (JUNE 2003) 52.219-5.

_____ (5)(i) 52.219-6, Notice of Total Small Business Set-Aside (JUNE 2003) (15 U.S.C. 644).

_____ (ii) Alternate I (OCT 1995) of 52.219-6.

_____ (6)(i) 52.219-7, Notice of Partial Small Business Set-Aside (JUNE 2003) (15 U.S.C. 644).

_____ (ii) Alternate I (OCT 1995) of 52.219-7.

_____ (7) 52.219-8, Utilization of Small Business Concerns (OCT 2000) (15 U.S.C. 637 (d)(2) and (3)).

Other sections of the regulations concern **convict labor laws, child labor laws, equal-opportunity and affirmative-action laws,** and so on. You are probably already aware of these regulations as they relate to your commercial business.

FAR 52,223-9

This regulation concerns **environmentally friendly**, recycled-content, and other regulations that may be relevant to your company's products. A more detailed discussion of the federal government's Environmentally Friendly, or "Green" purchasing program is found in the chapter on the Defense Logistics Agency's DIBBS site.

Buy American Act—FAR 52.225-1

The Buy American Act and the North America Free Trade Agreement place restrictions on certain foreign purchases. If your product is made outside of the United States, Canada, or Mexico, you must be aware of the restrictions that the government places on purchases of foreign-made products (FAR 52.225).

As a general rule, the Buy American act restricts the purchases of supplies that are not domestic-end products. Domestic-end products are those that are manufactured in the United States, Canada, or Mexico. At least 51 percent of the cost of producing the finished product must be incurred domestically in order for it to be considered as a domestic-end product.

You may import component parts from outside the United States/Canada/Mexico, and assemble the finished product domestically, as long as at least 51 percent of the final costs are incurred domestically. For example, a manufacturer may import component parts from outside the United States and assemble them here. As long as the cost of assembly is at least twice the cost of component parts, the item is considered to be domestic-end.

In January 2009 the Department of Defense issued an interim ruling, allowing Commercial-Off-The-Shelf (COTS) products to be treated as domestic-end products, if they are manufactured in the United States, without the need to track the origin of the item's components (Federal Register/Vol. 74, No. 10/15 January 2009).

Under certain conditions the Buy American requirements may be waived to allow foreign end products, including:

- **Trade Agreements:** Certain agreements such as the World Trade Organization Government Procurement Agreement (WTO GPA), Free Trade Agreements (FTAs) with various countries (including the Caribbean Basin Trade Initiative (CBTI), Memorandum of Understandings (MOUs) with Qualifying Countries, (DFARS 225.872), and the North American Free Trade Agreement (NAFTA).

- **Non-availability:** If the item is not available in sufficient commercial quantities, or is not of a satisfactory quality (FAR 25.104 and DFARS 225.104).

- **Unreasonable Costs:** If purchasing the item domestically would burden the government with an unreasonable cost (FAR 25.105/Subpart 25.5 and DFARS 225.105/Subpart 25.5).

- **Resale:** Foreign-end products may be purchased specifically for commissary resale.

- **Commercial Information Technology** items: See Federal Acquisition Regulation (FAR) 25.103 and the Dept. of Defense Supplemental Regulation (DFAR) 225.103.

52.232-30 Payments by Electronic Funds Transfers

As we discussed in Chapter 1, you must be registered in the Central Contractors Registration. You will be paid via Electronic Funds Transfer (EFT) into the account listed in your CCR registration. Make sure your bank details and account information in CCR is correct!

52.222-4 Fair Labor Standards, the Service Contract Act, and Minimum Wage Regulations

The regulations in this section refer to Minimum Wage laws and Fair Labor Standards. We will discuss this in more detail in Chapter 6.

Section J: List of Attachments

This section includes a list of any relevant drawings, meeting schedules, parts lists, and so on that are included as attachments. Here is an example, showing some Contract Data Requirements as separate attachments.

Exhibit A Contract Data Requirements List 10-July-2006

Attachment 001   ATPD 2277, Improved Bridge, Floating Ribbon, Interior Bay and Ramp Bay

Attachment 002   Graphic Representation of the IUID Plates,

Attachment 003   Projected IRB Fielding Schedule for the IRB thru FY11,

Attachment 004   Government Configuration Management Plan

Attachment 005   Listing of Parts under CLIN 1013AA

Section K: Representations, Certifications, and Other Statements of Offerors

This section contains the Representations and Certifications clauses that we discussed in Chapter 1, "Important Business Codes and Numbers"; specifically the section about registering at the new **Online Representations and Certifications Application (ORCA)** site. The **Place of Manufacture Clause** requires you to declare if your product is produced within or outside of the United States. This information is for statistical purposes only, and is not the same as the Buy American or Trade Agreement acts.

Section L: Instructions, Conditions, and Notices to Offerors

Federal Acquisition Regulations may be referenced either in full or in part in this section. Of course, we cannot include every regulation that may appear in this section, so you will need to carefully read each regulation that appears in the solicitation document. You will *also* need to check those regulations that are only referenced in the document, by searching at the FAR and/or the FarSite Websites, in order to make sure that you understand how they apply to this offer.

FAR: *acquisition.gov/far/index.html*; (45) FarSite: *http://farsite.hill.af.mil*. (46)

This section may contain clauses such as:

- 52.211-2: **Availability of Specifications.** As we discussed earlier, many unclassified Defense specifications and standards may be downloaded from the ASSIST Website at *https://assist.daps.dla.mil*, (27) or they may be ordered from the Department of Defense Single Stock Point (DoDSSP) at *http://dodssp.daps.dla .mil*. (133) This regulation gives you exact details on how to obtain them.

- 52.211-14: **Notice of Priority Rating For National Defense Use.** This regulation concerns the **Defense Priorities and Allocations System (DPAS)** we discussed earlier in the book. If this regulation is cited, then any contract awarded would be a DX-Rated Order, and you would need to follow the instructions concerning this regulation. We discussed this regulation earlier in this chapter, under Section A. For more information on this program, go to: *www.ml.afrl.af.mil/dpas/default. html*. (132)

- 52.214-34: **Submission of Offers in the English Language**; and 52.214-35: **Submission of Offers in U.S. Currency.** You must submit your offers in the English language, and in U.S. dollars.

- 52.216-1: **Type of Contract.** This is a Firm Fixed Price (FFP) contract—there can be no adjustments to the price during the life of the contract. At other times contracts may be Fixed Price With Economic Price Adjustments, Fixed Ceiling Price Contracts, Level of Effort Contracts, Cost Reimbursement Contracts, Cost-Sharing Contracts, Contracts with Incentives, Time & Materials Contracts, Labor Hour Contracts, and so on.

- 52.211-4047: **Notice to Offerors Intending to Offer Other Than New Material.** This section discusses whether you may offer a remanufactured or re-conditioned product, or whether the item must be new.

- 52.245-4002: **Acquisition of New Facilities**, Special Test Equipment, or Special Tooling. The agency will not reimburse you for the cost of any new facilities, special test equipment, or special tooling as a separate item. However, you may choose to amortize any of these costs in your submitted price.

- 52.245-4003: Use of Existing **Government-Owned Property.** At times the agency may furnish you with an item in order for you to fulfill your contract; for example, if a service contract involves the repair or upgrade of a particular piece of government-owned equipment. At other times you may request use of government-owned facilities, tools, or other special test equipment. In that case you would need to include the written permission of the contracting officer when you submit your offer.

Section M: Evaluation Factors for Award

The agency will evaluate all the offers it receives, and base its award decision on what it determines is in the best interests of the government. Your proposal will be evaluated in three areas: (1) Past Performance, (2) Technical/Management, and (3) Price.

In some cases price alone is the determining factor. At other times the agency may give equal weight to other factors. In this section of the solicitation document the agency will clearly state how it will make its evaluation, and how price, technical ability, past performance, or other factors will be weighed when making its decision.

In cases in which technical requirements are critical, the agency may convene a **Technical/ Management Evaluation Panel**, which will analyze each Technical/Management Proposal that is submitted, and will then rate each element, giving the highest rating to the best overall approach. In these cases the Technical/Management and Past Performance factors become significantly more important than price.

In some cases the agency will assign a rating to each factor, depicting how well you meet the requirements in each area. For example, your evaluation will be rated highest if your proposal meets or exceeds the requirements of the solicitation, if you show a very good solution for meeting the needs and objectives of the program, if you have significant strengths in certain critical areas, and so on.

The **Past Performance evaluation** tries to determine whether your company will successfully complete the requirements of the contract, based on your previous performance in both current and past contracts. The agency will look at past contracts that are relevant to the current requirement, and are as up-to-date as possible. The agency will look at previous contracts with federal, state, or local governments, as well as commercial contracts when making their evaluation. If there were any problems with the contract, the agency will take into consideration whether they were appropriately and effectively addressed— not just what was promised or planned!

If you have no record of past performance, or if Past Performance information is not available, then the agency will give you a "neutral" rating in this area. That is, you will not be evaluated favorably or unfavorably on Past Performance.

The **Past Performance Information Retrieval System** is the site where government agencies note how well you performed on any awarded contract, and this information is shared among other government agencies. You can have access to your own records, and may comment upon anything in the report, but you do *not* have access to the records of other contractors. Since July 2009, agencies are required to post *all* contractor performance evaluations at this site.

Website: *www.ppirs.gov*. (39)

Combined Synopsis/Solicitation

In some cases you may come across a Combined Synopsis/Solicitation. In these instances there is no solicitation package. The combined synopsis/solicitation will not contain any administrative paperwork, but will reference all the rules and regulations pertaining to this proposal. The regulations are referenced by a Federal Acquisition Regulation (FAR) number, followed by a subject name. For example: FAR 52.212-3 Offeror Representation and Certifications.

You will need to look in the FAR Website to find the details for each regulation that has been referenced: *http://acquisition.gov/far/index.html*. (45)

Because there is no solicitation standard form in this case, you will be required to submit your offer on your company letterhead. Remember to include:

- The date of your offer.
- The agency or department's name and address listed on page 1 of the solicitation.
- Attention: The name of the contracting officer listed on page 1 of the solicitation.
- The Solicitation Number.
- The Nomenclature—in other words, the description of the item requested.
- Your total delivered price.
- A statement that you have read and agree to all the regulations that apply to this offer.
- A copy of your Online Representations and Certifications document—FAR 52.212-3.
- All amendments, signed and acknowledged.
- Your signature, your printed name and title in the company, and the date signed.

Submitting Your Offer

Once your quote is completed and signed, be sure to include the complete solicitation document, signed and dated; any amendments, which must also be signed and dated; any other additional information (catalogues, sales sheets, price lists); and Past Performance references if required.

In the bottom left-hand corner of the envelope, write the Solicitation Number, and the Bid Opening Date and Time. This will allow your bid to be sent to the correct department as quickly as possible, and will avoid any delays. *Make Sure Your Quote Arrives On Time!*

Help!

If you have any questions about this chapter, we would be happy to try to help you. Go to our Website, *www.sell2gov.com*, and at the Contact tab you can send us an e-mail with your questions. Please put "Definitive Guide" in the subject line.

Chapter 6

Service Contracts

Are you a Landscaping company?

A Public Relations firm?

A Temporary Staffing agency?

A Construction firm?

A Computer Programming company?

A Janitorial/Facilities Management agency?

Or any other type of Service-Oriented Company?

If so, then this chapter is for you! Although much of the information in the previous chapters applies to both product and service contracts, there are some special requirements you will need to be aware of if your company provides a service. Of course there are enormous differences between different types of service companies—a landscaping company looking to be awarded a contract for grounds maintenance at a particular agency site will need to cover a specific set of criteria, whereas a public relations firm will need another, very different approach. However, there are still some general rules that apply in *any* service contract, regardless of type. In many cases the solicitation document for a service contract will require you to submit your proposal in three distinct parts:

1. The Price Proposal.
2. The Technical Proposal.
3. Past Performance Information.

The **Statement of Work (SOW)** or the **Performance Work Statement (PWS)** sections of the solicitation document will state clearly how to complete each one of these parts, and you will need to pay attention to the details in these sections. In many cases failure to follow the requirements set out here can result in your proposal not even being given consideration!

Understanding the Structure of a Typical SOW or PWS

A **Statement of Work** should identify and emphasize the critical elements the agency is looking for. The agency will state exactly what is required, including the deliverables and the due dates that must be met.

145

A **Performance-Based Work Statement** (PWS) is written in such a way that allows you to determine how to meet the government's performance objectives.

The SOW or PWS contains the following sections:

- **Background:** Describes the project in general terms; its purpose, and how it relates to any other projects. If necessary it may include a brief summary of statutory authority or any applicable regulations. This section may also provide details of any relevant background documents, either as a reference or as an attachment.

- **Objectives:** Gives an overview of the project and how the results or end products will be used. It contains the agency's goals and objectives for the project.

- **Scope:** Covers the general scope of the work you will be required to perform.

- **Tasks or Requirements:** Gives detailed work and management requirements, and spells out more precisely what is expected in the performance of the work.

- **Selection Criteria:** Identifies the objective standards of acceptable performance that you must provide.

- **Deliverables or Delivery Schedule:** This section describes exactly what you will be required to provide, identifies your responsibilities, and gives details of any specialized expertise, services, training, or documentation that may be required. This section will clearly state the deliverables, the delivery schedule (in calendar days from date of award), quantities, and delivery location. It will also indicate the exact type of documentation (printed and electronic) to be provided, as well as any quality indicators the agency wants from you.

- **Government-Furnished Equipment and Information:** Identifies any equipment or information that will be provided by the agency.

- **Security:** States the appropriate security requirements.

- **Place of Performance:** Specifies whether the work is to be performed at a government site or at your site.

- **Period of Performance:** Lists the performance period of the contract, in terms of hours, days, weeks, or months.

Preparing a Service Contract Proposal

In many ways preparing a government proposal can be quite similar to the way you submit proposals to your commercial clients.

The following may sound obvious, but—please read the solicitation package very carefully, and take time to completely understand the agency's requirements. Understand the entire contents of the bid package, not just the Statement of Work section. In Chapter 5 we discussed the Uniform Contract Format, which allows you to more easily find specific sections of the contract. Again, these are:

Section A: Solicitation/Contract Form

Section B: Supplies or Services and Prices/Costs

Section C: Description/Specifications/Work Statement

Section D: Packaging and Marking

Section E: Inspection and Acceptance

Section F: Deliveries or Performance

Section G: Contract Administration Data

Section H: Special Contract Requirements

Section I: Contract Clauses

Section J: List of Attachments

Section K: Representations, Certifications, and Other Statements of Offerors

Section L: Instructions, Conditions and Notices to Offerors

Section M: Evaluation Factors

Initially you will read the Statement of Work (SOW), Performance Work Statement (PWS), or Statement of Objectives (SOO), in Section C. This will give you an idea of whether you can consider submitting a proposal.

However, once you have decided that this *is* something to consider, you will also need to look carefully at all the other sections, including Section L for Instructions, Conditions, and Notices; Section J for any attachments; and Section M to see the evaluation factors the agency will use to determine their award.

Pricing

In this area you must be the best judge of what is considered to be fair and reasonable pricing in your industry, as well as the typical pricing structure to use.

Pricing History

Obtaining pricing history for a service contract may be difficult. In many cases the agency may not have had that service performed in the past, or the scope of work for the solicitation may be different from any previous contracts, so a fair comparison could be difficult. But you may be able to find out some indication of the previous history of this contract—if a particular company has been awarded a contract for this service at this agency in the past, finding out those details may help you to make some decisions on costs and pricing structure. You may wish to ask the contracting officer if there is any information on past contracts for this service. For example, is there an incumbent contractor? If so, you may be able to get an award number. The award document can tell you the total award amount, and the length of the contract. If this particular company has been performing this service at this agency or base for several years, is the buying office more likely to award another contract to that company? Perhaps the company cannot compete this time around; perhaps the agency is looking for a more competitive offer? Armed with this knowledge, will you decide not to compete, or can you offer something better? Remember that you are in this market to make a profit, *not* just to win a government contract at any price.

Hidden Extras

Be aware of possible details in the Statement of Work or other areas of the solicitation document that may add up to extra, unanticipated costs. Will you need security clearance to perform the service at an Army base? Army contracts include a Contractor Manpower Reporting (CMR) clause, which requires you to track and report the number of personnel (including subcontractors) and the number of hours used in the service of the contract each year. This could be an additional "hidden" administrative cost to be aware of. Perhaps the agency requires certain certifications or quality assurance provisions, in addition to labor and material costs.

If the solicitation is a **Request for Proposal**, the agency will give details of the requirement and ask you to propose a method to fulfill it. You will need to give details of how you plan to meet the requirements—perhaps detail your managerial approach, and how you plan to keep the project on time and budget—and show the agency that you understand what it is looking for, and can meet its requirements.

Notice if the document is a **Request for Information (RFI)**, **Sources Sought**, or **Market Research**. In this case the agency does not yet have a specific proposal in mind. Just as the name implies, the agency is taking an initial look at the marketplace to see what may be available to fill its needs in the future. There is no guarantee that if you respond to an RFI there will be a solicitation for the work issued at a later date. Of course you may still decide to respond—letting the agency know who you are and your capabilities is a great way to get exposure—but be aware that you will not be reimbursed for the work you put into this request.

The Technical Proposal

This section is probably the one that will take most of your time to prepare. Remember, however, that you will probably be able to use this information again in future submissions, with only minor changes each time to reflect the requirements of a particular contract document.

In many instances the agency will set a limit of the number of pages you may submit in this section, and they will often require you to submit these documents in a particular format and font style, using double- or-single spaced type, and so on. Pay particular attention to this—you don't want your carefully prepared proposal to be rejected because of a minor error like this. Also, because the agency will often limit the number of pages you can submit here, you want to make the best use of each page, and make sure you cover each requirement thoroughly.

Color Inside the Lines

Stay within your capabilities; don't be tempted to respond to a solicitation that is outside the core of your business strengths. Are the requirements listed in the solicitation a good match for your company? Do you have the technical capability to fulfill the requirements? Have you had experience with similar contracts?

Read through the requirements of the **Technical Proposal** carefully before you begin to gather information. You may be able to find a lot of the information you need in your existing marketing literature—company brochures, Website pages, and previous proposals for commercial clients. These could all become the starting point for your proposal, which you then tailor to meet the specifics of the requirements. In many cases this section will reflect the way you submit offers in the commercial environment.

The first thing here is to read through the Statement of Work (SOW), the Performance Work Statement (PWS), or the Statement of Objectives (SOO) section carefully. Often the agency will describe what it needs line by line, so make sure that your proposal fully covers each requirement listed.

If the project requires it, you may be asked to describe your overall project-management plan, the functions of each team member on the project, and the procedures you will put in place to ensure that deliverables are met, including cost-control measures, project schedules, staffing requirements, and so on. If you are planning a teaming or subcontracting approach to this project, you should show how you will maintain a unified effort, and how the team will interact with the agency.

In many cases the requirements of the Statement of Work (SOW) will be broken down into smaller tasks, and a specific timetable for delivery of each task will be laid out, as we can see in the following example. Keep in mind that this example shows you a *general* look at a Statement of Work, but because there are so many different agencies, and so many variables on the type of work to be performed, the overall look of any Statement of Work section will vary greatly.

Deliverables

SOW Paragraph Reference	Deliverable Description	Delivery Date (no later than)
General	Deliverables—All deliverables become the property of the United States Government. Unless otherwise stated, all deliverables will be submitted in both hardcopy and electronic media in Microsoft Word/PowerPoint/Excel format.	NLT=No Later Than

1.0	Completed analysis or assessment—Completed draft analysis or assessment in the appropriate Joint Staff Study format. Presented in briefing, written report and/or white paper format.	NLT 5 days prior to suspense
3.0	Briefing describing strategies and analysis campaign plans—Summarize current analysis strategies and campaign plans for the major department processes.	NLT 10 days after government tasking
4.0	Briefing summarizing results of literature searches—Briefing identifying the general issue area to be researched.	NLT 10 days after government tasking
5.0	Research and decisional meeting briefings—Draft briefing to scope requirements.	NLT 10 days after government tasking
6.1	Analytic Tools Briefing—Draft briefing and point papers assessing new analytic tools/methodologies/emerging technologies.	20 days following technology ID
6.2	CCB Briefs and Tool Management Reports—Draft briefing and information package for Configuration Control Board meetings; draft CM plans and process reports.	5 pays prior to board
7.1	Scoping research briefings—Draft briefings and papers summarizing research to scope analytical requirements, tools, and methodologies.	NLT 20 workdays following tasking
7.2	M&S Topic Report—Draft written response to M&S issues in standard Joint Staff format.	10 workdays following task ID
8.1	Status Tracking Report—Monitor, track, and compile database spreadsheet representations of the status of studies based on their timelines, milestones, and progress reports.	10 workdays prior to end of each month
8.2	Reports, summaries, and briefings—Prepare draft reports, study summaries, formal briefings, and supporting graphic material in written or oral form. All documentation shall be provided in hard copy and electronic format and shall be rendered in the current Joint Staff version of Microsoft Office applications.	NLT 5 days prior to suspense

8.4	Meeting Support—Provide support by organizing technical interchanges and support discussions, preparing meeting minutes and after-action reports, coordinating and integrating study results with other organizations, and distributing materials. This includes offsite government-sponsored conferences and seminars.	NLT 5 days after event
8.5	Scheduling Support—The contractor shall provide support scheduling issues for the FM FCB. This includes monitoring JCIDS documents and milestones in order to develop and provide recommendation summaries and status reports to the government.	3 workdays following task ID
9.0	Quality Control Plan	10 days after contract award
1.0, 2.0, 3.0, 4.0, 5.0	Monthly Status Reports	By the 5th workday each month

In your proposal you should:

- Demonstrate a complete understanding of the requirement.
- Show that you are qualified to complete the task. Include staff experience and qualifications, as well as previous work that was similar in nature.
- Respond carefully to the criteria for evaluation in Section M.
- Follow the format required. Sometimes the solicitation will state a maximum number of pages, and even a specific font and size for the proposal. Don't lose the opportunity to be considered just for a simple oversight like this!
- Show good management and cost accounting practices. Provide adequate cost and pricing data; show how you will keep the project on time and budget.
- Proofread. Check grammar and spelling. Rewrite if necessary. Take the time to make your proposal as professional and complete as possible. Beware of in-house or industry-accepted abbreviations or acronyms. Don't assume the person reading your proposal is aware of these terms.
- Keep copies of everything you submit. You may be able to use much of this proposal as a basis for your next one!

> **~Once Upon a Time~**
> When a small construction company realized it needed to prepare business, technical, and financial proposals in order to submit an offer, it seemed like a great deal of work! But once the proposals were completed the company realized that it could use them as a basis for a lot of other proposals in the future.

Past Performance Evaluation

The agency is looking for clear evidence that you have performed work of a similar nature in the past, and that your previous work was satisfactory. To this end you will be asked to supply information on previous customers, so that the agency can contact them and evaluate your performance. You may be asked for any customer surveys that demonstrate customer satisfaction with overall job performance and the quality of the job that was completed. If there were any problems or delays in these contracts, how well did you resolve them? You may be asked for details of any federal contracts you have previously completed, as well as any recent commercial projects.

If you plan a subcontracting arrangement with another company you will need to provide complete information on how this will work, and whether you have teamed with this contractor on previous occasions.

Submitting a No-Bid Response

If you decide *not* to submit a proposal for a specific reason, you may wish to inform the contracting officer of this, so that the agency understands you are still interested in future requirements, but in this particular instance you cannot submit. Keep your company name on the list of those who are interested in future opportunities.

Contracting Regulations for Services

Federal Acquisition Regulation (FAR) Part 22 describes how existing labor laws apply to government contracts: Federal agencies must encourage contractors to cooperate with federal and state labor requirements such as safety, health and sanitation, maximum hours and minimum wages, equal employment opportunity, child and convict labor, age discrimination, disabled and Vietnam-veteran employment, and employment of the handicapped.

Wage determinations are available at the Dept. of Labor's Wage Determination Online Website, *www.wdol.gov*. (134) At this site federal contracting officers can find the appropriate wage determinations for their particular contract. You will often find the wage determination listed or referenced in the solicitation document. You can also research the prevailing wage determinations for your company's area of expertise here.

The Davis-Bacon Act ensures fair minimum wages for all employees in a building construction, or alteration or repair contract. Contractors and subcontractors must make sure that their employees are given at least the same wages and benefits that they pay for other similar contracts. The Dept. of Labor determines the local prevailing wage rates. This requirement also applies to other related areas such as transportation, housing, air and water pollution reduction, and health.

The **Service Contract Act** also sets standards for compensation, safety, and health protections for employees

Other acts include the **McNamara-O'Hara Service Contract Act**, which covers service employees; the **Contract Work Hours and Safety Standards Act**, which requires you to pay time-and-a-half over 40 hours as well as prohibiting unsanitary, hazardous, or dangerous working conditions; the **Copeland Anti-Kickback Act**, prohibiting you from inducing an employee to give up any compensation to which he or she is entitled, and requiring you to submit a weekly statement of the wages paid to each employee; and the **Walsh-Healey Public Contracts Act**, which requires you to pay minimum wage rates and overtime pay on federal contracts to manufacture or furnish materials, supplies, or equipment.

Manpower Reporting

As we discussed earlier in this chapter, if your contract is with the Army, you must report annually on all manpower required to perform a service contract. The Contractor Manpower Reporting Application (CMRA) Website is: *https://cmra.army.mil*. (135)

You will need to provide details on the contracting office, the contract number, the date of the reporting period, your company information (name, address, telephone), the estimated number of labor hours and the estimated dollar amount paid, the Federal Service Code that applies to this contract, your estimated data-collection costs, the location where the contract is performed, and the number of employees involved.

Insurance (FAR 52.228-5)

You are responsible for making sure that you have the required insurance for any contract. Refer to Part 28 of the Federal Acquisition Regulations, which can be found at the FAR Website, *http://acquisition.gov/far/index.html*. (45) This section covers Bonds and Insurance, including such things as Workers Compensation and Liability Insurance requirements. This regulation does not always apply to all service contracts.

Site Visits (FAR 52.237-1)

In many cases it will be either suggested or required that you perform a site visit, so that you can see the conditions that may affect the cost of the contract. Failure to inspect the site cannot be grounds for a claim after the contract has been awarded. A site visit may be a great opportunity for you to see who your competitors may be! If any questions come up during the visit, these will be posted to FedBizOpps in order that any potential offeror may view them.

The Federal Travel Regulation (FTR)

The Code of Federal Regulations (CFR) 41, Chapters 300–304, contains the policies that concern travel by federal civilian employees and others authorized to travel at government expense. This is known as the Federal Travel Regulation, or FTR. If travel is a necessary part of any contract, the solicitation will describe exactly what is covered.

For more information on the Federal Travel Regulation (FTR) go to the General Services Administration Website at *www.gsa.gov/ftr*. **(136)** You can also find information on the Defense Travel Management Office (DTMO) Website, *www.defensetravel.dod.mil*. (137)

Safety and Security Requirements

If you will be performing all or part of the work at a secure location, for example on an Army base, then you will need to be aware of any specific security requirements that will affect you or your employees. You may have to register your employees and/or your company vehicles in order to gain access to the base, wear security ID badges, or be escorted to the work site. You will also need to be aware of any specific safety regulations, and may be required to attend a brief safety meeting.

In addition, for some types of contracts you may be required to get security clearance. If you notice this is listed in the solicitation document, you will need to find out more about the exact requirements. There are several levels of security clearance:

- **Confidential:** The simplest security clearance to get, this takes anywhere from a few weeks to a few months.
- **Secret** (Collateral Secret or Ordinary Secret): This takes anywhere from a few months to a year. It may take longer if you have changed your address a lot in the past, if you have a residence abroad or have significant ties outside the United States, if you have filed for bankruptcy or have unpaid bills, or if you have a criminal record.
- **Top Secret:** This type of clearance can take anywhere from six to 18 months, and sometimes takes as long as three years to obtain.
- **Eyes Only:** Reserved for the highest-ranking officials.

Evaluating Your Offer

FAR 52.212-2 describes how the agency will evaluate the offers it receives. The award will be made to the best overall (best value) proposal; that is, one that it considers to be the most beneficial to the government. The agency will look at four evaluation factors:

1. Technical Approach.
2. Management Approach.
3. Past Performance.
4. Price.

In the solicitation document the agency will list these factors in their order of importance; in some cases the Technical Approach will be significantly more important, and at other times Management, Price, or Past Performance may take precedence. Remember that the award may not necessarily be made to the lowest price offered.

Technical Approach

The agency is looking for clear evidence that you fully understand the technical requirements necessary to complete the tasks or objectives laid out in the solicitation (Statement of Work [SOW] or Performance Work Statement [PWS]). Your proposal will need to show that you have the skills, knowledge, and capabilities to successfully perform all the required tasks—in-depth knowledge of the field in question, understanding of regulations and codes that may apply, familiarity with the applications commonly used in this field, and so on.

Management Approach

The agency will be looking for evidence that you can provide personnel who are qualified in the field, and that your management plan will ensure that the contract is completed on time and budget. Does your management plan allow you to properly oversee your personnel and ensure quality deliverables? You must be able to demonstrate sound business practices, stable fiscal control, and so on.

The agency will assign an adjectival rating to the technical and management approaches of your submission, as shown in the following table.

Adjectival Rating	Definition
Outstanding	A proposal that satisfies all of the government's requirements with extensive detail to indicate feasibility of the approach. Shows a thorough understanding of the problems and offers numerous significant strengths, which are not offset by weaknesses, with an overall low degree of risk in meeting the government's requirements.

Good	A proposal that satisfies all of the government's requirements with adequate detail to indicate feasibility of the approach. Shows an understanding of the problems and offers some significant strengths or numerous minor strengths, which are not offset by weaknesses, with an overall low to moderate degree of risk in meeting the government's requirements.
Acceptable	A proposal that satisfies all of the government's requirements with minimal detail to indicate feasibility of the approach. Shows a minimal understanding of the problems, with an overall moderate to high degree of risk in meeting the government's requirements.
Marginal	A proposal that satisfies all of the government's requirements with minimum detail to indicate feasibility of approach. Shows a minimal understanding of the problem with an overall high degree of risk in meeting the government's requirement.
Unacceptable	A proposal that contains a major error(s), omission(s), or deficiency(ies) that indicates a lack of understanding of the problems, or an approach that cannot be expected to meet requirements, or involves a very high risk. None of these conditions can be corrected without a major rewrite or revision of the proposal.

Past Performance

The agency will look at how well you performed on recent similar contracts, either in the federal or commercial areas. You should include all your relevant past contracts, and show how you handled any problems as they arose. If you have no available past performance information, this section of the evaluation will be regarded as neutral—neither favorable nor unfavorable.

The agency will assign an adjectival rating to the past performance section of your submission, as shown in the following table.

Adjectival Rating	Description
Low Risk	Little doubt exists, based on the offeror's performance record, that the offeror can perform the proposed effort.
Moderate Risk	Some doubt exists, based on the offeror's performance record, that the offeror can perform the proposed effort.

Adjectival Rating	Description
High Risk	Significant doubt exists, based on the offeror's performance record, that the offeror can perform the proposed effort.
Unknown Risk	Little or no relevant performance record identifiable; equates to a neutral rating, having no positive or negative evaluation significance.

Price

In many service proposals your proposed price will be less important than your technical and management approaches and your past performance. Your proposal must demonstrate reasonable pricing that is aligned with the technical and management approaches.

A-76 Competitions—Competitive Sourcing

In 1998 the Office of Management and Budget's Circular No. A-76 established a Competitive Sourcing Program, which aimed to increase efficiency and reduce government costs. The guidelines encouraged competition and provided a level playing field between private industry and government organizations.

Examples of these service competitions could include computer facilities management services, data entry services, database management and IT services, office administrative services (mail clerk or file clerk, for example), various support services, and facility management and operations services.

The Federal Activities Inventory Reform (FAIR) Act requires agencies to make an annual inventory of the commercial activities that are currently performed by federal employees and submit them to the Office of Management and Budget.

There are two different types of A-76 competition:

1. Standard Competition.
2. Streamlined Competition.

In a **Standard Competition** an agency issues a solicitation and selects a service provider based on the offers it receives. At the same time the agency develops a "most efficient organization" that will form the basis for the agency's offer in the competition. This typically involves streamlining the existing organization, and aims to place the government in the best competitive position against private sector offers. A standard competition is usually completed within 12 months of a public announcement.

In a **Streamlined Competition** an agency determines an estimated contract price for performing the work by an outside contractor. The agency may either solicit proposals from prospective contractors or it may conduct its own market research, (for example by looking at current multiple award schedule contracts). The agency then determines how much it costs to perform the function in-house, using the organization either as it currently exists, or as it will be configured after proposed streamlining has taken effect. After the costs for both the public and private sectors are compared, the best-value organization wins. A streamlined competition is usually completed within 90 days from public announcement.

In order to determine the in-house cost of a particular function the agency must follow certain regulations or guidelines, listed in Attachment C of OMB Circular A-76. The agencies also use a software program called COMPARE, which you can find at this Website: *www.comparea76.com*. (138)

UPDATE

In **March 2009** the program was suspended for the remainder of the fiscal year, and in **October 2009** it was again put on hold in order to allow a review of procedures, costs, oversight, and so on.

More Resources

- The Acquisition Center for Excellence (ACES)—Services: *https://acc.dau.mil/ace*. (139)
- Acquisition Central: *www.acquisition.gov*. (140)

Help!

If you have any questions about this chapter, we would be happy to try to help you. Go to our Website, *www.sell2gov.com*, and at the Contact tab you can send us an e-mail with your questions. Please put "Definitive Guide" in the subject line.

Chapter 7

Fulfilling the Terms of Your Contract

Congratulations: You have been awarded the contract! Now it is up to you to make sure that you fulfill the terms of the contract, and that you deliver a satisfactory product or service on time, following the terms laid out in the contract.

In this chapter we will discuss in detail:

- Post-Award Orientation Conferences.
- Packaging, Marking, and Shipping.
- Inspection and Acceptance.
- Invoicing, including Web Invoicing Systems and Wide Area Work Flow.
- Contractor Review Reports and Performance Reports.
- Reporting Requirements—VETS100 and E-Verify

Many of the regulations discussed in this chapter refer to those required by the Department of Defense and its Supply Centers in Richmond, Philadelphia, and Columbus. Of course, other agencies may have different rules and regulations, so you are always advised to read the solicitation document carefully so that you understand the requirements.

The Post-Award Orientation Conference

After the contract has been awarded the agency may contact you at your place of business, usually through a phone call or a letter. This is known as a Post-Award Orientation Conference. Alternatively, if you wish, you can contact the agency directly and request a conference.

The **Administrative Contracting Officer**, or **ACO**, will work with you to answer any questions you may have concerning the fulfillment of your contract. (Remember, however, that this is *not* a substitute for taking the time to understand the contract requirements before you make your offer, and it cannot change any terms of the contract once it has been awarded.)

The administrative contracting officer will discuss with you any technical aspects of the contract, how to prevent any problems before they arise, and agree with you on common issues. He or she will identify and review specific key requirements and milestones that were identified in the contract. This conference could be particularly useful to you if this is your first government contract.

Often the aim of these conferences is simply to establish a good working relationship with you, and give you a specific point of contact for any issues you may wish to discuss.

Packing and Marking Requirements

Commercial Packaging

The federal government uses the term *commercial packaging* to describe any packaging that is developed by the supplier. The American Society for Testing and Material (ASTM) develops and maintains commercial packaging standards that are widely followed and referenced throughout the commercial packaging arena. The Department of Defense has adopted the **ASTM D 3951** (Standard Practice for Commercial Packaging) as its commercial standard. Other commercial standards may also apply, based on the product involved, and the agency's particular needs. You can find this standard at the ASTM Website, *www. astm.org*. (141)

Performance-Based Packaging

The agency may specify a performance-based packaging requirement—that is, the agency will describe the required outcome and provide criteria for measuring and verifying performance, but will not dictate the specific methods to be used to achieve those outcomes. In this case you would propose an appropriate packaging plan, and work with the agency involved to agree on a mutually acceptable plan of action.

Agencies generally prefer to use commercial packaging and performance-based specifications whenever possible—that is, when it is cost effective and will withstand anticipated conditions.

Military Packaging

The term *military packaging* is used to describe the standard packaging requirements developed by the Dept. of Defense, known as **MIL-STD-2073-1**. Traditional packaging methods, which would normally serve a commercial customer well, can be unsuitable for the more severe conditions that arise when that same product is shipped to a military customer. In these instances more stringent military packaging requirements may be appropriate. You can find this standard at the ASSIST Website: *https://assist.daps.dla.mil*. (27)

Liability for Damage Caused by Inadequate Packaging

If the contract has specified Commercial Packaging, then, if the damage is the result of faulty packaging, you will assume liability for items packaged in accordance with normal commercial practices.

However, the government accepts full responsibility for items packaged in accordance with military specifications. It is your responsibility to follow exactly the requirements of the military specifications listed in the contract, but the agency will be responsible for any losses incurred if the packaging does not provide adequate protection. Naturally you are still liable for other defects or deficiencies in the delivered item—that is, defects that are *not* caused by inadequate military packaging or handling.

Packaging and Marking Codes

In the solicitation document you may come across a series of packaging and marking codes. Here's how it might look in a solicitation document:

> **PACKAGING DATA—MIL-STD-2073-1D (15 DEC 99)**
> QUP= 001: PRES MTHD= 41: CLNG/DRY= 1: PRESV MAT= 00:
> WRAP MAT= CA: CUSH/DUNN MAT= JC: CUSH/DUNN THKNESS= X:
> UNIT CONT= D3: OPI= O:
> INTRMDTE CONT= EC: INTRMTE CONT QTY= 024: PACK= U:
> MARKING SHALL BE IN ACCORDANCE WITH MIL-STD-129.
> SPECIAL MARKING CODE= 00—NO SPECIAL MARKING.
> DOD BAR CODE MARKING REQUIRED IN ACCORDANCE WITH
> MIL-STD-129 (LATEST REVISION) MARKING AND BAR
> CODING IN ACCORDANCE WITH AIM BC1

Alternatively it could be in a table format, like this:

Quantity Unit Pack (QUP)	CODE	001
Preservation Method	CODE	41
Cleaning and Drying Procedures	CODE	1
Preservative Material	CODE	00
Wrapping Material	CODE	CA
Cushioning and Dunnage Material	CODE	JC
Cushioning and Dunnage Thickness	CODE	X
Unit Container	CODE	D3
Optional Procedure Indicator	CODE	O
Intermediate Container	CODE	EC
Intermediate Container Quantity	CODE	024

FOR DLA STOCK:		
Pack	CODE	U
FOR OCONUS PRIORITY 9 THRU 15 AND FOREIGN MILITARY SALES (FMS):		
Pack	CODE	Q
Packing	CODE	B
MARKING AND BAR CODE REQUIREMENTS:		
ALL SHIPMENTS FOR DLA STOCK, OCONUS PRIORITIES 9-15, AND FOREIGN MILITARY SALES (FMS) SHALL BE MARKED AND BARCODED IN ACCORDANCE WITH MIL-STD-129P AND AIM BC1 (UNIFORM SYMBOLOGY SPECIFICATION CODE 39).		
Special Marking Code: 00 (NO SPECIAL MARKING)		
FOR NON-FMS AND NON-STOCK ORDERS FOR CONUS DELIVERY AND OCONUS PRIORITIES 1 THRU 8:		
MARKED AND PACKAGED STANDARD COMMERCIAL IAW ASTM D 3951 AND BAR CODED IAW AIM BC1.		

Looks pretty intimidating, doesn't it? Don't worry; there is a way to interpret what you see.

Code Lookup

There are several Websites that allow you to interpret the different packaging and marking codes you may come across.

At the Website shown on the next page you can enter the codes that you find in the solicitation document, and get the information you need: *www.palm.saic.com/code_lookup.nsf.* (142)

If we enter some of the codes listed in the previous example, we can see the following packaging information:

Method of Preservation:	41	Method 41 (formerly Submethod IA-8)—Watervaporproof bag, sealed. The item, wrapped and cushioned as required in 5.2.3.6, shall be enclosed in a close fitting heat sealed bag conforming to MIL-B-117, Type I, Class E, Style 1, 2 or 3; or Type I, Class F, Style 1; or Type III, Class E, Style 1. (Note: For electrostatic protection refer to 5.2.4.1.) When specified in the contract or purchase order, a designated bag, other than noted herein, shall be furnished. (Note: When specified in the contract or purchase order, a carton or box shall be required to complete the unit container and the primary cushioning specified in the contract or purchase order shall be placed between the outside of the bag and the inside of the carton or box.)
Cleaning and Drying:	1	Any applicable process.
Wrapping Material:	CA	A-A-203, kraft wrapping paper.
Cushioning Material:	JC	Domestic fiberboard meeting the requirements of ASTM-D4727 used as pads, cells, die cuts, or sleeves.
Cushioning Thickness:	X	As required to protect the item or elements of the package.

U/I Container:	D3	PPP-B-566, A-A-2807, PPP-B-676, or ASTM-D5118, folding, metal edged, setup or fiber-board box.
Optional Procedures:	O	Options can be exercised as to specific method of preservation or DoD approved packaging materials to be used. However, basic preservation method shall be retained, supplemental data shall be complied with, and unit package dimensions shall not be increased by more than one inch. Equal or better protection shall be given the item and there shall be no increase in the package cost.

Preservation Methods

There are five basic Methods of Preservation:

1. Method 10— Physical Protection
2. Method 20—Preservative Coating
3. Method 30—Waterproof Protection
4. Method 40—Water Vapor Proof Protection
5. Method 50—Water Vapor Proof Protection with Desiccant

Packing Levels

There are two levels of protection:

1. Level A—Protection required to meet the most severe worldwide shipment, handling, and storage conditions.
2. Level B—Protection required meeting moderate worldwide shipment, handling, and storage conditions.

Marking and Packaging Codes can be found at this Website: *www.dscc.dla.mil/Offices/Packaging*. (143)

Unique Identification of Items—Bar Codes and RFID Tags

The Department of Defense must establish accountability records for all items with a unit acquisition cost of $5,000 or more, as well as for *all* sensitive or classified items, or items furnished to third parties. The Unique Identification of Items (UII) uses machine-readable data (bar codes, RFID tags, and so on) to allow the Dept. of Defense to distinguish one item from all other like and unlike items.

More information on this requirement can be found at the Dept. of Defense Packaging Site: *www.dscc.dla.mil/Offices/Packaging*. (143)

Bar Codes

For the Defense Supply Centers, bar code markings are required on all containers and loose or unpacked items. At one time the military standard for bar codes was known as LOGMARS, but this no longer applies. Now the military has adopted the commercial bar code standard **ISO/IEC 16388** for all its bar code requirements.

You will need to apply a bar code containing the National Stock Number (NSN) on all unit packs and intermediate containers. Any exterior container should be bar coded with both the National Stock Number (NSN) and the contract number. This is required even for small items, which would need to have the bar code on an attached tag.

If you are *not* shipping the item to a Distribution Depot (known as DVD, or Direct Vendor Deliver), you will also need to include other relevant information such as the document number, Routing Identifier Code, unit of issue, quantity, condition code, distribution code, and unit price information. This information should be put onto labels that are then attached to DD Form 250, the Material Inspection and Receiving Report. We discuss this form later in this chapter.

Bar Code requirements can be found at this Website: ***www.dscc.dla.mil/offices/ packaging***. (143)

Radio Frequency Identification (RFID) Tags

The Department of Defense requires you to use passive Radio Frequency Identification (RFID) tags, at the case and palletized unit load levels, when shipping certain items. By using your CAGE code information you will be able to generate serial numbers that are unique to your shipping facility.

You will be required to provide information about the shipment in advance, via the Wide Area Work Flow system (WAWF). WAWF uses EDI Transaction Set # 856 for Advance Shipment Notices, where you will provide information including the contract number, the shipment date, the NSN and item description, the quantity, and the RFID tag number. We discuss WAWF later in this chapter.

If your company does not already use RFID tagging, don't despair! You may choose to use a third-party provider to complete this work, or you may purchase pre-programmed DOD compliant tags. Alternatively, if you are expecting multiple shipments to the DOD, you may choose to purchase a printer with blank tags for you to program and print in-house.

You can view **RFID Requirements** at this Website: ***www.dodrfid.org***. (144) Your local Procurement Technical Assistance Center (PTAC) will also offer free training and assistance.

Wood Packaging Material

Wood Packaging Material includes wooden pallets or skids, wooden boxes or crates, and so on. It does not include fiberboard, plywood, particleboard, or veneers. Since 2006, the Department of Defense has required that any wood packaging material used in shipping must meet certain international standards that are designed to block the movement of pests from one nation to another. If you are going to use any wood packaging material to ship items to the Dept. of Defense, you must meet these standards.

Website: ***www.dscc.dla.mil/offices/packaging***. (143)

More Information

- **Mil-Std 2073-1** contains the standards for military packaging.
- **Mil-Std 129-P** provides information on standard military marking requirements.
- **Fed-Std-313-D** contains information on Material Safety Data Sheets and Hazardous materials.
- The **DLA's Packaging, Specifications, Standards** Website has more detailed information at **www.dscc.dla.mil/Offices/Packaging/specstdslist.html**. (145)
- Packaging and Marking Requirements can be found at the **ASSIST** Website: **https://assist.daps.dla.mil**. (27)
- **DoD 4140.1-R** is the Dept. of Defense Material Management Regulation.
- **ASTM D 3951** is the Standard Practice for Commercial Packaging.

Shipping Your Product

You must provide the proper shipping documentation when you ship your products. You must complete the **Distribution Data Report (DD250)** before first shipment for each deliverable item. This information is used by the government for estimating shipment costs, storage planning, and transport security. You will be told where the report should be e-mailed, and if any other copies of it are required.

The form requests such information as the item size and weight, and a description of the unit packaging, shipping container, and Unitized Load. You will also need to indicate any special requirements; for example, any licenses or security needed for transporting the item, whether the item is considered dangerous goods for transport, if the item requires electrostatic- or magnetic-sensitive marking. You should also indicate if the shelf life of the item is less than one year from the date of manufacture (such as food, medicines, batteries, paints, sealants, adhesives, film, tires, chemicals, packaged petroleum products, hoses/belts, o-rings, and Nuclear/Biological/Chemical equipment and clothing).

Form DD 250, a commercial packing list or the Wide Area Work Flow Receiving Report must be attached to the outside of the shipping container. (See later in this chapter for details of Wide Area Workflow.)

Inspection and Acceptance

Inspection

When the product reaches its destination, it is inspected to make sure that it complies with the contract requirements. There are several levels of inspection, depending on the contract involved.

When the contract does not exceed the simplified acquisition threshold ($100,000), the agency will generally rely on you for overall inspection, unless the contracting officer decides that some form of government inspection and testing is necessary (FAR 52.246-1).

FAR 52.212-4 includes information about the inspection and acceptance of commercial items. You must ensure that the items or services you supply conform to the requirements of the contract. The government reserves the right to inspect or test any items.

FAR 52.246-2 is the **Standard Inspection Requirement**. In this case the agency requires that you set up an inspection system that is acceptable to them.

The **Higher-Level Contract Quality Requirement** (FAR 52.246-11) is used when the contract has more stringent technical requirements. If this clause is cited in the contract, you must agree to comply with more stringent government inspection or quality assurance procedures. An example of this type of higher-level quality control standard is ISO 9000 (FAR 46.202-4).

Acceptance

Once it has been inspected, the agency will officially accept the product or approve the specific service rendered. If the item or service does not conform to the requirements, you must correct the deficiency by a specified date. Supplies or services that do not conform to the contract requirements are classified in one of three ways:

1. **Critical Non-Conformance** is likely to result in hazardous or unsafe conditions for those who use or depend on the supplies or services.

2. **Major Non-Conformance** will result in the failure of the supplies or services, or make them unusable for their intended purpose.

3. **Minor Non-Conformance** will not render the supplies unusable, and the defect has little bearing on their effective use or operation.

No matter how slight a defect, strictly, the government is entitled to reject an item if it does not conform to all the specifications in the contract. Normally, however, the government will only reject a product if the defect affects safety, health, reliability, durability, performance, or any other basic objective. (**Mil-Std 1916** is the **Military Standard for Acceptance of Products**.)

Invoicing

How you prepare and submit your invoice will vary, depending on the requirements of the particular purchasing agency involved.

You may simply be given an address to send your invoice, with no other specific requirements. However, many agencies have expanded the use of electronic invoicing systems, in order to more easily track and pay their suppliers.

The federal government is required to pay their suppliers in 30 days. This actually means that they will pay you **either** 30 days from the date the paying office receives notification that the product has been accepted or the service has been performed satisfactorily, **or** 30 days from the receipt of a **correct** invoice, whichever is later. In practice, if there is a problem with acceptance of the product or service, or a delay in the acceptance office sending the information to the paying office, or if your invoice is not completely and correctly filled out, your payment could be delayed.

Remember that the **buying office** (the agency purchasing the item), the **receiving office** (the department responsible for inspection and acceptance), and the **paying office** (responsible for receiving invoices and making payments) may all be in different locations. Make sure your invoice goes to the correct office, to avoid payment delays!

Payment will be sent by **Electronic Funds Transfer** (EFT) to the account you listed in your Central Contractors Registration (CCR). Make sure the information in CCR is correct!

Invoicing via the Web Invoicing System (WINS)

WINS is a free service of the Defense Finance and Accounting Service (DFAS) that allows you to invoice the Department of Defense quickly, cheaply, and accurately, which can dramatically speed up the time it takes for you to receive payment.

Web Invoicing allows you to submit invoices and vouchers electronically. You can enter your invoices into the system, and the system checks to be sure that the information you submit is correct the first time. This significantly cuts down much of the paperwork involved, and gets your invoice into the DFAS system usually within 24 hours. Web invoicing is free to vendors doing business with the government.

The system can be used from any Windows computer that has Internet access—there's no need to save any files on the computer, and you don't need to supply any personal certificates in order to log in to WINS. Dial-up access and AOL are also okay.

You can control the login for your WINS account and share it with as many or as few employees as you like. If you have more than one facility (and therefore more than one CAGE code) you can see and perform billing for all of them without having to log in and out for each one.

- WINS Website: **https://ecweb.dfas.mil**. **(146)**
- DFAS Vendor/Contract Payments Website: ***www.dod.mil/dfas/contractorpay .html***. **(147)**

> **Important!** The Web Invoicing System (WINS) is being gradually phased out, soon to be replaced by Wide Area Workflow (WAWF). Unlike WINS, WAWF includes Inspection, Acceptance, and Approval of invoices and receiving reports.

Invoicing via Wide Area Workflow (WAWF)

What Is WAWF?

Wide Area Work Flow (WAWF) is a Web-based invoicing and reporting system that allows both you and the agency to track an item through its contract lifecycle. Using WAWF you will be able to quickly check the status of your contract and payments. In October 2006 the Department of Defense made the use of this system mandatory for all its vendors, and other government agencies are quickly following suit.

For each step of the way—from shipping, receiving, acceptance, and invoicing to payment—you and the agency will be able to check the status of your documents. If a document is rejected for any reason, it will be easy for you to correct and resubmit it electronically. All this means a faster turnaround time, and quicker payment of your invoice. You will be able to submit invoices and receive reports electronically, track the status of any document, receive updates via e-mail whenever the status changes, and resubmit rejected documents.

Getting Started

First check that you are registered at the **Central Contractors Registration** (CCR) site, (discussed in Chapter 1). Then decide on who in the company will be the **Electronic Business Point of Contact** (EB POC) and the Alternate Electronic Business Point of Contact (AEB POC). These people will determine which of your employees will be authorized to have access to the system to track, submit, and modify data on your behalf. You will need an e-mail account for sending and receiving the documents—you will be notified via e-mail whenever there are any changes.

Each person who will be using the system will need to register at the site, and will gain access to the system using either a **user ID and password** or a **Public Key Infrastructure** (PKI) certificate. If you wish, you may allow certain employees to have "view only" access to documents.

Wide Area Workflow is a system that includes the complete lifecycle—shipping, receiving, inspection/acceptance, *and* invoicing. Therefore, you must submit a report to the system *as soon as you ship* your item. This way the receiving office already has the information it needs when the items arrive. The solicitation document will give you the details of the various departments you will need to include in your report. Here is an example, listing the Dept. of Defense Activity Address Codes (DODAAC) of the various offices involved in the process.

```
[ X ]   Pay DoDAAC*: HQ0303
[ X ]   Issue DoDAAC: W911PT
[ X ]   Admin DoDAAC*: W911PT
[ X ]   Inspect by DoDAAC*: W16H1F
[ X ]   Contracting Officer*: W911PT
[ X ]   Ship To Code*: W16H1F
```

The paying office and mailing addresses will be located on the front of your award. You can track your payment information on the Website.

Submitting Invoices via WAWF

You will be able to submit Invoices and Receiving Reports electronically using an Interactive Web Application, Electronic Data Interchange (EDI), or Secure File Transfer Protocol (SFTP).

EDI and SFTP are suitable if you will be submitting many invoices or reports. The interactive Web application is suitable if you do not have a lot of invoices or reports to submit at any one time. Most vendors use the manual, Web entry method to input their documents directly into WAWF. This is a good method if you have a small volume of payment documents to create, or if you have a small number of lines on your contract.

You will also need to register for **Electronic Document Access**, in order to be able to view details of contracts your company has been awarded. The Website is *http://eda.ogden.disa.mil*. (148)

Once you have submitted your Invoice or Receiving Report, your designated Point of Contact will receive e-mails whenever any action is taken by the agency. For example, if a Receiving Report or an Invoice is rejected for any reason, you will be able to quickly correct the data and resubmit. You will also be able to view previously submitted documents and check on their status.

Wide Area Workflow Training

Free Web-based training is available at ***www.wawftraining.com***. (149)

Also at this site, if you click on the Resources button in the top-right corner, you can find many links to other information sites specifically for vendors using this system:

You can practice using the system at these training sites before you submit your first "live" invoice. **Using Wide Area Workflow for Vendors—A Student Guide** is also available for download. This is quite a large file to download, at more than 250 pages, but it is full of useful information about the system: ***www.dod.mil/dfas/contractorpay/electroniccommerce/ECToolBox/WAWFVendorGuide3.pdf***. (150)

Vendor Tools
Practice Using WAWF
Use WAWF
Vendor Decision Tools
WAWF Users Manual
Instructor Led WAWF Training
PKI Certificate Site
UID Help
RFID Help
Navy Vendor Guide
DCMA WAWF Web site
DFAS Vendor Getting Started Guide
DFAS Vendor Student Guide
DFAS End Users Tool Box
DFAS Payment Information
WAWF Technical Support

More Electronic Data Interchange (EDI) Information

- EDI formats: ***www.X12.org***. (151)
- EDI implementation guides: ***www.dfas.mil/contractorpay/electroniccommerce/edi.html***. (152)

Other Invoicing Systems

Several other agencies have alternate systems for invoicing, so you will need to look carefully at the solicitation document to determine the method that is used.

Some examples are:

- The **Treasury Department** uses an Internet-based system called **PAID**. Information can be found at ***http://fms.treas.gov/paid***. (153)
- The **General Services Administration** (GSA) has a **FedPay** system, which can pay vendors in as little as 10 days! We will discuss this in more detail later in the book.
- The **Department of the Interior** uses an electronic invoicing system called **GovPay**: ***www.govworks.gov***. (154)
- The National Institute of Health (NIH) invoice query site is ***https://silk.nih.gov/adb/billpay***. (155)
- The **Coast Guard** Web invoicing is at ***www.fincen.uscg.mil***. (156)

Progress Reports

Progress Reports may be required to ensure that you remain on schedule, and to check on any possible delays. Sometimes the contract requires a Production Progress Report. These reports must be submitted by you on time. The contracting officer is authorized to withhold payments to you, up to 5 percent of the total contract amount, or a maximum of $25,000 if these reports are delayed.

Quality Assurance

Contracts for commercial items usually rely on the contractor's existing quality assurance system, as a substitute for government inspection and testing. However, remember that even in commercial contracts the government *never* waives its rights to conduct its own inspection.

Performance Reports

Agencies keep reports on how well you fulfill the terms of your contract, and share this information with other agencies. They will be looking at the quality of the product or service you provide, whether you delivered on schedule, your cost control, your business relations, your customer satisfaction, and so on. Ratings can range from Excellent through to Good, Fair, Poor, or Unsatisfactory. Some agencies will use a numeric score.

You will be provided with a copy of the agency's report as soon as possible after the evaluation is completed. You will be allowed at least 30 days to comment on the report, and if necessary refer the evaluation to a higher level. However, the agency makes the final decision. Reports are completed annually during the life of the contract. The agency will keep copies of the report, your response, and any comments for a maximum of three years after the end of the contract. Departments and agencies will share information with other agencies and departments on request, in order to support future award decisions.

Significant or recurring problems that may be included in the report are:
- Failure to perform the work in accordance with the terms of the contract.
- A history of repeated failure to perform, or an unsatisfactory performance.
- Violations of certain laws such as the Drug-Free Workplace Act or the Buy American Act.
- Unfair trade practices, lack of integrity, or failure to observe standard business ethical practices.

Past Performance Information Retrieval System (PPIRS)

The Past Performance Information Retrieval System (PPIRS) is the site where government agencies note how well you performed on any awarded contract, and this information is shared among other government agencies. You can have access to your own records, and may comment upon anything in the report, but you do not have access to the records of other contractors.

Website: *www.ppirs.gov*. (39)

Reporting Requirements

Veteran Employment Report (VETS-100)

Federal Acquisition Regulation (FAR) 52.222-35 forbids any form of discrimination against any veteran or disabled veteran. Any contractor or subcontractor who receives a federal government contract that is valued at **$100,000 or more** must file the Federal Contractor Veteran Employment Report (known as the **VETS-100 Report**) on an annual basis. The requirement applies to *all* employment openings (full-time, part-time, and temporary) except for:

- executive and top management positions
- positions that will be filled from within your organization
- positions lasting 3 days or less

Under the terms of this regulation you must list all your employment openings during the duration of the contract at an appropriate local public employment service office of the State—for example at the U.S. Department of Labor's America's Job Bank. You must post employment notices stating the employees' rights, your obligations, and so on.

Website: *https://vets100.vets.dol.gov*. (157)

Employee Immigration Status Report (E-Verify)

Since **September 2009**, federal contractors must verify the immigration status of any employees working on government projects. However, there are several exceptions to the E-Verify rule. It does not apply to:

- contracts worth less than $100,000
- contracts for commercially available (COTS) equipment
- subcontractors in projects valued under $3,000
- contracts outside the United States

Contractors have 30 days to sign up to the system, and 90 days to verify their employees' employment status.

More information is available at the U.S. Citizenship & Immigrations Services Website, *www.uscis.gov/everify*. (158)

Help!

If you have any questions about this chapter, we would be happy to try to help you. Go to our Website, *www.sell2gov.com*, and at the Contact tab you can send us an e-mail with your questions. Please put "Definitive Guide" in the subject line.

Chapter 8

An Introduction to the GSA Contract

As a small business owner you may have heard of a General Services Administration (GSA) Federal Supply Schedules (FSS) contract, more commonly known as a **GSA contract**, but what is it exactly? How does it work? Is it difficult to obtain? Is it worth your time and effort?

In this chapter we set out to answer these questions. We describe **how** the GSA contract works, and explain **why** it can benefit your business. We also list several factors that could stop you from going any further—better to find this out right now, before you invest any more time in the process!

We show you how to do some preliminary **research** into the schedules program to determine whether your company can be competitive in this market. We give an overview of the work you will need to do in order to **prepare a submission**, and we detail the work you will need to do *after* **the contract** has been awarded, in order to keep the contract current. Take a good look at the **investment of time and personnel** you will need to make in order to submit, market, and manage your GSA contract; understand the **benefits** that a GSA contract can give your company, and then make an **informed decision** to go ahead with the submission.

If you decide to go ahead and submit a contract proposal to GSA, then Chapter 9 becomes your **Do-it-Yourself Manual**! This chapter takes you by the hand through every part of the submission process, so that you can be confident in your proposal—it shows you where to download the solicitation package, how to complete each section in turn, where to go for more information, and some pitfalls to avoid.

Finally, Chapter 10 works as a **Post-Award Manual**, to which you will turn time and again. It shows you how to upload your contract details to GSA's online ordering Website, so federal agencies can see the details of the products and services you are offering. We also discuss how to modify the contract, how to submit reports, and much more.

In 2008 we wrote a successful book on government contracting, which discussed federal procurement in a more general way, looking at how small businesses could find and secure federal government contracts up to $100,000. We referred briefly to GSA contracts, but didn't discuss them in any detail. *Winning Government Contracts* is available at Amazon (*www.amazon.com*) (159) and Barnes and Noble (*www.barnesandnoble.com*) (160) stores, and is a good general reference guide to the federal contracting process.

Although a GSA contract is not an absolute requirement in government procurement, it is becoming more and more common to see contract actions that either require or prefer the offeror to have a GSA contract.

Assisting companies to submit their GSA contract proposal has been the core of our business for many years. Preparing and submitting these proposals for many different types of small businesses has given us the hands-on knowledge of the actual process that you need—these real-life examples cannot be compared to a simple reading of the rules and regulations.

What Is a "GSA Contract"?

Picture yourself on bended knee, proposing to the GSA. Tell it all about yourself... what you do, your terms and conditions, how the two of you will make a great team! As long as your proposal meets its standards it *will* award you a contract, as this is a non-competitive proposal. The GSA contract proves to a potential federal buyer that you are a responsible vendor.

Remember: A GSA contract is *not* a guarantee of sales. It has been compared to getting a hunting license—you still have to go out there and hunt for the sales, but you now have some legitimacy in the eyes of procurement officers. You have proven your willingness to dedicate time and resources to getting Approved Vendor status.

Patience and Perseverance

How long do you think it would take you to become a vendor to Wal-Mart or IBM or General Electric or any other Fortune 500 company? How hard would it be to even get an appointment to make your sales pitch? Once you get the coveted appointment, how long would it take you to prepare the presentation? Fly to the corporate offices? How many *more* appointments with people higher up the chain of command would you attend before you get any results?

The federal government is the biggest customer in the entire world for what you do. It has opened the door and asked you to make your presentation from the convenience of your office. The government is mandated to pay its bills on time, it offers staff to assist you, it is fair and impartial, and you *never* have to take it to lunch!

Don't try to rush through this process; remember, this is an open enrollment contract, and it is in your best interests to take the time to read, understand, check, and double-check the paperwork.

Know the Rules of the Game! This is the federal government and its agents you are working with: It is *their* ball, *their* glove, *their* bat, and *their* field! You play by their rules or you do not play. Make sure you understand the rules of the game before you step onto the field!

The General Services Administration's Federal Supply Schedules Program

The General Services Administration (GSA) manages one of the largest marketplaces in the world, bringing together business contractors and hundreds of thousands of government customers. The **GSA Schedules Program** gives government agencies a simplified process for obtaining commercial services and products. Because each contract holder has **Approved Vendor** status, the buyer is assured that he or she is getting the best pricing, delivery, and terms; each company has already negotiated pricing and terms with GSA.

GSA contracts do *not* guarantee sales. Schedule contractors are awarded an Indefinite-Delivery Indefinite-Quantity contract to provide services and/or products to government agencies. The contract gives commercial companies Approved Vendor status for an initial two-year period, followed by three one-year options, then followed by three five-year options, for a possible total of 20 years!

The Schedules

The commercial products and services sold via GSA contracts are separated into more than 40 distinct schedules. There are currently more than 17,500 existing GSA contracts in place, covering more than 11 million products and services. Every year several thousand firms submit the necessary paperwork in order to be awarded a GSA contract. GSA estimates $40 billion in sales in FY2007 via GSA schedule contracts. Of that, 38 percent will go to small businesses—make sure some of that business goes to you!

The GSA Schedule Program allows government agencies to buy directly from the commercial marketplace; everything from Advertising to Zoo Keeping; from Animals to Zippers! The government buys a huge assortment of commercial products; approximately 20 percent of all the products sold in the United States! Government agencies also purchase a wide range of services—landscaping, construction, software design, management, public relations, maintenance and repair, training, staffing, renting or leasing equipment, and so on. The GSA also provides government agencies with vehicles and fleet-management services.

The GSA's online ordering system, called **GSA *Advantage!***, allows agencies to order more than 3 million of these products and services via the Internet.

How Does the GSA Schedules Program Work?

There is no guarantee of sales. It is very important to understand that GSA contracts do *not* guarantee sales. Schedule contractors are awarded Approved Vendor status, with an Indefinite-Delivery Indefinite-Quantity (IDIQ) Contract to provide specific services and/or products. Each schedule contains many contractors who supply similar products or services.

There is a Minimum Sales Requirement. You will *not* be awarded a GSA Schedule contract unless the contracting officer estimates that your sales to GSA will exceed $25,000 in the first 24 months and $25,000 in sales for each subsequent 12-month period.

Each of the GSA schedules covers a specific type of industry and is further subdivided into many **Special Item Numbers** (SINs). For example, Schedule 874, which is Management, Organization, and Business Improvement Services (MOBIS), has nine SINs:

1. 874-1, Consulting Services
2. 874-2, Facilitation Services
3. 874-3, Survey Services
4. 874-4, Training Services
5. 874-5, Ancillary Supplies and/or Services
6. 874-6, Acquisition Management Support
7. 874-7, Program and Project Management
8. 874-8, Acquisition Workforce Training
9. 874-9, Off-the-Shelf and Customizable Print, Audio, and Instructional Training Devices

How Does This Program Benefit the Government Agencies?

Streamlining

Because much of the paperwork has already been completed by the GSA contract holder, the agencies are able to streamline their acquisition process, avoid red tape, and reduce the time it takes to purchase the products or services they need. Conversely, a competitive bid posted to FedBizOpps can be a time-consuming process—the buyer must post the bid, wait for submissions, sort through the offers, award the contract, and then wait for delivery. Items can be purchased more quickly and easily via GSA—the buyer can search GSA's online shopping site called GSA *Advantage!* for the item he or she needs, request quotes from three GSA contract holders who offer the item, and award the contract quickly, while still fulfilling his or her obligations for competitive acquisition.

Flexibility

Because there are numerous contractors in any given schedule, the agencies have the flexibility to select the products or services that best meet their particular needs. In many cases, even though price may be a factor in awarding a contract, it is often not the only factor that is considered. Delivery times, extended warranties, environmentally friendly attributes, or technical expertise also play an important part in deciding where to place an order. This is known as Best Value purchasing.

Competitive Pricing

Because the GSA has already negotiated the prices with each contract holder, the agencies know that schedule orders are priced competitively. Schedule holders agree to offer GSA customers *at least* the same price that they currently offer to their **Most Favored Customers**. Agencies also expect to be able to negotiate a discount for quantity or volume purchasing, and may also look for additional one-time spot price reductions.

Contracting Goals

As we explained in earlier chapters, federal agencies have contracting goals requiring them to **Set Aside** a certain percentage of their contracting business to particular business groups, such as Small, Minority-Owned, Disadvantaged, or Veteran-Owned businesses. When you submit your company details to the GSA, you will be asked whether you qualify for any of these set-asides, and if so your business will be designated as such. Federal agencies can then use this knowledge to award contracts to specific set-aside categories of businesses, in order to achieve their mandated goals.

Revenue

It should be noted that it is to the benefit of GSA to award contracts, because the agency receives revenue not only from the Industrial Funding Fee (currently 0.75 percent) that it receives from contractors, but also by payments it receives from the agencies that purchase from this program. Through the administration of the schedules program, GSA has become a federal agency that actually makes a profit!

How Agencies Make Awards

For orders at or below $3,000, known as the **Micro-Purchase Threshold**, an agency does not need to solicit offers from more than one vendor, but can simply place the order with the vendor that best meets its needs.

For orders over this amount the buyer must survey **at least three schedule contractors.** Typically the buyer will browse the GSA's *Advantage!* Website, where vendors post their catalogs. Buyers may choose to ask a vendor for an additional one-time price reduction, especially if they are buying in any quantity, but you are not obligated to give one. Once he or she has reviewed the catalogs, the contracting officer will make a Best Value selection, based on a combination of price, delivery, warranties, and so on.

Each schedule contract lists a **Maximum Order Threshold** for each Special Item Number (SIN). The maximum order threshold is *not* the maximum the agency may order, but is the point at which the agency must request additional quantity/volume price reductions from the vendors.

How Does a GSA Contract Benefit My Business?

Stability: Once awarded, your GSA contract is valid for a period of five years (two initial years, with three one-year options). After that, the contract may be extended with three five-year options—a total of 20 years!

Teaming: You will be able to form team arrangements with other Schedule contractors, in order to provide solutions to large or complex requirements. These **Contractor Team Arrangements** allow you to work with another Schedule contractor who complements your company's capabilities, so that you can compete for orders as a team, when you may not be able to qualify independently.

Exposure: Once you have been awarded a contract, you will be required to submit details of your products and services, including pricing, to the government's Website known as GSA *Advantage!*. This gives contracting agencies around the world access to information about your company's products and services. In addition, your company will be listed in the Schedules e-Library online, which identifies you as an approved vendor for specific products or services.

If you are in the **Information Technology** industry, the e-Government Act of 2002 established a program that allows state, city, and local governments to use the GSA Schedules to acquire information technology products and services.

Disaster Purchasing: State and local government agencies may purchase a variety of products and services from GSA Schedule contractors in advance of a major disaster or in the aftermath of an emergency event. Schedule contractors who wish to participate in this program are designated by an icon in the GSA *Advantage!* Website.

Marketing: You will be able to market your company through the magazine known as *MarkeTips*. This magazine is the key to the federal marketplace. With a mailing list of more than 100,000 federal buyers, *MarkeTips* provides you with an opportunity to promote your products or services to federal agencies, free of charge. (We discuss marketing your contract later in the book.)

Am I Eligible?

Before making an award, the contracting officer will ensure that:

- Your Company is considered to be **responsible**.
- The pricing structure agreed upon is fair and **reasonable**.
- You are able to meet any other contract **terms and conditions** that apply.

Furthermore, the contracting officer will ensure that a **responsible** prospective contractor:

- Has adequate financial resources to perform the contract, or has the ability to obtain them.

- can fulfill the required delivery or performance schedule.
- has a satisfactory business performance record.
- has a satisfactory record of integrity and business ethics.
- has the organization, experience, accounting and operational controls, and technical skills necessary to complete the contract, or has the ability to obtain them.
- has the necessary production, construction, and technical equipment and facilities, or the ability to obtain them.
- is qualified and eligible to receive an award under applicable laws and regulations.

For details, see Federal Acquisition Regulation FAR 9.104

Any responsible offeror can be awarded a contract as long as the requirements of the solicitations are followed, and as long as the **prices are fair and reasonable**. In order to determine this, contracting officers use their understanding of the commercial marketplace together with information you submit in your offer concerning your commercial pricing structure. The contracting officer's goal is to ensure that the prices you submit in your offer are comparable to that which you offer your **Most Favored Customer** (MFC). This allows the contracting officer to be sure that the contracts that are awarded are competitive. If necessary, the contracting officer will negotiate with you in order to obtain acceptable prices, or to resolve any other issues related to your proposal. Pricing is one of the key contract elements covered in most negotiations, but it is not the only issue. Negotiations may cover a variety of other contract terms and conditions, depending on the situation.

Information Technology Government-Wide Agency Contracts (GWAC)

There are several key differences between a GWAC for Information Technology (IT) and a Multi-Agency Contract (MAC) like Schedule 70.

- **Scope:** Schedule 70 is aimed at a broad range of general IT products and services, whereas the GWACs are specifically designed for a **solutions-based contract** that can combine hardware, software, and services.
- **Opportunity:** For purchases under Schedule 70 the agency can ask for quotes from three contractors for a product or service, and use Best Value criteria to award the contract to one of these companies. GWACs operate a little differently, because they are required to comply with **Fair Opportunity purchasing**. This means that the agency must give all contractors within a specific functional area a "fair opportunity" to be considered for each order. The agency may issue a brief description of the requirement to all of the contractors, and then request full proposals only from interested firms. Or it may request written or oral proposals from all of the contractors. Each contractor within a defined contract functional area must be considered for each task order. (There are four specific exceptions to this

requirement: urgent need for the services, specialized or unique services that can only be provided by one contractor, work that is a "logical follow-on" to work already competed, or if the agency needs to satisfy a minimum guarantee provision in a contract. In addition, the 8(a) GWAC is of course restricted to small disadvantaged 8(a) IT companies.)

- **Contract Type:** Multi-Agency Contracts like Schedule 70 allow fixed-price, labor-hour, and time-and-materials orders. GWACs can also issue cost-reimbursement contracts.
- **Submissions:** Multiple Agency Contracts like Schedule 70 are "standing" solicitations that allow submission of proposals at any time. By contrast, GWACs have a cutoff date, after which proposals will no longer be accepted. (Exceptions to this can be made if it is in the best interest of the government to do so.)
- **Range:** Multi-Agency Contracts have a large pool of contractors, and a buyer will do some research to find those who can perform a particular task. There are fewer contractors in the GWAC pool, and all of them are capable of performing the work. The buyer does not have to perform further market research to narrow the field.
- **Worldwide:** Multi-Agency Contracts like Schedule 70 allow companies to offer domestic only coverage, but GWAC contractors must be able to offer their services worldwide.

There are several other distinctions besides these. If you need more information, go to the GSA Website at *www.gsa.gov* (161) and enter "GWAC" in the search bar, or go to *www.gsa.gov/gwacs*. (162)

The GWAC contracts are:

8(a) STARS	Set-Aside for 8a disadvantaged businesses.
Alliant Alliant SB	Worldwide IT solutions to federal agencies. SB is the small business set-aside
ANSWER	Applications 'N' Support for Widely Diverse End User Requirements
HUB-Zone	For Historically Underutilized Business Zone small businesses.
ITOP II	Information Technology Omnibus Procurement II

Millennia Millennia Lite	Large system integration and development projects. IT capital planning, studies, and assessments; high-end IT services; mission support; legacy systems migration; enterprise systems development. Typical projects include biometrics, nanotechnology, capital planning and investment control, information assurance and security, critical infrastructure protection, knowledge management, systems engineering, application development, software development, Computer Aided Design, Engineering, Management and business analysis, and systems analysis.
VETS	Service-disabled veteran-owned small business set-aside.
ACES	Access Certificates for Electronic Services.
Smart Cards	ID, building access, property control, biometrics.
Virtual Data Center Services	Data processing and support services.

* Note: Some GWACs that will expire in 2010 (Answer, Millennia, and Millennia Lite) will not be renewed because they have been replaced by the Alliant and Alliant Small Business contracts.

GSA and the American Recovery and Reinvestment Act (ARRA) of 2009

GSA is well positioned to offer buying agencies the products and services they need to implement the Recovery Act. The fact that contractors are already approved allows agencies to acquire the products and services they need quickly and efficiently.

GSA Schedule contractors who have accepted the terms, conditions, and reporting requirements of the Recovery Act will be identified with an **ARRA** symbol next to their items on GSA *Advantage!*. Buyers can indicate that their purchases will be a Recovery/ Stimulus Acquisition when they request quotes from approved vendors, via GSA's E-Buy system.

One of the main goals of the Recovery Act is to modernize many kinds of federal structures and managed communities: military facilities, borders stations, ports of entry and barracks; federal buildings, courthouses, and prisons; air traffic control centers; research facilities; hospitals, medical facilities, health facilities, family housing, and child development centers; Indian reservations; and national parks, wildlife refuges, and fish hatcheries. There are several GSA schedules that can be used, either together or separately, to provide Recovery support, including:

- **O3FAC**, Facility Maintenance/Management Services; Marine
- **84**, Alarm and Signal, Fire and Security
- **56**, Pre-engineered and Prefabricated Buildings and Structures
- **871**, Construction Management Support
- **51V**, Supporting Equipment and Services
- **66**, Scientific Equipment and Services
- **73**, Food Service, Hospitality, and Cleaning
- Various schedules for Office, Household, Quarters, Special Use, and Packaged Furniture

More information on GSA and the American Recovery and Reinvestment Act (ARRA) can be found at *www.gsa.gov*. (161) Click on Recovery Act for more details. More information on the specific reporting requirements for contracts awarded under this act can be found at *www.FederalReporting.gov*. (163)

Special Programs for State and Local Agencies

The following are several programs that allow state and local agencies to purchase products and services from GSA schedules under certain circumstances.

- **Cooperative Purchasing:** Under this program, state and local governments may purchase information technology (IT) products, software, and services from contracts awarded under Schedule 70, as well as alarm and signal systems, facility management systems, firefighting and rescue equipment, law enforcement and security equipment, marine craft and related equipment, special purpose clothing, and related services from contracts awarded under Schedule 84. If you agree to participate, this means that you will allow state and local governments to purchase these items from you *for the same terms and prices* that are in your GSA contract. Your company will be flagged with an icon in the GSA e-Library, and on *Advantage!*, the agency's online shopping program.

- **Disaster Recovery Purchasing:** This program allows state and local governments to purchase certain items from GSA Schedule contracts to facilitate recovery from a major disaster, terrorism, or attack, as well as in advance of a major disaster declared by the president, or in the aftermath of an emergency event. Schedule contractors participating in this program are identified with an icon in the GSAs e-Library and on GSA *Advantage!*

- **Public Health Emergencies:** Since August 2009, state, local, territorial, and tribal governments may access all Federal Supply Schedules as authorized users for goods and services when expending Federal grant funds in response to Public Health Emergencies (PHE) declared by the Secretary of Health and Human Services.
- **The 1122 Program:** This program allows state and local governments to purchase law enforcement equipment from GSA schedules, provided it is used for **counter-drug** activities. In 2009 an expanded pilot program *also* allows state/local purchases for **homeland security and emergency response** activities. Currently only six states are participating in this expanded pilot program: North Carolina, Georgia, Florida, Nevada, California, and Arizona.
- **The Wildland Fire Program:** GSA supplies wildland fire protection equipment both to federal agencies and to U.S. Forest Service agencies. Most of these items are covered by very rigid Forest Service specifications.
- **The Computers for Learning Program:** This allows schools and educational nonprofit organizations to obtain excess computer equipment from federal agencies.
- **The Federal Surplus Personal Property Donation Program:** This allows certain organizations such as nonprofit educational and public health agencies to obtain personal property that the federal government no longer needs.

Some Other Federal Contracting Vehicles

Although a GSA contract is probably the best known of the Multi-Agency Contracts (MAC) or Government-Wide Agency Contracts (GWAC), it is not the only one. There are many other procurement vehicles used by agencies for their specific requirements, particularly in information technology.

This list contains some of them, and the acronyms they love to use!

- Air Force AF Way: *https://afway.af.mil*. (164)
- Air Force Network-Centric Solutions (NETCENTS): *http://public.gunter .af.mil/aq/NetCents*. (165)
- Army-Air Force Exchange Program (AAFES): *www.aafes.com/vendors*. (166)
- Army Small Computer Program (CHESS): *https://ascp.monmouth.army.mil/scp/ index.jsp*. (167)
- Department of Defense E-Mall: *www.dlis.dla.mil/emall.asp*. (168)
- Defense Information Technology Contracting Organization (DITCO): *www .ditco.disa.mil*. (169)
- Department of Energy Utility Energy Services Contracts: *www1.eere.energy.gov/ femp*. (170)

- Department of Homeland Security (DHS): *www.dhs.gov/xopnbiz*. (171)
- Enterprise Acquisition Gateway for Leading Edge Solutions (EAGLE): *www.sra-eagle.com*.
- Department of Justice (DOJ—Includes Dept. of Alcohol, Tobacco, and Firearms [ATF]; Drug Enforcement Administration [DEA]; Federal Bureau of Investigation [FBI]; Federal Bureau of Prisons; Prison Industries): *www.usdoj.gov/jmd/irm/sts/itss2001/itss-3.htm*. (172)
- Internal Revenue Service—Total Information Processing Support Services (TIPSS-3): *www.irs.gov/opportunities/procurement*. (173)
- Federal Aviation Administration—Broad Information Technology and Telecommunication Services (BITS II): *www.faa.gov* (174) (search BITS).
- NASA—Scientific and Engineering Workstation Procurement (SEWP): *www.sewp.nasa.gov*. (175)
- National Institute of Health Technology Acquisition and Assessment (NIHTAAC): *http://nitaac.nih.gov*. (176)
- Navy—Seaport-e: *www.seaport.navy.mil*. (177)
- U.S. AID Indefinite Quantity Contracts: *www.usaid.gov/business*. (178)

What Are My Responsibilities Once the Contract Is Awarded?

The GSA contract can offer your company a great deal of opportunity, but you must also be aware of certain obligations and responsibilities you will have. Now is a good time to look briefly at some of these obligations, so that you can consider them as you make a decision to pursue a GSA Schedule contract.

After the contract has been awarded you are required to submit a **Schedule Price List** document to the contracting officer within a specified time period. This price list must follow a very specific format, which is detailed in the solicitation. (We will discuss this requirement in detail later in the book.) Once the price list has been approved you must agree to distribute your Schedule price lists as required by the contract.

You must submit your prices, terms, and conditions to the government's online ordering system, **GSA *Advantage!*** You may also submit photographs of your products at this point. You will usually have six months after the contract award to complete this task, but this time period may vary from schedule to schedule. We will discuss this requirement in detail later in the book.

You must submit a **Quarterly Sales Report** within 30 days of the close of each calendar quarter (January, April, July, and October). You must have a system in place that allows you to keep track of your GSA contract sales separate from other federal agency sales, as well as separate from your commercial sales. You must be able to separate the sales made via your GSA contract from those sales made outside of the contract.

You must submit your **Industrial Funding Fee** (IFF) based on your reported quarterly sales. The Industrial Funding Fee allows the Federal Supply Services (FSS) to administer the Schedules Program. The GSA prices that you negotiate with the contracting officer *must* include this fee. The rate is established by the FSS and is not negotiable. The current rate is 0.75 percent.

Remember that GSA does not market or promote specific contracts, does not distribute products of individual firms, and does not steer business to any individual contractor. Once you receive your contract, you *must* be prepared to **market your products or services** to the federal community—do not expect the agencies to come beating down your door!

Return on Your Investment

No doubt about it, a GSA contract can be a wonderful opportunity for your company, but before you go any further, be aware of the investment of time and effort you will need to make in order to submit, maintain, *and* manage your GSA contract. Remember that a GSA contract does *not* guarantee sales. If you make the effort to submit the proposal but do not subsequently work to market and manage it, your contract could be withdrawn (if you make less than the required $25,000 in sales during the first two years). If you make few sales under this schedule then the amount of time you spent submitting it will be wasted. Be prepared to do some initial research into the contracts and find out if there is a demand for your products and services, and who your competition will be. Later in this chapter we will show you how to do this. Your competitors may not have had *any* GSA contract sales, if they did not make the effort to market their contract.

At this point a very brief overview might be a good place to start. Look at this as a roadmap to your success! Begin to think about these basic questions:

- **Products and Services:** Which products and/or services will you offer?
- **Delivery:** What delivery times will you offer? Can you offer expedited delivery? Will you offer overseas delivery, or just within the Continental United States (CONUS)?
- **Warranties:** Will you offer a standard commercial warranty or something better?
- **Production Points:** Where are your products made? What will be the point of origin of your services? You will need to provide this information in your proposal.
- **Pricing:** What prices will you offer? You must offer GSA *at least* the same pricing as your Most Favored Customer (MFC). You will need to document your commercial prices, and your pricing structure, and show the pricing you offer your MFC.
- **Discounts:** Will you offer any quantity or volume discounts to GSA?

- **Financial Details:** You will need to give GSA details of your average sales in the last three financial years, and your expected sales to GSA.

- **Customer References:** You will need to gather and submit a list of past customers who will be prepared to respond to questions about your products and services, and the quality of your services.

- **Training:** You may need to complete a basic online training module designed to help you understand the process, and include the certificate with your submission.

- **Receiving Orders:** How will you receive orders? Who will be the point of contact for GSA contract orders? GSA buyers will send e-mail requests for pricing to you via a system known as e-Buy. Who will receive these requests? Will you have a system in place so that you can reply quickly and accurately with a quote?

- **Invoicing and Payments:** Who will be responsible for sending invoices and tracking payments?

- **Sales Reporting:** You must keep records of any sales made under this contract separate from other sales. Then you must report these quarterly to GSA and pay the appropriate Industrial Funding Fee. Who will be responsible for this?

- **Pricelist Preparation:** After the contract is awarded you will need to prepare a Schedule Contract price list in a specific format, and upload this information onto the GSA *Advantage!* Website. Who will be responsible for this task?

- **Maintaining the Contract:** You will need to make regular modifications to your contract in order to add or delete products or services, change administrative details (point-of-contact information and so on), and increase or decrease your contract prices. Any reductions in your commercial prices or terms may *require* you to make equal reductions in your GSA contract. You will not be able to increase prices for a certain period of time after the contract is awarded (which will be specified in the contract), and then you may only increase prices a certain number of times a year, with a maximum percentage price increase. You will have to submit a formal modification request to the contracting officer whenever you wish to add products/services or increase prices, and once they are approved you must then update your prices both in your Schedule pricelist and on the GSA *Advantage!* site. Who will be responsible for this?

- **Marketing the Contract:** Because the contract is no guarantee of sales, it will still be essential to market your catalog to federal agencies. Other companies will also sell products or services similar to yours, and they will also be listed on GSA *Advantage!* Will you be competitive? Later in this chapter we show you how to do some of this market research to find your potential customers, identify the competition, compile a list of agency buyers, and look at Contractor Team Arrangements or subcontracting opportunities. Remember that price is not the only factor a buyer will consider when he or she makes a purchase. Consider how other factors may make you more competitive, such as a faster delivery time, a longer warranty, extra accessories, quantity price breaks, environmentally friendly attributes, and so on.

Don't Panic! You don't have to spend hours thinking about this right now; just keep these things in your mind as you read through this book, and try to understand how these questions could be resolved as you begin the work to research, submit, market, manage, and sell your products and services to the federal government via your new shiny GSA Schedule contract!

Other Opportunities in Federal Contracting

Remember that *you do not have to have a GSA contract* in order to begin selling your products and services to the federal government; a GSA contract is just one of the many options available to you. If you feel you are not ready to submit right now, you can look at other avenues to begin exploring opportunities in the federal marketplace, and then decide to submit your GSA proposal at a later date.

Stop! Go No Further If...

- **You are not willing to commit time and personnel to this project.** You must be prepared to submit, manage, *and* market your contract.
- **You have been in business less than two years.** If this is the case I suggest you read this book carefully to understand the benefits of a GSA contract, and be ready to make your submission at the appropriate time.
- **You expect to make less than $25,000 in sales to the federal government.** GSA will not award a contract to a company that cannot make $25,000 in sales in the first two years of the contract, and $25,000 in each subsequent year.
- **You sell products imported from restricted countries such as China.** If you only sell a finished product imported from certain countries you will not be awarded a contract. You will need to study the list of designated countries to see if this applies to you.
- **You do not accept credit cards.** GSA makes extensive use of government-issued payment cards. Their SmartPay® card is used by more than 350 agencies and organizations, spending more than $26 billion annually. GSA contract holders are *required* to accept payment via these purchase cards for orders under the Micro-Purchase Threshold (currently $3,000), and are "strongly encouraged" to accept payment card orders above that amount.
- **You are an architectural design company.** The GSA Schedules Program may *not* be used to acquire services that are subject to Federal Acquisition Regulation 36.6, the Brooks Architect-Engineer Act which requires A/E design service contracts to be negotiated on the basis of competence and qualification. Rather than price being

an essential factor in evaluation, competition relies almost exclusively on technical factors. This is known as Qualifications-Based Selection (QBS). Although there are a lot of opportunities for you in the government marketplace, there is not a specific schedule for your services. Check the FedBizOpps Website for contracting opportunities at **www.fbo.gov**. (20)

Market Research at the GSA E-Library

Website: *www.gsaelibrary.gsa.gov*. (179)

This Website is a great place to begin your initial research. Use this site to do some pre-contract market research on your direct competitors. Find out which suppliers have a contract and what items are available, by using various search options. You can also link directly to the GSA *Advantage!* online ordering Website and see the products or services that are listed, with pricing details and product information. Search by the name of the manufacturer, the name of a specific contractor, or a particular contract number.

Which Schedule Is Right for Me?

You will need to take some time to look at the various schedules to decide which is right for you. You may find that there is only one schedule that fits your company's products or services, but sometimes a little research can lead to several different options. You will need to be aware of several things at this point:

Many companies have **more than one GSA Schedule**, with various products and services on each. If you offer a range of products or services, some research at this site should help you decide with which schedule you should begin. Which of your company's products or services are most likely to succeed in government sales? Once you have experience in submitting a schedule, you may decide to submit a proposal for a second schedule at a later date. Remember that a lot of the information that you need to gather will be the same for any schedule.

Even though a GSA contract has no guarantee of sales, each schedule does give an **estimate of the annual sales**, based on previous purchases. You may decide to focus on your core product or service, on the one with the largest profit margin, the schedule where most of your competitors are listed or perhaps the schedule where you feel you have the least amount of competition!

You cannot put the exact same product or service into two separate schedules. If you find that there is more than one schedule that seems appropriate, you will need to **decide carefully which schedule best fits your needs**, and where you might best market to the government. At this point a little more research at this site could confirm your best choice. Using the e-library as a research tool, you should be able to find companies that sell the same or similar products or services, and you will be able to see which schedule was used.

Remember that you will not be awarded a GSA Schedule contract unless the contracting officer **estimates your sales to be $25,000** in the first two years, and $25,000 annually in subsequent years. Some market research at this point will show you the types and quantities of products/services that have been purchased by the agency in the past.

A good way to begin your research may be to select View Schedule Contracts on the right-hand side of the page. This will give you a complete listing of the current Federal Supply Schedules, including the schedule number, and a brief description of the services or products included in that schedule. For example, Schedule 03FAC, Facilities Maintenance and Management, is primarily concerned with building maintenance and repair services. As we said earlier in the book, schedules are subdivided using Special Item Numbers (SIN). If you click on the schedule number you can see all the services that are covered under this schedule as well as their Special Item Number, including energy management (SIN 871 202), building commissioning (SIN 871 206), fire inspection, pest control, grounds maintenance, landscaping, tree trimming, snow removal, elevator inspection and maintenance (SIN 541 001), fire alarm system maintenance and repair, laundry services, janitorial/custodial services, roofing repair, plumbing and pipefitting, electrical, HVAC, and much more.

Schedule 51V is known as the **Hardware Superstore**. This schedule operates in much the same way as your local big-box hardware store, with various "aisles" such as Domestic Appliances (SIN 639 001), a Hardware Store (flooring, fencing, building materials, paint), Power Tools, Lawn and Garden (SIN 341 100 is used for mowers), and much more.

Search Contractor Listings

If you go back to the Schedules e-Library Home Page, you will see other options open to you. For instance, you can search an alphabetical list of **current GSA Contractors**.

This would be a good place to find out whether any of your direct competitors already have a GSA contract, and which schedule (or schedules) applies to them.

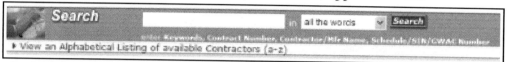

Let's look at the type of information you can find by clicking on a specific contractor listing. In this example I clicked on a company called **Minuteman Trucks**.

Here is the company's address and Website link. We can also see that it is listed as a Small Disadvantaged Business. You can see the schedule number (23 V Vehicular Multiple Award Schedule) and the contract number. The contract end date is listed, and because a GSA contract is for a period of five years, we can tell how long Minuteman has had its GSA contract. It has products under category 271 108—Spare Parts and Equipment. Click on the category and you can see that there are 30 different contractors who also have a GSA contract under this category.

Here is a partial list of the contractors under that category. We can see their contract numbers, their places of business, and their business status—Small, Veteran-Owned, Disadvantaged (8a); Woman-Owned, and so on.

The **Disaster Recovery** icon identifies a business that is willing to supply state and local organizations with supplies under the terms of this contract, in the event of a natural disaster or emergency. The **American Recovery and Reinvestment Act** (ARRA) icon indicates that the company has agreed to the terms of doing business with agencies using ARRA funding, including Recovery Act reporting requirements.

Click on the **Contract Terms** icon to see more details of that particular company's terms.

Click on the *GSA Advantage!* icon to see the full list of products it offers, along with price details, delivery times, options, and accessories.

Click on the **Mfg Part Number** to see more details of the product, as well as details of delivery times, any volume discounts that are offered, and more.

In some instances several different companies may offer the same manufacturer part number. In that case the buyer can make direct comparisons between these companies' offers. Remember that price may not always be the deciding factor—if one company offers a better delivery, for example, the buyer may choose to order from them, even though their prices are slightly higher. Other factors that may influence the buyer include socio-economic status (minority or Veteran-Owned for example), warranty details, and minimum order requirements. Also notice that the delivery details for each company show whether it will deliver to Alaska, Hawaii, and/or Puerto Rico, in addition to the Continental United States (CONUS).

The **Advanced Search** option (underneath the shopping cart icon) allows the buyer to search for items in specific environmental categories.

These are the boxes you can check here:

- **UNICOR mandatory items:** from the Federal Prison Industries (see the details on this agency in Chapter 4.)
- **Ability One/NIB/NISH mandatory items.** (We discussed these requirements for purchases from the National Institutes for the Blind [NIB] and Severely Handicapped [NISH] in Chapter 2.)

- **CPG Compliant items:** refers to the Environmental Protection Agency's Comprehensive Procurement Guidelines for the purchase of recycled items. (We discussed this in Chapter 3.)
- **FEMP Energy Efficient items:** (These were also discussed in Chapter 3, in the section on environmentally friendly procurement.)
- **Prime Program items:** refers to the Navy's Plastics Removal in Marine Environment (PRIME).
- **HSPD-12 Certified:** refers to the Homeland Security Presidential Directive number 12, concerning secure and reliable forms of identification for federal employees and contractors.
- **Section 508 Regulations** require Federal agencies to make electronic and IT accessible to people with disabilities.

Buyers may also search for other environmental attributes such as **Recycled** items, **EnergyStar** compliant, or **Biobased** items. The **EPEAT** program helps buyers evaluate, compare, and select electronic products based on their environmental attributes.

Market Research at the Schedule Sales Query Website

Website: *http://ssq.gsa.gov.* (180)

As we mentioned earlier, schedule contractors must report their GSA contract sales on a quarterly basis. At this site you can get detailed information on GSA contract sales. There are several different types of report available, including sales for a particular schedule, listings of all the contractors in a specific schedule and their dollar sales per quarter or Fiscal Year, or contract sales for a particular company.

At the home page, click on **Create a Report**. Step one asks for your name, address, and telephone numbers, but you need not enter that information; simply click on the Proceed button. Here are the sales report options you have available:

For this example I selected Report # 10—total sales by contractor for a specific schedule. Select the schedule, the fiscal year, and the format in which you want to see your report. Once the report has been generated you will see an example of the report's format, and you will be able to see the *actual* report by clicking on the Download button.

1. All Schedules by Fiscal Year
2. All Schedules by all Available Fiscal Years
3. SIN & Schedule Totals by Fiscal Year
4. All Contract Sales by Schedule by Fiscal Year
5. Schedule Sales Grand Total by Quarter by Fiscal Year
6. Total for All Quarters by Contractor by Fiscal Year
7. Total by Quarter & SIN by Contract Number and Fiscal Year
8. Total for Each Quarter for a Specific SIN by Fiscal Year
9. Total by Quarter & Contract for a Specific Contractor and Fiscal Year
10. Total by Contractor for a Specific Schedule and Fiscal Year
11. All Sales by Fiscal Year for a Specific SIN Number

Market Information at the Federal Procurement Data Center Website (FPDS)

This Website can give you vital information about the government's spending patterns. The information is free, and covers more than 12 million contracts from many different government agencies. You can find detailed information on contracts of more than $25,000 and summary data on procurements of less than $25,000. Via this Website you can identify who brought what, from whom, for how much, when, and where. There is also information on subcontracts (through the Subcontracting Data Systems) as well as foreign sales (via the Foreign Trade Data System). You will need to register at this site, and create a username and password, in order to have access to the information.

Website: ***www.fpds.gov***. (181)

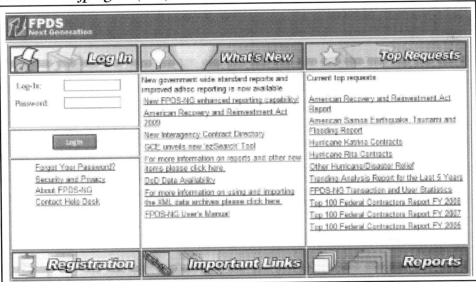

There are more than **50 Standard Reports**, with up to 12 months' worth of data on each agency. **Published Reports** show the spending patterns across the federal government, as well as Small Business Goaling Reports. You can also create your own **Custom Reports**, should you need them. However, certain information is *not* available, such as:

- Copies of complete contracts.
- Statements of Work.
- Subcontracting information.
- Sales made using a government credit card, or purchase card, if less than $2,500.
- Information from certain agencies that are exempt from reporting.
- Information on grants, cooperative agreements, training authorizations, and so on.

Taking the Next Step

Once you have taken some time to research the schedules, check out the competition, and decide upon the schedule that is right for you, you will be ready to download the entire set of schedule documents and begin to put together your proposal. In the next chapter we take you step by step through the process.

Help!

If you have any questions about this chapter, we would be happy to try to help you. Go to our Website, *www.sell2gov.com*, and at the Contact tab you can send us an e-mail with your questions. Please put "Definitive Guide" in the subject line.

Chapter 9

Preparing Your Submission

Overview

Okay. You've used the information in the previous chapter to help you do some initial research. You also:

- Have looked at the various schedules available, and decided which one is right for you.
- Have researched the other companies that are already "on schedule" and have decided that you can compete with them—either in terms of pricing or with other factors such as delivery, warranty and so on.
- Understand the commitment of time and effort you are going to make to submit, market *and* manage your proposal…

Now the work begins: preparing your proposal for submission!

Don't Panic! This chapter takes you step by step through a typical proposal, and helps you understand what is needed.

Downloading the Schedule Documents

You can download your schedule from the FedBizOpps Website at *www.fbo.gov*, (20) or you can go to the GSA's e-library and find the link there: *www.gsaelibrary.gsa.gov*. (179)

In the Quick Schedule section in the top right of the screen, use the drop-down arrow to find the schedule you wish to download, then link to FedBizOpps to find the latest version of the documents.

Download *all* the documents.

Here's an example of the various documents contained in the **Schedule 56** download, Buildings and Building Materials. As you can see, there are often many different documents

to download—but take heart, they will not all be relevant to your submission!

Several attachments are relevant only **after the contract has been awarded**. The Modifications attachment is used to request price increases, known as Economic Price Adjustments (EPA), or to add new products or services to your contract. The Options attachment is used when the agency wishes to exercise its option to extend your initial contract. A Novations attachment is used to notify the agency of any change of name to the company, and so on.

Some attachments are **only relevant in certain instances**, such as the requirement to submit a Subcontracting Plan or a Marketing Plan, which may only be relevant to large businesses.

There will be several attachments that **may not be relevant** to the product or services you are offering. For example, in this particular schedule, Attachment 12 is used if you are offering Leasing or Rental Services. You will only need to complete those attachments that are relevant to your proposal.

Because there are more than 40 schedules, and they are all different in some way, you must download *all* the files in order to look at them carefully and decide which ones need to be included in your submission.

Several Schedules include a **Read Me First** document that gives an outline of the requirements, and often a **Checklist** document to ensure that you submit all the documents required.

The Basic Solicitation Document

The Basic Solicitation document is the best place to begin to prepare your schedule. *Always* read the document thoroughly from beginning to end—I know it seems like a lot of work, but it is essential that you fully understand the terms and conditions of the schedule, your responsibilities, and the government's requirements *before* you submit your proposal.

At the beginning of this document you will find an overview of any changes that have been made since the last Refresh. Schedule documents are updated, or refreshed, on a regular basis, and you must always submit the latest version of your schedule.

It may take you several months from when you begin to work on the proposal until you are ready to submit your offer, and you may find that a new refresh document has been issued in the meantime! *Always take the time to check that you have the latest version before you make your submission!*

In this example, Schedule 51V—the Hardware Superstore, the basic solicitation document tells you exactly which of the attachments you must submit with your offer.

Attachment 1. Commercial Sales Practice (CSP-1). (A SEPARATE CSP-1 MUST BE COMPLETED FOR EACH COMMODITY/SIN OFFERED)
Attachment 2. Subcontracting Plan Format. This **MUST** be completed by large business offerors.
Attachment 3. Hardware Store Department
Attachment 4. Commercial Coatings, Adhesives, Sealants, Fuels And Lubricants
Attachment 5. Household and Office Appliances Department
Attachment 6. Tools Department
Attachment 7. Lawn and Garden Department
Attachment 8. Woodworking and Metalworking Machinery and Equipment Department
Attachment 9. Guidelines for developing your marketing plan (required by all offerors)

In this example, you are required to submit the following documents:

- The basic solicitation document.
- Attachment 1, the Commercial Sales Practices form.
- The specific attachment(s) relevant to your offer—numbered 3 through 8.
- Attachment 9, the Marketing Plan.
- Attachment 2 is a Subcontracting Plan document that only needs to be submitted by large business offerors, so it will not be relevant if you are a small business. However, we will briefly discuss subcontracting plans later in the book, so that you have an understanding of the process.
- In some cases there may also be a **Vendor Response Document**. This document consolidates the relevant information you must submit to GSA, and the schedule *may* allow you to submit this shorter document in lieu of the solicitation document.

The Contracting Officers

You will find names and telephone numbers of the contracting officers who will be responsible for answering any of your questions. In many cases you will also see an e-mail address so that you can get in touch with them quickly and easily. These contracting officers will be your best friends in this endeavor—they are always willing to answer questions and help you make the best submission possible.

The Checklist

In the example on the next page the GSA has provided a checklist to help ensure that all the information you need to submit is included in your offer. If your schedule does not contain one, it might be a very good idea to create your own, as you read through the solicitation document.

THE FOLLOWING OFFER CHECKLIST IS USED BY THE CONTRACTING OFFICERS TO REVIEW YOUR OFFER. IT IS PROVIDED HERE TO ASSIST YOU IN SUBMITTING YOUR OFFER.

REFRESH 11 – July 2009

Vendor Response Document/Offer Response Document (eOffer) Complete?		Y	N
G-FSS-900-C – Contact for contract administration complete?		Y	N
If offering overseas, is an in-country POC provided?		Y	N
K-FSS-1, Authorized Negotiators completed?		Y	N
Good & Services: Applicable SINs information completed?		Y	N

Information-Gathering

At this point it might be a good idea to have an overview of exactly what information you are going to need to gather together before you begin. It will make the submission process much easier! We will discuss these areas in more depth later, but a basic roadmap at this point can help you to understand the process.

Basic Company Information

Gather together basic information about your company. We discussed these codes and how to obtain them in Chapter 1. They include:

- Central Contractors Registration (**CCR**)
- Online Representations and Certification (**ORCA**)
- Commercial and Government Entity (**CAGE**) code(s)
- Dun & Bradstreet Number (**DUNS**)
- Company **name, address, telephone** number, and **fax** number
- Tax Identification Number (**TIN**)
- North American Industrial Classification (**NAICS**) codes
- Federal Supply Classification codes (**FSC**)
- Product Service Codes (**PSC**)

Points of Contact

Who will be responsible for the administration of the submission? Who will be authorized to negotiate with GSA concerning terms, conditions, and pricing? Who will be responsible for invoicing and payments? Who will be the point of contact for electronic business? It is a good idea to have a main and an alternate point of contact for each of these areas. If your company is small you may list the same person, but remember that if someone is not listed in the submission as either a point of contact or an authorized negotiator, GSA will *not* discuss the contract with them. You will need:

- **Administrative** Point(s) of Contact
- **Payment and Invoicing** Point(s) of Contact
- **Electronic Business** Point(s) of Contact, and
- **Authorized Negotiators**

Products or Services

Gather together some basic information about the products or services you will be offering to GSA:

- Will you be using any **other facilities** to perform this contract? If so, you must provide a list of their names and addresses.
- Are any of the products **manufactured outside the United States?** If so, you will need to compile a list of the Production Points where the items are manufactured, with addresses for each.
- Are any of your products classified as **environmentally friendly?** Check out the earlier chapters of the book where we discussed these factors. You will be able to indicate this when you submit your contract to GSA's *Advantage!* online catalog.
- You will need to include a copy of your current **commercial catalog**, or a spreadsheet that describes your company's products and/or services, including prices, delivery times, warranties, and country of origin. If you do not currently have a printed commercial catalog that you can include with your offer, you will need to create a spreadsheet containing the relevant information. In this case you will need to include invoices or other documents that confirm this pricing. We will discuss this later in this chapter.
- What are your standard **delivery times** after receipt of an order? Do you offer expedited delivery?
- Will you offer just **domestic** delivery, or will you also offer **overseas** delivery? For overseas delivery, what countries or geographical regions will you include? Will your domestic delivery prices include delivery to Alaska, Hawaii, and/or Puerto Rico?
- Are there any **hazardous materials** involved? If so, you will have to supply Material Safety Data Sheets (MSDS). Are there any safety standards that apply to your product?
- What **warranties** do you offer? What about **service** or repair?
- If you are a dealer that will be supplying products from an Original Equipment Manufacturer (OEM) you will need a formal **Letter of Supply** from each of them,

guaranteeing a regular supply of the product in sufficient quantities so that you can fulfill the terms of the contract. This letter takes a specific format, and will need to be on the manufacturer's letterhead and signed by an officer of the company.

The **Letter of Supply** from your Manufacturer could be a stalling point; a large manufacturer could take a while to respond to your request, which could hold up the whole submission process—get this ball rolling as soon as possible!

- **Pricing and Discounts** is a critical area for you to consider, and we will devote more time to it later, but at this point you will need to start thinking about your commercial pricing structure, and consider the pricing structure you will offer GSA.

- What are the terms and conditions that you currently offer your **Most Favored Customer** (MFC)? This will include not only pricing, but also any discounts you offer on quantity or volume purchases, as well as concessions on delivery (free shipping?), warranties (extended warranties?), or any other special discounts or concessions.

- What are the terms, conditions, and discounts you are going to offer GSA? These must be *at least* as good as those you offer your MFC.

Financial Information

This information will be needed when you complete the important **Commercial Sales Practices Form**, known as the CSP-1. We will discuss this in detail later in the book, but begin to gather some of this information now.

- What is the company's **dollar value of sales** made to the general public, based on an established market price, during the last 12 months, or last fiscal period?

- What are your **projected annual sales** for each Special Item Number (SIN) in this contract?

Orders and Invoices

How will you **accept orders**? Via Fax? Via **Electronic Data Interchange** (EDI)?

You *must* accept payment via a **government purchase card** (credit card) for orders up to the Micro-Purchase Threshold of $3,000. Will you also accept government credit cards for orders above this minimum amount?

GSA buyers may use an electronic Request for Quote system called **e-Buy** to send out notices to GSA contract holders. You will need to respond to the RFQ within a stated number of days. Even if you do not wish to submit a quote it is a good idea to send a No Bid reply. This indicates to the buyer that you are still active in the market. How will you keep track of this? Whose e-mail will receive these requests, and make sure they are responded to in a timely manner?

GSA also uses a **Purchase Order Portal** to notify you of orders, and receive invoices and payments. Someone in the company will have to learn how to use this system, and keep track of sales, invoices, and payments.

You may need to use **Wide Area Workflow** (WAWF) or another specific invoicing system to submit invoices and receive payments. Think about how this might be implemented. We discussed WAWF in an earlier chapter. GSA also has a voluntary **FedPay®** invoicing system that you may wish to use—this system can allow GSA to pay you in as little as 10 days! More on this later, but for now, think about who is going to learn about and manage this new system.

Your prices to GSA must include an **Industrial Funding Fee** (currently 0.75 percent). You will need to keep track of sales made via your GSA contract, separate from any other sales, so that you can submit a **Quarterly Sales Report** and then submit the appropriate Industrial Funding Fee. Again, we will discuss this in more detail later in the book, but for now you should begin to think about how you will keep track of your GSA sales, and who will need to be trained to understand this system

References and Certifications

GSA requires you to submit several documents and reports that show you are a company in good standing, and that you understand the obligations of your GSA contract.

Open Ratings

Open Ratings is a report generated by Dun & Bradstreet, and is essentially your company's reference. You will need to gather contact information on at least six and up to 20 of your **previous customers**. Dun & Bradstreet will ask them to comment on your performance—satisfactory quality, timely delivery, good customer service, and so on. This report will be sent to you and to GSA. You must include a copy of the report in your submission. You are responsible for the cost of the report (as of March 2010 the report costs $185). Begin to gather contact information for past customers who will be willing to give you a favorable report.

Pathways to Success

Someone in the company who is listed as a Point of Contact or Authorized Negotiator must take this **online course**, which explains the GSA contract process and your obligations. After the video presentation you will take a multiple-choice test. Once you have completed the test you will be issued a certificate of completion, which you must include with your GSA submission. There is no cost to take the course or the test, and you can take it as many times as necessary until you pass.

The Basics—Standard Form (SF) 1449

This two-page document forms the basis of your proposal. As you can see, you do not have to complete the entire form, but certain sections; namely, blocks 12, 17, 23, 24, and 30.

SOLICITATION/CONTRACT/ORDER FOR COMMERCIAL ITEMS *OFFEROR TO COMPLETE BLOCKS 12, 17, 23, 24, & 30*		1. REQUISITION NUMBER		PAGE 1 OF
2. CONTRACT NO.	3. AWARD/EFFECTIVE DATE	4. ORDER NUMBER	5. SOLICITATION NUMBER	6. SOLICITATION ISSUE DATE

7. FOR SOLICITATION INFORMATION CALL: ▶	a. NAME	b. TELEPHONE NUMBER *(No collect calls)*	8. OFFER DUE DATE/ LOCAL TIME

9. ISSUED BY CODE	10. THIS ACQUISITON IS
	☐ UNRESTRICTED OR ☐ SET ASIDE: % FOR: ☐ SMALL BUSINESS ☐ EMERGING SMALL BUSINESS ☐ HUBZONE SMALL BUSINESS NAICS: SIZE STANDARD: ☐ SERVICE-DISABLED VETERAN- OWNED SMALL BUSINESS ☐ 8(A)

11. DELIVERY FOR FOB DESTINA-TION UNLESS BLOCK IS MARKED ☐ SEE SCHEDULE	12. DISCOUNT TERMS	☐ 13a. THIS CONTRACT IS A RATED ORDER UNDER DPAS (15 CFR 700)	13b. RATING
			14. METHOD OF SOLICITATION ☐ RFQ ☐ IFB ☐ RFP

15. DELIVER TO CODE	16. ADMINISTERED BY CODE

17a. CONTRACTOR/ OFFEROR CODE FACILITY CODE	18a. PAYMENT WILL BE MADE BY CODE
TELEPHONE NO.	
☐ 17b. CHECK IF REMITTANCE IS DIFFERENT AND PUT SUCH ADDRESS IN OFFER	18b. SUBMIT INVOICES TO ADDRESS SHOWN IN BLOCK 18a UNLESS BLOCK BELOW IS CHECKED ☐ SEE ADDENDUM

19. ITEM NO.	20. SCHEDULE OF SUPPLIES/SERVICES	21. QUANTITY	22. UNIT	23. UNIT PRICE	24. AMOUNT
	(Use Reverse and/or Attach Additional Sheets as Necessary)				

25. ACCOUNTING AND APPROPRIATION DATA	26. TOTAL AWARD AMOUNT *(For Govt. Use Only)*

☐ 27a. SOLICITATION INCORPORATES BY REFERENCE FAR 52.212-1, 52.212-4. FAR 52.212-3 AND 52.212-5 ARE ATTACHED. ADDENDA	☐ ARE	☐ ARE NOT ATTACHED
☐ 27b. CONTRACT/PURCHASE ORDER INCORPORATES BY REFERENCE FAR 52.212-4. FAR 52.212-5 IS ATTACHED. ADDENDA	☐ ARE	☐ ARE NOT ATTACHED

☐ 28. CONTRACTOR IS REQUIRED TO SIGN THIS DOCUMENT AND RETURN _____ COPIES TO ISSUING OFFICE. CONTRACTOR AGREES TO FURNISH AND DELIVER ALL ITEMS SET FORTH OR OTHERWISE IDENTIFIED ABOVE AND ON ANY ADDITIONAL SHEETS SUBJECT TO THE TERMS AND CONDITIONS SPECIFIED	☐ 29. AWARD OF CONTRACT: REF. _____ OFFER DATED _____ . YOUR OFFER ON SOLICITATION (BLOCK 5), INCLUDING ANY ADDITIONS OR CHANGES WHICH ARE SET FORTH HEREIN, IS ACCEPTED AS TO ITEMS:
30a. SIGNATURE OF OFFEROR/CONTRACTOR	31a. UNITED STATES OF AMERICA *(SIGNATURE OF CONTRACTING OFFICER)*
30b. NAME AND TITLE OF SIGNER *(Type or print)* 30c. DATE SIGNED	31b. NAME OF CONTRACTING OFFICER *(Type or print)* 31c. DATE SIGNED

AUTHORIZED FOR LOCAL REPRODUCTION
PREVIOUS EDITION IS NOT USABLE

STANDARD FORM 1449 (REV. 3/2005)
Prescribed by GSA - FAR (48 CFR) 53.212

Block	
1	Requisition Number—For government reference only.
2	Contract Number—Completed by the contracting officer upon award.
3	Award Date—Completed by the contracting officer upon award.
4	Order Number—For government use.
5	Solicitation Number—Reference this number in any correspondence.
6	Solicitation Issue Date—Make sure you use the most recent "refresh."
7	The name and contact information of the contracting officer.
8	Due Date—Not applicable here.
9	The Issuing Office (GSA) and the address to submit your offer.
10	This Acquisition Is Unrestricted—There are no set-aside programs.
11	Delivery is to the FOB destination address, unless marked.
12	**Discount Terms—Usually this will be "Net 30 days."**
13	Rated Order—see more details on the Priority Allocation Program later in this chapter.
14	Method of Solicitation—RFQ, RFP, IFB.
15	Delivery Address—Each agency that places an order under this GSA contract will issue a delivery address.
16	Administered By—The GSA offices.
17	**Insert your company name, address, phone and fax numbers, and DUNS number. If you wish payments to be made to a different address, check this option and include the remittance address with your offer. The box marked "Code" is for your CAGE code, and the "Facility Code" box is for you to identify different locations, if your company operates from more than one office.**

18	Payment Will Be Made By—Payment will be made by the individual agency that places the order under this contract.
19-24	**Block 19 through 24—Insert "See Attached" Details of your products/services, and pricing will be given later.**
25	Accounting Data—For government use.
26	Total Award Amount—For government use.
27	If there are any attachments, these boxes will be checked.
28	This notes the number of copies of every document that must accompany your offer. If it is not checked here, these details will appear later in the solicitation.
29	Award Details—For government use.
30	**You must sign here, and include your full name and title, and the date you signed this document.**
31-end	The contracting officer will sign here when the contract is awarded.

The Solicitation Document

The solicitation document (shown on the next page) contains a great deal of information about the GSA contract and the regulations that apply. In addition, there are several places where you must complete some basic information about your offer to GSA. There is a *lot* to read here!

Although many of the regulations are akin to standard commercial business practices, there are areas that are specific to government contracting. The following pages give you a *brief* description of *some* of the regulations you need to be aware of, and also indicate those sections where you are required to fill in detailed information.

Remember that these pages are no substitute for a detailed reading of the documents, but they will give you an overall sense of the terms and conditions of this contract.

You MUST take the time to read and fully understand the terms and conditions of this contract before you submit your offer. (I know, we have said this before, but it is *definitely* worth repeating!)

Be Aware of These Important Regulations

We discussed many of these regulations earlier in the book.

- 52.204-7 **Central Contractor Registration** (CCR). You must be registered at the CCR site, which was discussed in detail in the first chapter of this book.

- 52.222-35 **Equal Opportunity for Veterans.** For contracts over $25,000 you will be required to list all your employment openings with the nearest State Job Service office, and each year you must submit Form Vets-100.

- 52.225-5 **Trade Agreements Act.** If your product is made outside of the United States, Canada, or Mexico, you must be aware of the restrictions that the government places on purchases of foreign-made products.

- 52.225-13 **Restrictions On Certain Foreign Purchases.** Most transactions involving Cuba, Iran, Libya, Sudan, and North Korea are prohibited. For a more complete listing, visit the Office of Foreign Assets Control Website at *www.treas. gov/ofac.* **(182)**

- 52.232-33 **Payment by Electronic Funds Transfer.** The government will make all payments to you by Electronic Funds Transfer (EFT), using the information from your CCR registration. You are responsible for making sure the information in CCR is correct.

- 552.211-15 **The Defense Priorities and Allocations System** (DPAS). This system gives preferential treatment for certain contracts and orders. If you receive a Rated Order you must give it preferential treatment in order to meet required delivery dates. There are two levels of ratings:

    1. All "DO" rated orders take preference over unrated orders.
    2. All "DX" rated orders take preference over "DO" rated orders and unrated orders.

    The rating designation is followed by a symbol that identifies the particular program involved. A list of Delegate Agencies, approved programs, and program identification symbols can be found in Schedule 1 of 15 CFR part 700. Additional information can be found at the DPAS Website, **www.bis.doc.gov/dpas**. (21)

- 552.216-70 **Economic Price Adjustment.** This section concerns price increases or decreases during the life of the contract. You may decrease your prices at any time. You may request a price increase after a specified amount of time after the initial contract is awarded. Your price increases must result from a modification of your commercial prices. There may be limits to the number of times you can increase your prices. When you request price increases the government may either accept or deny your request, or it may choose to negotiate more favorable terms with you. We will discuss this in more detail later in this chapter.

- 552.232-74 **Invoice Payments.** This regulation gives details of invoice payments, which we described earlier. An invoice will be paid either 30 days from the date the paying office receives notification that the product has been accepted or the service has been performed satisfactorily, or 30 days from the receipt of a *correct* invoice, whichever is later.

- 552.232-77 **Payment by Government Commercial Purchase Card.** The government's commercial purchase card is a credit card issued to government employees to pay for official government purchases. You *must* agree to accept payment via this card up to the micro-purchase threshold (currently set at $3,000). You *may choose* to accept orders for more than this amount, up to an established limit. If you choose not to do so, you must notify the agency within 24 hours of receiving the order. You must not process the payment until after the supplies have been shipped or the services are performed. You must credit a cardholder's account for items returned as defective or faulty.

- 552.238-71 **Submission and Distribution of Federal Supply Schedule Authorized Pricelists.** When you are awarded the contract, you will have a specific amount of time to prepare your Authorized Schedule price list, listing your GSA prices, and terms of your contract. You will send copies to the contracting officer, as well as to a central site listed in the solicitation document. You will send potential buyers either a copy of your authorized price list or a self-addressed, postage-paid envelope or postcard so that they can request a copy of the price list. You must also advise them that your pricelist information is available online at GSA *Advantage!*. The price list must follow a very specific format, which is discussed later in this book.

- 552.238-74 **Industrial Funding Fee and Sales Reporting.** You must report the dollar value of all sales (including "zero" sales) under this contract each quarter, throughout the term of the contract. The reported contract sales value must include the Industrial Funding Fee (IFF). You may record the sales at the receipt of an order, on shipment or delivery of an order, once an invoice is issued, or once you receive payment, but the reporting method you choose to use must be consistent. When you are awarded your GSA Schedule contract, you must register at the Vendor Support Center, and you will be given the Website address, registration instructions, and reporting procedures. Within 30 days of submitting your report, you must send your Industrial Funding Fee payment, which is currently set at the rate of 0.75 percent of reported sales. The Industrial Funding Fee is used to cover the costs of operating the Federal Supply Schedules Program.

- 552.238-75 **Price Reductions.** If you reduce prices in your commercial price list, or grant more favorable terms to another customer, you *must* offer the same price reduction to the government, with the same effective date and time. You may offer a government-wide price reduction at any time. You must notify the contracting officer of any price reductions as soon as possible, but no later than 15 days after its effective date.

- 552.243-72 **Contract Modifications.** You must contact the contracting officer if you wish to make any changes to the contract. This includes requests to add or delete products or services from the contract, or to reduce or increase the prices. We discuss modifications later in the book.

- 552.246-73 **Warranties.** Unless you specify otherwise, your standard commercial warranty will apply to this contract. In addition, if you are offering overseas delivery you must also provide a 90-day warranty on all non-consumable parts, you must supply the parts and labor needed free of charge, and you must also agree to bear the cost of returning the product for 90-days.

- I-FSS-40 **Contractor Team Arrangements.** You will be able to form team arrangements with other schedule contractors, in order to provide solutions to large or complex requirements. These Contractor Team Arrangements allow you to work with another schedule contractor who complements your company's capabilities, so that you can compete for orders as a team, when you may not be able to qualify independently. All contractors who participate in such an arrangement must abide by the terms of their respective contract. For example, you will each be responsible for your Industrial Funding Fee and Sales Reporting.

- I-FSS-163 **Option to Extend the Term of the Contract.** This is known as the Evergreen clause. At the end of the initial contract the government has the option to extend your contract for an additional five-year period, and it may exercise this option a maximum of three times.

- I-FSS-597 GSA *Advantage!*. You *must* agree to participate in the GSA's *Advantage!* online shopping service. Once your price list has been approved you will have a certain amount of time to upload the catalog to the GSA *Advantage!* system, including photographs, pricing and delivery details, warranties, and so on. This requirement is discussed in more detail elsewhere in this book.

- I-FSS-599 **Electronic Commerce—FACNET.** In 1994 the government established the Federal Acquisition Computer Network (FACNET) in order to do business using Electronic Commerce (EC) and Electronic Data Interchange (EDI). If you choose to do business via EDI, you must adhere to the requirements set out here. The Value Added Network (VAN) you choose to use must be certified by the Department of Defense, and must be connected to FACNET. All EDI transactions must comply with the Federal Implementation Conventions (ICs), which are available for common business documents such as Purchase Orders, Price Sales Catalogs, Invoices, and so on.

- I-FSS-639 **Contract Sales Criteria.** You will not be awarded a contract unless the GSA believes that your sales are expected to be at least $25,000 in the first 24 months of the award, and $25,000 each year thereafter. If you do not reach these sales levels, the government may choose to cancel your contract.

- I-FSS-644 **Dealers and Suppliers.** If you are a dealer rather than a manufacturer of an item, you may be required to submit a letter of commitment from the manufacturer, which assures your source of supply, or give other evidence that your supply will be sufficient to satisfy the requirements of the contract.

- 52.212-1 **Instructions to Offerors—Commercial Items.** This section gives details on how to submit an offer. One important thing to notice is that you must agree to hold the prices in your offer firm for a certain number of days. Because a GSA contract is an open solicitation with no closing or due date, the section on late submissions is not relevant. Just remember to check that you have the latest Refresh version of the solicitation document before you make your submission!

  This section also explains where you can obtain federal Specifications, Standards, and Commercial Item Descriptions, as well as Department of Defense Specifications and Standards, if you need to refer to them.

  Because the GSA Schedule contract is non-competitive, the section about post-award debriefing does not apply. This is only available for certain competitive contract awards.

- 52.212-3 **Offeror Representations and Certifications, Commercial Items.** This section is now completed online at the ORCA Website, and was discussed in detail in Chapter 1. Website: *http://orca.bpn.gov*. (19)

- 6FEC-552.216-70 **Economic Price Adjustments.** Price adjustments include both price increases and decreases. This section details exactly how and when you may alter your prices. Briefly:

  - Price decreases may be submitted at any time.
  - If you decrease your commercial prices you *must* also decrease your GSA prices.
  - Each schedule will indicate the maximum percent you may increase your prices each year.
  - To request a price increase you will need to submit your commercial price list, showing the price increase and effective date. If the information in your Commercial Sales Practices form (CSP-1) has changed, that will need to be noted also. You will also need to provide documentation of some kind to support the price increase.
  - The contracting officer may either approve or deny your request, or negotiate more favorable terms with you.

- 552.212-70 **Preparation of Offer.** In this section you can find detailed instructions on how to prepare your offer for submission to GSA. For each Special Item

Number (SIN) you include in your offer you will need to provide two copies of your current commercial catalog or price list. Next to each item you will indicate the SIN under which this item is offered, and clearly exclude or cross out items you are not offering to GSA. You will indicate the discounts you are offering GSA, including prompt payment discounts, quantity or volume discounts, and so on. You must indicate any concessions you will grant to GSA that you do not grant your commercial customers, such as extended warranties or additional services. If dealers are involved in this contract, you must describe the functions they will perform. For clarity, you may wish to prepare a price list specifically for this contract, using your commercial catalog prices. We will give an example of this later.

- I-FSS-125 **Requirements Exceeding the Maximum Order Threshold.** The Maximum Order Threshold is *not* the maximum amount that may be ordered under this contract. It is the price point at which the contracting officer will generally request an additional price discount from you.

Complete Company Information in These Sections

In several sections of the document you must fill in information about your company and about the products or services you intend to offer.

- 552.211-78 **Commercial Delivery Schedule.** In this section the government has inserted its minimum delivery requirements, and you will insert your normal delivery schedule for each SIN you will be offering, as well as any expedited delivery schedules you are willing to offer. In addition, if you can offer overnight or two-day delivery on some items, you are encouraged to detail these here. ARO means "After Receipt of Order."

ITEMS OR GROUP OF ITEMS (Special item No. or nomenclature)	GOVERNMENT STATED DELIVERY TIME (Days ARO)	CONTRACTOR'S NORMAL COMMERCIAL DELIVERY TIME
Attachment 01 - 260-01 - 260-98 & 260-99 - All other SINS -	365 DARO 30-120 DARO 120 DARO	————

- 552.216-73 **Ordering Information.** In this section you choose how you will receive orders—whether via mail, fax, or Electronic Data Interchange (EDI), and you list the appropriate details. If you choose to receive orders via EDI you will include the name, address, and telephone number of the person in your company who can be contracted about setting up the interface.

  Dealers: This section also asks whether you will be marketing through dealers, and if they will be participating in this contract. If this is the case you must supply two copies of a list of your participating dealers.

- 552.232-82 **Contractor's Remittance (Payment) Address.** List the address where the government can mail payments, if Electronic Funds Transfer is not available for any reason. Include the addresses of any authorized participating dealers.

- 52.215-6 **Place of Performance.** In this section you must check whether you intend to use a different plant or facility from the address on page one, for performance of the contract. If you do intend to do so, you must list that facility's name and address here. You may attach a separate sheet if needed.

- C-FSS-411 **Fire/Casualty Hazards or Safety/Health Requirements.** If any of your products involve fire or casualty hazards (for example, electrical items), or if they have safety or health requirements, they must conform to nationally recognized safety standards. If any of these standards are applicable, you must list them here. You should submit proof of conformance—a label, a listing, or acceptance by an approved organization. If no safety standards are applicable, then you must indicate that here.

- F-FSS-202-F **Delivery Prices—Overseas.** If you are offering overseas delivery, your prices must cover delivery either directly to the country involved, or to an overseas assembly point specified by the agency. In this section you must list all the areas or countries where you are able to provide delivery. If you wish, you can simply list "Worldwide" here, or you can list certain specific geographic zones or countries.

  Caution! It is important to note that if you wish to offer overseas delivery you *may* be required to have a person physically in that location to take orders and service the contract. Alternatively you may prefer to ship to a consolidation point within the United States.

- F-FSS-202-G **Delivery Prices—Domestic.** If you are not offering overseas delivery, you will list "United States, Domestic Delivery Only." The prices you offer must include delivery to the 48 contiguous states and the District of Columbia. This regulation concerns the specific details of delivery. You must indicate here whether or not your prices include delivery to Alaska, Hawaii, and Puerto Rico. If you do not wish your prices to include delivery to these specific states, then you will deliver to a specified point, and the government will pay the remaining charges.

- G-FSS-900-C **Contact for Contract Administration.** In this section you should designate someone in the company who will serve as the Contract Administrator. You may list the same person for both domestic and overseas contracts, or you may prefer to list a contact person for each. The contract administrator is responsible for overall compliance with contract terms and conditions, as well as for issues concerning the Industrial Funding Fee and Sales Reporting regulation, and reviews of your company records concerning this contract. If there are any changes to the point of contact information, you must notify the contracting officer.

- I-FSS-103 **Scope of Contract—Worldwide.** In this section you are asked to check whether you are offering delivery to the United States, to overseas destinations, or to both. Domestic delivery includes all 50 states (including Alaska and Hawaii) as well as Puerto Rico and Washington D.C. This section also lists the agencies that may choose to order via this contract. You are *not* obliged to accept these orders, except in the case of orders from the Executive branch of the federal government. If you choose not to accept an order, you must return it within five days, or within 24 hours if the order is placed with a government purchase card.

- I-FSS-594 **Parts and Service.** If you are offering overseas delivery you must be able to also offer parts and services, including warranties, from dealers or distributors in that country. You must supply the names and addresses of all the supply and service points in each country where you will deliver. If you are offering domestic delivery only, then you should insert "Not Applicable" here.

- K-FSS-9 **Section 8(a) Representation.** Indicate here whether or not you are an 8(a) Business Development Program participant. This SBA program helps small disadvantaged businesses to compete in the federal marketplace. Individuals may be designated as either socially or economically disadvantaged: Socially disadvantaged individuals are usually minorities (Black-American, Hispanic-American, Native-American, and Asian-American). Economically disadvantaged individuals have trouble securing financing or credit opportunities for their businesses. In order to be eligible for 8(a) status, at least 51 percent of the company must be directly and unconditionally owned by a socially and economically disadvantaged individual. We discussed this in an earlier chapter.

- K-FSS-1 **Authorized Negotiators.** In this section you must list the names of at least two people in your company who are authorized to negotiate with the government concerning this contract. List their names, titles, telephone numbers, and e-mail addresses. Remember that if someone is not listed as a Point of Contact or Authorized Negotiator, GSA will not be able to speak to him or her about this contract.

The Commercial Sales Practices Form (CSP-1)

This is a critical section of the proposal, which looks in detail at your commercial price structure and discounting practices, and ties these to the prices/discounts you will offer GSA. You will need to provide information for each Special Item Number (SIN) you propose or for each group of SINS.

Current and Projected Sales Data

You must provide the dollar value of sales made to the general public, based on an established market price, during the last 12 months, or last fiscal period. If you feel that this is not an appropriate measure of your sales, you may provide an alternative. Also you must provide your projected annual Schedule sales for each SIN covered. Remember that you will not be awarded a GSA contract if the agency does not expect you to make at least $25,000 in sales in the first two years of the contract, and $25,000 annually in subsequent years.

Discounts and Concessions

At this point you are asked to give details of the various discounts and concessions you offer to your commercial customers. You may offer several different types of discounts to different categories of customers. Are the discounts and concessions you are proposing to offer GSA *at least equal to* those you offer your **Most Favored Customer** (MFC)?

A discount may be a rebate, a quantity discount, a purchase option credit, or any other term that will ultimately reduce the amount of money a customer pays for that item. If a net price is lower than the list price, this is considered to be a discount. A concession can reduce the overall cost of an item, or it can encourage a customer to purchase. Examples include a freight allowance, an extended warranty, extended price guarantees, free installation, or bonus goods.

You must identify and explain any instances in which a commercial customer is offered a better pricing structure than your proposed offer to GSA.

Complete the table that is provided in the CSP, giving details of the various categories of customers, and their discounts or concessions.

Column 1 Most Favored Customer Category	Column 2 Basic Discount Granted to MFC	Column 3 Quantity/ Volume Discounts	Column 4 FOB Terms	Column 5 Concessions

If there are ever any deviations from these policies that result in better discounts or concessions, you must explain them here. For example, perhaps you offered a larger, one-time discount to a customer for a specific reason that no longer applies.

Dealer/Reseller Information

If you are a dealer or a reseller who does not have any significant sales to the general public, then you will be asked to provide information about the manufacturer. This will include the manufacturer's name, address, point of contact, and telephone and fax number. For each manufacturer you must list the manufacturer's part number, your corresponding part number, a product description, the manufacturer's list price, and your percentage discount from list or net prices.

The Most Favored Customer (MFC) and the Basis of Award Customer

When you submit your proposal you will need to establish which customer or group of customers will form the Basis of Award. This could well be fairly straightforward—

if the majority of your sales are to a single category of customers, then the pricing and discounting policies for this class of customers will form the basis for your GSA pricing structure.

Why is this important? As we stated earlier, GSA expects to receive the same pricing and discounting structure that you offer your **Most Favored Customer** (MFC), but this should be for the class of customer that most closely resembles GSA. For example, if you and GSA agree that the Basis of Award is the general category of "commercial end user," or is a specific customer; your GSA pricing structure will be tied to that category. If you reduce your prices to that customer, you will be *required* to give the same reduction to GSA. If you offer this commercial customer an additional discount, an extended warranty, or a faster delivery time, you will be *required* to offer the same to GSA. Discounts offered to customers who do *not* form part of your Basis of Award do *not* affect your GSA contract.

Example: A distributor of a product may get a substantial discount, but in exchange it must keep a certain level of stock, provide warranty service, attend training sessions, or have minimum sales requirements. You should be able to convince the agency that this type of customer is very different from GSA, and not have to use this as your Basis of Award customer.

Example: Your best customer orders a large quantity of an item on a regularly scheduled basis, and everything is delivered to the same address—although you *may* receive orders from GSA for a large number of these items, they could be from many different agencies, at indefinite times, with many different shipping addresses. In this case perhaps you could offer a quantity discount only when the order is from a single agency.

Your Pricing Structure

GSA expects you to provide them with a copy of your **standard commercial price list,** so that they can compare it to your proposed GSA pricing. (It need not be a published price list; it could simply be an internal company document, but you will need to be able to prove that these prices are valid, via invoices, or another form of documentation.)

GSA also expects you to have established **discounting and concessions policies**; again, so that they can make comparisons with the discounts you are proposing to GSA. This may pose a problem, because many small companies do not have a formal discounting policy; rather, they will offer discounts based on current market conditions—whatever they need to offer in order to close the deal!

GSA pricing must be an established fixed unit price. Although you are allowed to make modifications after the award (discussed in the next chapter), the contract places restrictions on when, how often, and how much you can raise your pricing. Model your commercial pricing structure in your GSA price proposal, including unit prices, quantity discounts, and so on. A service company may price using hourly rates, square foot, geographic regions, and service wages—how ever you price your jobs in the commercial field.

Best Scenario: A company with a published commercial price list, stable prices, and strict discounting policies (for example, a simple quantity or volume discount), and that only offers better discounts under very specific conditions.

More of a Problem: A company with fluctuating prices and a loosely regulated discount policy used to "seal the deal."

Remember: You will need to work with the contracting officer in a professional manner. Don't be adversarial in the negotiations—keep the relationship courteous and professional, and be prepared to offer a paper trail in order to document that your pricing and discounts are fair and reasonable.

A Note on MFC Pricing

In June 2009 an advisory panel recommended that GSA vendors should no longer be required to offer federal agencies their lowest prices. Instead they recommended that agencies obtain at least three bids and document the steps that were taken to ensure maximum competition. This would place the competition at the task-order level rather than being written into the GSA contract. Sounds great, doesn't it?! However, a recommendation by a panel is a *long way* from a change in the regulations! So MFC pricing is here to stay—at least for the foreseeable future. **The Advisory Panel's final report was issued in February 2010.**

For more information go to *www.gsa.gov*. (161) Click on Policy and Regulations, then on Acquisitions, and find the Multiple Award Schedules Advisory Panel.

Preparing Your GSA Pricing Document

You may wish to prepare a simple pricing document showing the relationship between your list price, your Most Favored Customer (MFC) prices and discounts, and the prices/discounts you are offering to GSA. In addition, you may wish to add information such as the part number, manufacturer, and production points (country of origin). Preparing this type of document could be especially helpful if you have a large number of products or services to offer. It can also be useful after the contract is awarded, when you need to upload your products/services to GSA *Advantage!*, because the information will be in a compatible format. Take a look at the next chapter to see why formatting a price list at this point could help later, once the contract is awarded.

On the following page I have shown an example of this. Although not a requirement, formatting a price list may clarify things for you and for the contracting officer—especially if you have a large number of products or services to offer.

Use this example as an idea of the information you would wish to include. This clarifies the relationship among your list prices, your MFC prices, and the prices you are offering GSA.

SIN	P/N	Mfg Name	List Price	MFC Discount	MFC Price	GSA Discount	GSA Price	GSA Price incl. IFF
Special Item Number	Manufacturer's Part Number (You may wish to add another column if you use a different p/n from the mfg.)	Manufacturer's Name	Commercial List Price	Most Favored Customer Percentage Discount from List Price	Most Favored Customer Price	GSA Percentage Discount from List Price	GSA Price	GSA Price inclusive of the Industrial Funding Fee (0.75 percent)

In addition you may wish to include the following information. Although you may not need it right now, it will be required after the award, and could be particularly helpful if you are planning to offer a large numbers of products or services.

U/I	Production Point	Product Description	Environmentally Friendly	Delivery	Warranty	NSN
Unit of Issue (Each, Box, Package of 12, etc.)	Country of Origin (Production Point)	Short description of the item	Any environmentally friendly attributes	Delivery period After Receipt of Orders (ARO)	Product warranty—standard commercial, or other	National Stock Number, if available

The Small Business Subcontracting Plan

Because this book is aimed at small businesses, the requirement to create a Small Business Subcontracting Plan does not really apply here. However, a basic overview of the plan will help you understand this obligation, and could help you place your small business in the subcontracting arena.

A Small Business Subcontracting plan is required unless:

- The business is classified as a Small Business.
- Total contract orders are estimated to be less than $500,000 based on the total of both the base and option periods.
- The business believes that no suitable subcontracting opportunities exist. In this case, supporting documentation must be presented to the GSA.
- The contract will be performed entirely outside the United States.

Types of Subcontracting Plans

The **Commercial Subcontracting Plan** covers the company's fiscal year and applies to the entire production of commercial items sold by either the entire company or by a company's division, plant, or product line. This type of plan is preferred by the GSA.

An **Individual Contract Plan** covers the entire contract period but applies only to a specific contract.

A **Master Plan** contains all the required elements of an individual contract plan, except goals. Once approved, this plan may then be incorporated into individual contract plans. A Master plan is effective for three years. GSA will only accept Master Plans that are part of an Individual Plan.

All subcontracting plans must meet the requirements of Federal Acquisition Regulation FAR 19.704, Subcontracting Plan Requirements. Also, each subcontracting plan must include the following information:

- How much the company plans to subcontract out, both in terms of dollar amounts and in percentages. Also the total amount the company plans to subcontract specifically to small businesses.
- The separate dollar and percentage subcontracting goals for various business categories. For example, how much subcontracting business is planned to go to woman-owned or veteran-owned businesses.
- How the company determined these dollar and percentage amounts—the method it used to reach these numbers.
- How the company will identify potential subcontracting sources.
- A description of the types of services and products that will be subcontracted. Again, this should show the breakdown by types of businesses, such as for small, woman-owned, or veteran-owned businesses.

- A statement on whether indirect costs were used to establish these goals, and the methods used.
- Contact information for a company employee who will administer this plan, and his or her duties and responsibilities
- How the business will ensure that various categories of small business have an opportunity to compete for subcontracts.
- An agreement to ensure that all subcontractors comply with FAR subcontracting clauses.
- An agreement to comply with survey and reporting requirements, including submitting Standard Forms SF294 and SF295.
- A description of the types of records that will be maintained to ensure that they comply with these requirements.

The Dun & Bradstreet Open Ratings Report

You must include a copy of the Dun & Bradstreet Open Ratings Report with your GSA submission, so allow plenty of time for it to be processed. The report usually takes about three weeks to complete, but the time period varies depending on how quickly your references respond to the survey.

You are responsible for the cost of generating this report. (As of March 2010 the cost was $185.) The report is valid for six months from the date it is issued.

Website: *www.ppereports.com*. (183)

You will be asked to provide up to 20 customer references. A customer reference is someone who has purchased products or services from your company in the past. If you have fewer than 20 customers, list as many *quality* references as you possibly can. In most cases Open Ratings requires at least four to six customer references. Supply as many good references as you can, so that you get the required number of responses as quickly as possible. Check with your references in advance to make sure they are willing to respond, and explain that they will receive an e-mail notice from Open Ratings asking them to complete an online survey. These days people are often swamped with e-mails, both at home and at work. Asking your references to look out for the survey makes it more likely that it will not be ignored. The report *cannot* be generated until the minimum number of contacts has responded.

You will need to list the first and last name of the person who will give the reference, the name of the company that person works for, a telephone number, and an e-mail address. (Remember to save a copy of the report for yourself before you leave the Website.) Open Ratings will contact your references directly, initially by e-mail. This is similar to when you give references at a job application—remember to include customers who will give you the best reference, and check in advance that this is okay with them before you include them in the report.

How the Report Is Evaluated

The Open Ratings report includes the feedback it has gained from your recent customers, as well as any other company information obtained from the Dun & Bradstreet databases. Key issues will include:

- The timeliness of delivery of your product or services.
- The overall quality of your product or services.
- The support your company offers its customers.

Your references' feedback is kept confidential—you will not be able to view their responses.

Once the order is closed, the Past Performance Evaluation report is generated; one copy is sent to you, and another is sent to GSA. You may request additional copies for another person if you wish when you make your order. The report generates a Performance Rating score for your company, and shows how that score compares to other companies within the same Standard Industrial Classification (SIC) code. Make sure you enter the correct SIC code when you request the report.

The report lists the questions that were asked in the survey, along with a list of the industries of the responding companies—but not the actual names of the companies themselves, in order to protect confidentiality. It also shows a Feedback Rating on a scale of 0 to 10. A score from 9 to 10 is considered positive feedback, 5 to 8 is neutral feedback, and 0 to 4 is considered negative feedback.

Information for Service Companies

The following example is from Schedule 03FAC, which requires a pricing structure showing Hourly Rates and Unit Prices. You are asked to provide a catalog, price list, or other relevant documentation showing your current pricing structure. There are also requirements about obtaining security clearances, permits, and so on. You will also need proof of workers compensation and liability insurance details. Other service schedules might be a little different, but this gives you a fair idea of the sort of thing you will need to do.

Technical Proposal Requirements: Schedule 03FAC—Example

Section	Information Required
Factor #1: Understanding of Requirements	Concise descriptions of the services offered and how they represent the SIN.

Factor #2: **Professional Staff**	A sampling of resumes of professional staff members to be assigned work resulting from this RFP. Resumes must be sufficiently detailed to permit an assessment of the capability of professional staff to do the work described in the RFP for all SINs proposed. Resumes must clearly show your staff members' education credentials, as well as successful experience in the specific area of expertise that will be required in order to work on the Special Item Number(s) (SINs) you are offering.
Factor #3: **Corporate Experience**	Summary descriptions of services proposed for SINs undertaken by the offeror and/or proposed subcontractors, within the last two years, in support of federal, state, or local government agencies. If insufficient experience with government agencies exists, descriptions of services provided in the commercial marketplace should then be included. Descriptions must include the following: A description of the service provided to an agency or firm. Show objectives, methodologies, and results. Indicate the nature of the organization for which services were provided, such as: civilian agency, military, postal services, etc. Identify the agency or firm, including names and telephone numbers of individuals in the agency's or firm's program office, as well as line managers for whom work was performed. This information may be used to verify information provided in the summaries. Project duration, which includes start date and completion date.
Factor #4: **Past Performance**	Complete the Dun & Bradstreet past performance evaluation forms and send them to Open Ratings, Inc. Offerors are reminded that they are responsible for payment of any fees. Include one copy of the completed evaluation forms, with your offer to GSA, clearly showing the date of submission to Open Ratings.

Pricing Proposal Requirements: Schedule 03FAC—Example

The pricing structure you propose to use for GSA must be representative of your current commercial pricing structure. You will need to show the best price at which you sell to your commercial customers or category of customers, and you must be able to substantiate these prices either via an established commercial catalog or by submitting cost or pricing information such as copies of contracts, invoices, or agreements.

222 THE DEFINITIVE GUIDE TO GOVERNMENT CONTRACTS

You should submit as many invoices as you can in order to show both the pricing and discounts that have been offered your Most Favored Customer. Any pricing that is not based on a standard commercial price list must show how you arrived at the final pricing—show hourly rates, cost markups, and why this method was used. **Remember that the contracting officer needs to be able to establish that these prices are fair and reasonable.**

Clearances, Safety, Insurance, Permits, and Licenses

If you will be performing a service you may need to address the following issues in your proposal:

- **Safety Standards:** How you will comply with safety requirements; dealing with potentially hazardous materials.
- **Security Clearances:** You may be required to obtain security clearances.
- **Permits and Licenses:** You are responsible for obtaining all permits and licenses.
- **Insurance:** You will need to show that you have the appropriate insurance documents, including workers' compensation, employers' liability, and so on.
- **Environmental factors:** You may be required to use environmentally friendly products in the performance of the service (such as grounds maintenance; janitorial).

Evaluation

Your proposal will be evaluated to see that you have a good understanding of these requirements:

- Your proposal is in line with the description in the Scope of Work.
- Your employees are capable of providing the services described.
- You have experience with similar work in the past.

Financial Statements

Sometimes the schedule will also require you to include a copy of your recent financial statements, in order to show the company's financial solvency. Check the solicitation document to see if this is a requirement for your particular schedule.

Marketing Plan

Some schedules (such as 51V, the Hardware Superstore, for example) require you to prepare a Marketing Plan that shows that your company is capable of marketing its products or services to government agencies. Because a GSA contract is no guarantee of sales, the agency wants you to show that you have given some thought to how you will market your products and services to various federal agencies after you have the award. It is to no one's benefit if you do not make any sales after you are awarded your GSA contract.

The marketing plan need not be overly long or complex, but should cover such things as:

- Your Target Market: The product or service that you sell will probably be purchased by some federal agencies more than others. Try to determine which agencies are most likely to become your target market.
- Your Marketing Plan: How do you plan to market your product or service to the federal customer?
- Do you know of any specific agencies that would purchase from your Federal Supply Service contract? Have you had any government sales in the past? If so you should include them here. Are there any federal agencies located in your area that could be potential customers?

We will discuss how to market your GSA contract in the next chapter.

Ability One

Website: ***www.abilityone.com***. (184)

This is a mandatory source program (formerly known as JWOD, or the Jarvit's Wagner O'Day program) that requires federal personnel to purchase certain products and services from agencies that employ those who are legally blind or have severe disabilities—that is, from the National Institutes for the Blind (NIB) and the National Institute for the Severely Handicapped (NISH). It is administered by the Committee for Purchase From People Who Are Blind or Severely Disabled, which determines which products and services are suitable for the program, and also establishes fair market pricing.

Essentially the Same

Several GSA schedules (for example 51V, the Hardware Superstore) offer items that are similar to those sold through this program. These schedules require you to determine whether your items are **Essentially the Same** (ETS) as those offered by Ability One, and if so, to develop a blocking system to ensure that agencies purchase these items from Ability One and not from you. The criteria of an Essentially the Same item is generally based on the principle of "form, fit, and function". That is, does the product or service perform the same function as the commercial item?

Your first step will be to go to the Ability One Website and look closely at the products and services that are offered. **Ability One products** include certain types of Chemical Supplies, Cleaning and Janitorial Products, Clocks, Clothing, Computer and Printer Accessories, Disposable Paper Products, Furniture, Hardware, Kitchen and Break Room Supplies, Mattresses and Bedding, Medical and Surgical Supplies, Office Supplies, Outdoor

Supplies, Paint and Paint Accessories, Personal Care and Personal Safety Products, Picture Frames, Shipping and Packaging Supplies, Thermometers, and Writing Instruments.

Ability One Services include certain types of Administrative Services, Call Centers, Facilities Management, Commissary, Promotional Items, Document Conversion, Secure Document Services and Destruction, Embroidery, Fleet Management, Food Services, General Support, Grounds Maintenance, Janitorial/Custodial, Laundry, Mail Centers, Recycling, Switchboard, Transcription, and Supply Chain Management.

If you feel that you supply any of these types of products or services you will need to look closely to determine if your items could be classed as "essentially the same." If so, you will need to go through your catalog and exclude them from your offer.

Remember that, although this program sells quite a wide range of products and services, your items may offer additional features, such as environmentally friendly attributes, a wider range of sizes, customized products, and so on. You would need to contact the Ability One program to get a determination.

~Once Upon a Time~

One of our clients sold handheld ink stamps, which at first glance appeared to be something that was sold through the Ability One program, under Office Supplies. However, a closer look revealed that the stamps from Ability One were pre-printed and did not allow any customization, unlike those offered by our client. We were able to get a determination from Ability One that our products were not essentially the same, and were able to offer them in his GSA proposal.

Again, if some of your items are in fact essentially the same as items sold through Ability One, you will need to remove them from your offer to GSA. In addition, you will need to set up a "blocking system" that identifies federal agencies and those items that cannot be sold to them.

Ability One Blocking System

You will need to describe how you will:
* identify those items that are Ability One equivalents in your catalog
* identify any federal customer, and let him or her know that these items cannot be purchased from your GSA contract
* train your employees in this system
* ensure compliance

Ability One Distributor

Alternatively, you may apply to become an official distributor of Ability One items. Your application will be evaluated on how you intend to maximize the availability, variety, and sales of these products or services. You will be asked to do the following:

- Estimate your sales to federal customers of these products or services.
- Agree not to sell any commercial products to federal customers if there is an equivalent Ability One item available.
- Demonstrate that the blocking system you set up will automatically block federal customers from purchasing the commercial equivalent, and substitute the Ability One item.
- Submit a marketing plan showing how you will promote Ability One items to your federal customers.
- Prepare a quarterly report showing sales of these products or services as well as your total government sales.
- Agree to charge prices that are acceptable to the Ability One committee. On the GSA Schedule, you will be able to list a percentage markup amount for these items.
- Supply an integrated government catalog if possible, but you may also offer your commercial catalog with the essentially-the-same items removed, and an Ability One insert. Your electronic or online catalogs must fully integrate these items and block ETS items.
- Obtain your Ability One products through an approved wholesaler.
- Be evaluated annually for compliance, for the percent of sales, on-time delivery, no substitution of commercial products, payment history, your catalog, input from federal customers, an effective blocking system, and so on.

Pathways to Success

Many GSA Schedules are now requiring you to complete this two-part online training program *before* you submit your proposal. The course gives you an outline about the GSA Schedules program and aims to improve the quality of the offers it receives. The course includes information on the proposal-submission process, the obligations involved in being a Schedule contractor, and ideas to help you become successful in the federal marketplace.

The certificates are valid for one year. The person who completes the course must be listed as an Authorized Negotiator or Point of Contact in your proposal, and must still be employed by the company when the proposal is submitted.

Go to the GSA Vendor Support Center at *http://vsc.gsa.gov*. (185)

The presentation explains how the GSA Schedules program works, what the requirements are, and so on. You may view the presentation as a video, or you may prefer to save a PowerPoint presentation of the slides, together with a transcript of the text. Following the presentation you will be required to complete a set of multiple-choice questions based on the information in the presentation.

Once you have successfully completed the course you will be issued a Certificate of Completion, which you will need to include with your Schedule submission.

The MAS Express Program—A GSA in 30 Days?

Website: *www.gsa.gov/masexpress*. (186)

The Multiple Award Schedule (MAS) Express Program is designed to simplify, streamline, and accelerate the process for companies to obtain GSA contracts. The program aims to have an approval for a completed offer in 30 days—but it is only appropriate for companies that meet very specific criteria.

Currently only certain schedules offer this option, and for only specific Special Item Numbers (SINs) within the schedule. If you have no more than 500 products or labor categories in the following schedules, you *may* be eligible for this program.

Schedule Number	Description
36	Office, Imaging, and Document Solutions
48	Transportation, Delivery, and Relocation Solutions
51 V	Hardware Super Store
58 I	Professional Audio/Video, Telemetry/Tracking, Recording/Reproducing, and Signal Data Solutions
67	Photographic Equipment—Cameras, Photographic Printers, and Related Supplies and Services (Digital and Film-Based)
70	General-Purpose Information Technology Equipment, Software, and Services
73	Food Service, Hospitality, Cleaning Equipment and Supplies, Chemicals, and Services
75	Office Products/Supplies and Services
78	Sports, Promotional, Outdoor, Recreational, Trophies, and Signs (SPORTS)
81 IB	Shipping, Packaging, and Packing Supplies

| 599 | Travel Services Solutions |
| 899 | Environmental Services |

If you wish to consider this option, you will need to look carefully at the criteria—these will be *in addition* to the regular proposal submission requirements.

When you download the regular solicitation package of documents for any of these schedules, it will include a MAS Express document that explains which SINs are eligible for this program, as well as the additional criteria you must meet in order to be considered for this "fast track" to award. Rather than submitting your proposal to the office that handles the regular submissions, you will submit it to the Schedule Program Express Evaluation Desk (SPEED) desk—the address will be in the solicitation package.

The evaluation and approval process is broken down into several phases, so that if any problems are indicated you can be notified of them straight away. The SPEED office will conduct an initial review of your proposal and will let you know quite quickly if you have met the minimum criteria. This does not guarantee you will receive an award—your proposal must still meet all the other requirements—but it will get the ball rolling, and let you know if there are any initial problems.

The Initial Review:

- You will need to submit an original and one copy of your complete offer.
- You will need to submit two copies of the **Express Program Vendor Checklist**. This indicates you have attached all the required documents, identified the SINs you are offering, agreed to the terms and conditions of the solicitation, and met all the criteria for Express evaluation.

Reviewers will confirm that your company is not listed in the **Excluded Parties List System** (EPLS), which is a registry of companies that have been debarred, suspended or declared ineligible to receive Federal contracts.

Core Criteria:

- You have been **in business for at least two years**.
- You have had a **minimum of $100,000 in sales** during the last two years. (You will need to submit documentation to support this—financial statements, invoices, etc.)
- You must have a **minimum current ratio of 1.5 of assets to liabilities**, based on your current year's financial statement. (You will need to submit documentation to support this—financial statements, income and balance sheets, etc.)
- You must have a positive or neutral rating on *all* elements of your **Open Ratings Report**. You will submit two copies of your application *and* two color copies of the final report.

In order to be considered for the MAS Express Program, you must be able to meet all these core criteria. If any of these criteria are not met, your offer will be rejected and returned to you, with an explanation of where the deficiency occurred. This does not preclude you from applying for a GSA contract for this schedule under the regular submission process.

Secondary Criteria:

- Your **Central Contractor Registration** is up to date.
- Your **Online Representations and Certifications Application** is up to date.
- You are only offering items under approved **Special Item Numbers.**
- Your **Pathway to Success** training has been completed.
- **Standard Form 1449** is completed and signed.
- All information in the **solicitation document** is filled in—scope of contract, ordering information, contact for contract administration, payment address, authorized negotiators, place of performance, and so on.
- You have a **current, dated, commercial price list/catalog**, or other information that establishes pricing.
- **Commercial Sales Practices Form** (CSP-1) is completed.
- You have provided at least one year of your most current **financial statements.**
- You offer no more than **500 products** or labor categories.
- You have provided **manufacturers' price lists** and **letters of supply**, if applicable.
- You guarantee **Most Favored Customer** pricing or better.
- You take no exception to any of the solicitation **terms and conditions.**
- You have a **Subcontracting Plan** (large businesses).
- You have completed **Technical and Price Proposals** (service companies).

If you had met the basic, initial requirements but are rejected at secondary criteria, GSA may work with you to address any problems. Your offer will still be subject to the normal negotiation process.

Some of these schedules may have other requirements, so you will need to look carefully at the MAS Express Program document in your particular schedule.

~Once Upon a Time~

A company heard about this program, and felt that he met all the criteria for Express evaluation. However, he had not looked closely at *all* the requirements, and his Express offer was ultimately rejected. Although he was still able to submit an offer via the regular program—and subsequently did receive his GSA contract—the initial false start cost him time and effort. A closer reading of the requirements may have prevented this delay.

Submitting a GSA Proposal Electronically—eOffer

Website: *http://eoffer.gsa.gov*. (187)

GSA's eOffer program allows you to submit your proposal electronically. This applies to both regular and Express offers. It is also designed so that after the award you may make contract modifications electronically, via the eMod program. In February 2009, electronic modifications via the eMod program became mandatory for three schedules (03 FAC, 66, and 874V), and will probably become the way forward for many other schedules in the future.

> **UPDATE**
>
> Several schedules have now made submission via the eOffer program mandatory; for example, **Schedule 56 (Building Materials and Industrial Services/Supplies)** in February 2010, and **Schedule 73 (Food Service, Hospitality, Cleaning Supplies, and Chemicals)** in March 2010). More schedules are sure to follow.

You will download and read all the solicitation documents, work through the responses, and create your attachments as normal. Once you have all the information you need you will log on to the eOffer site to submit your proposal.

Obtaining Digital Certificates

You will need to obtain a digital certificate in order to submit your offer via this program. A digital certificate confirms your identity and allows you to sign the documents electronically. It also allows you to transfer information securely. You are eligible for two free digital certificates per DUNS number from the eOffer program. Two people in your company should have a digital certificate. If you need more than two certificates you will need to purchase them. Digital certificates are issued to individuals (not to companies), and are not transferrable. A digital certificate usually takes one to two weeks to be issued, and they must be updated every two years. The people who get the digital certificates must be listed in the proposal as Authorized Negotiators.

Submitting via eOffer

Once you have the digital certificate, you will be able to log in and complete the submission process, adding attachments as necessary. Once everything is completed, you can submit the proposal documents to GSA.

Completing Negotiations

After your proposal has been reviewed, the contracting officer will contact you in order to begin the normal Final Negotiations process. Once the negotiations are complete the contracting officer will notify you to go into eOffer and retrieve your final contract package.

Signing the Proposal

You will then sign the final contract, using your digital signature, and return it to the contracting officer, who will also sign. You will then be able to download the completed, signed contract for your records.

Checklist

Many schedules include a checklist that clearly shows all the documents you must submit with your offer. Although there are variations from schedule to schedule, certain documents are required in almost all cases.

If the schedule you wish to submit does not include its own checklist, you may wish to create your own as you work through the documents, so that you are sure not to miss anything.

This table shows many of the commonly required documents you should submit with your GSA—but be sure to check your specific schedule for detailed requirements!

CCR	Central Contractors Registration completed.
ORCA	Online Representation and Certifications completed.
SF1449	Standard Form 1449 completed, signed, dated.
Solicitation or Vendor Response Document	All information in solicitation document completed, or Vendor Response Document completed if applicable.
Attachments	Any required attachments completed.
Pricing Information	Commercial price list or documentation included. Most Favored Customer pricing and discounts listed. GSA pricing at least equal to MFC pricing and discounts. Manufacturer's price list included if applicable. Letters of Supply from Manufacturer included, if applicable. Commercial Sales Practices Form (CSP-1) completed.

Product Information	Production Points listed. Use a separate sheet if necessary. List other facilities used in production, if necessary. Any applicable Material Safety Data Sheets, hazardous materials, or safety standards documented. Warranty information included.
Services Information	Technical and Price Proposals included if applicable.
Delivery Information	Delivery days After Receipt of Order (ARO) listed. Expedited delivery listed if applicable. Delivery Areas listed. CONUS? Alaska/Hawaii/Puerto Rico? Overseas?
Receipt of Orders	Details for receipt of orders listed (fax, e-mail, EDI).
Payments	Electronic Funds Transfer information in CCR correct. Alternate Remittance Address listed.
Points of Contact	Authorized Negotiators listed. Points of Contact (POC) listed for Contract Administration, Invoicing and Payments, Orders, and Electronic Business. Alternate POCs for each.
Pathways to Success	Certificate of Completion included.
Open Ratings	Open Ratings Report included.
Subcontracting Plan	Subcontracting plan included, if applicable.
Marketing Plan	Marketing Plan included, if applicable
MAS Express Checklist	Included if applicable.
Financial Information	Included if applicable.

Help!

If you have any questions about this chapter, we would be happy to try to help you. Go to our Website, *www.sell2gov.com*, and at the Contact tab you can send us an e-mail with your questions. Please put "Definitive Guide" in the subject line.

Chapter 10

After the Award

Congratulations! After a lot of hard work you have finally been awarded your GSA Contract!

...So what happens next?

In this chapter we will discuss how you will manage your contract once it has been awarded. This will include:

- Uploading your products and services to GSA's *Advantage!* online shopping site, so that agencies can view your catalog, terms, and conditions.
- Creating your **schedule price catalog,** known as the FSS-600.
- Tracking contract sales, completing the **Quarterly Sales Reports**, and paying the **Industrial Funding Fee**.
- Making **modifications** to your contract—this includes price increases and decreases, adding or deleting product or services, administrative changes, or changes to your terms and conditions.
- Receiving orders from GSA, via **e-Buy** or the **Purchase Order Portal**.
- Sending Invoices via **Wide Area Workflow (WAWF)** or **FedPay**.
- **Contractor Team Arrangements**.
- **Marketing** your contract.

Contracting Officers

You will be given details of your points of contact at GSA. The Procuring Contracting Officer and the Administrative Contracting Officer will ensure that you are in compliance with the terms of the contract. They will be the people to contact for any day-to-day administrative matters, including contract modifications.

Uploading Your Contract to GSA *Advantage!*

This is one of the first places to begin once you are awarded your contract. Getting the details of your products/services onto this Website will allow agencies to see what you have to offer.

You will have a specific amount of time to get this task done (check the details of your Schedule solicitation), often about six months. Depending on the number of products/ services you offer, this task could be quite time-consuming, so start as soon as possible after you have the award.

The Vendor Support Center

Website: *http://vsc.gsa.gov*. (185)

Register Your Contract

At the Vendor Support Center site you will first need to register as a new vendor and receive a password. At the Getting on *Advantage!* tab along the top of the screen click on Getting Started—Register Your Contract. Have your contract number and your Dun & Bradstreet (DUNS) number available.

You may use Electronic Data Interchange (EDI) to upload your information, if you use this system, or you may use a program known as the Schedule Input Program (SIP). At the registration page choose MAS Contract and enter your contract number.

You will give the name and e-mail address of the person who will upload the catalog. This person must be listed as an Authorized Negotiator or Point of Contact in your proposal. The Vendor Support Center will send an e-mail to that person, with a password which will be used later to upload your catalog. Keep the password safe!

Download the Schedules Input Program (SIP)

If you are planning to use the SIP program, you will first need to download it to your computer. At the Getting on *Advantage!* tab along the top of the screen click on Getting Started—SIP-Download Software. This section also has an SIP Training option to help you with this process. The program will download several folders into your computer's C drive.

Preparing the Files

There are several ways to use the SIP program to upload your files:

- If you do not have a large number of line items, you can choose to go into the program and manually input the information.
- If you have a larger number of products or services, you may prefer to prepare several Microsoft Excel spreadsheets to import into the SIP program.
- If you are a service company you may prefer to create a text file describing your services and upload that as an alternative.

Entering Your Contract Information in SIP

Go to the SIP program now installed on your computer (in your C drive), and you will see this home page:

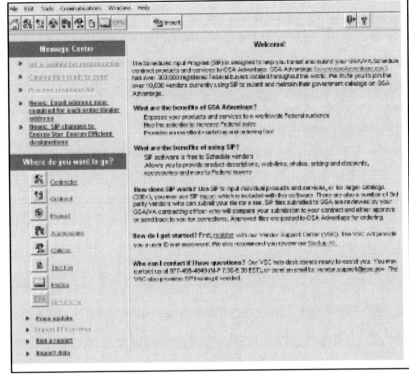

Under the **Where Do You Want to Go?** heading, you will need to complete the information in each screen, as we explain in the following paragraphs.

At the **Contractor** screen you will need to add your company name, address, and Website, as well as an e-mail address and telephone/fax number for the person who will receive the orders. You will also need to add the password you received from the Vendor Support Center when you registered. When you have filled in the information, click the Save button before you close the screen.

At the **Primary Contract Information** screen, you will need to click on the Add button that appears above and outside of the window in order to complete it.

Scroll down below the question about minimum orders to complete more information before you can click Save, and then close this screen.

Important! Remember that all the information you enter into this SIP program *must* be the same as the terms of the contract. For example, if you agreed to a 30-day delivery time in the contract, the same information must be entered here.

Once you save and close this screen, a window will pop up that asks for your maximum order amount for each Special Item Numbers (SIN) that is in your contract. Use the drop-down arrows on the screen to indicate a SIN and its corresponding Maximum Order amount. If you have additional SINs click the Add Next button until you have entered all the applicable SINs. Then Save and Close the window.

You will be asked to indicate whether you have any dealers or other sales offices that will be receiving orders; whether pricing is structured by geographical zones; if products have color or fabric options; and whether there are any special charges applicable. If you answer yes to any of these questions, the SIP program will take you to the appropriate screens.

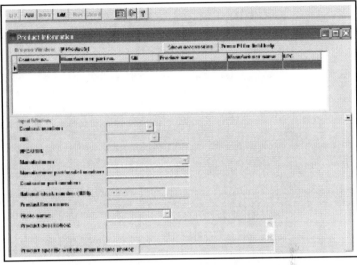

At the **Product Information** screen you may add your products line by line. Click on the Add option above the window, and complete all the information, exactly as it appears in your contract.

In the Product Description field, add as much as you can to best describe the product and its features.

You are encouraged to add product **photographs** at this point. All photographs should be in .jpg format and no larger than 70k. The photograph file names should contain no special characters, but you should be able to easily cross-reference them to the item (for example, use the part number, with no dashes or asterisks). Put these photographs in the Photos folder located in the SIP program download files (on the C drive of your computer). Use the drop-down arrow at the Photo Name bar on this window, view all the photographs that are stored there, and identify the appropriate one.

You may also include a link directly to the product information if you wish. This should not simply link to your main company Website, but directly to this particular product.

You will not need to complete information in the Product Dimensions section (length and weight) unless your shipping terms were FOB Origin.

Complete the Unit of Issue, Delivery, Warranty, and Production Point sections, then click Save. At this point a window will pop up where you can enter **Price Information**. Click the Edit option, then enter your Commercial List Price (catalog price) and the price you are offering GSA. Then click Save.

Now the **Qty/Vol Discount** button will be enabled. If you are offering any discounts, click on this button to list any quantity or volume price breaks you are offering GSA. Again, click Save, then Close.

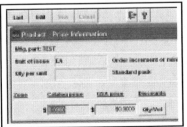
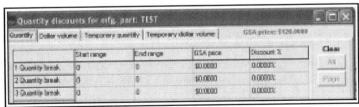

Now an **Environmental Features** window pops up. Click on any that apply and close the window. (We discussed the federal government's emphasis on environmentally friendly purchasing in a previous chapter.)

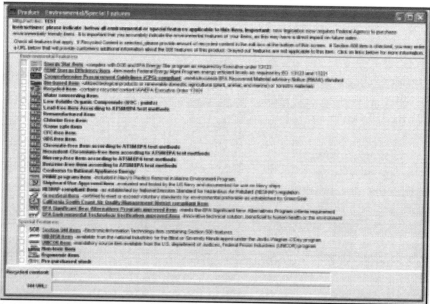

Click the Add button to add another product.

~

As you can see, this is quite a tedious process that is really only appropriate if you have few line items. Later in this chapter we will discuss the option of uploading all this information via a series of Excel spreadsheets.

Some Schedules and Special Item Numbers are not really suitable to the type of manual input we just described, particularly if you are offering a service. In this case you may decide to create a suitable **text file** that can be viewed online. Agencies cannot make direct purchases from this option, but they may view the files and contact you for a quote.

Preparing Spreadsheets for Import into SIP

This option works well if you have more than a few line items to enter.

When you first downloaded SIP, the program placed various folders into the C drive of your computer. In the Import folder you will find the templates for the various spreadsheets you will need to create. At a minimum, you must create:

- ICONTR.xls—information about your GSA contract.
- ICORPET.xls—information about the company.
- IPROD.xls—product descriptions (for product companies only).
- IPRICE.xls—your commercial list prices and your GSA prices.

- IMOLS.xls—Maximum Order Thresholds for each SIN awarded.
- IREMITOR.xls—payment information.

There are several additional spreadsheets you may also need to complete, depending on the terms of your contract:

- IZONE.xls—if your contract listed different prices across geographic shipping zones.
- IACCXPRO.xls—for any accessories to your products that you are offering.
- ICOLORS.xls—if your products have different color options.
- IFABRICS.xls—if your products come in a variety of fabric choices.
- IBPA.xls—if your products are being offered under a Blanket Purchase Agreement (see note below).
- IQTY/VOL.xls—if you are offering quantity or volume price breaks.
- IMSG.xls—for any environmentally friendly attributes to products.
- IOPTIONS.xls—for any options you are offering.

Note: A Blanket Purchase Agreement (BPA) is used to supply products that need to be purchased frequently, such as office supplies. A BPA allows the agency to restock the items as needed, without having to place a new Request for Quote each time. The agency issues a BPA for a specific period of time, and the items may be purchased without the need for additional competition.

Once you have created all the spreadsheets, copy them to the Import folder in the SIP program. Make sure you have all the photographs in the Photos folder.

Creating Your Terms and Conditions Document

In addition to the spreadsheets, you will also need to create and upload a Terms and Conditions document, using a specific format.

In your Schedule solicitation document you will find a section known as the FSS 600, which describes the format you must use. Each company's Terms and Conditions document follows the same format, so that contracting officers can more easily make comparisons between companies' offerings. For example, the delivery terms for each company will always be in the same place.

Your **Schedule Catalog Price List** will use this same document as a cover sheet, with the addition of your GSA prices. Because your products, services, and prices will already be listed in GSA *Advantage!,* the Terms and Conditions document does not need to include prices.

On the following pages we have an example of the information needed on the cover sheet of the document, followed by two examples of the required information that follows afterward—one as simple text, the second in a table format. As long as the information is listed in the correct order, it can take any format you wish. You can "make it pretty" by using different fonts, adding your company logo, and so on, as long as the essential information appears in the stated order.

Your *Company Logo (optional)*

General Services Administration
Federal Supply Service
Authorized Federal Supply
Schedule Price list

Online access to contract ordering information, terms and conditions, and up-to-date pricing are available through GSA *Advantage!* a menu-driven database system. The INTERNET address for GSA *Advantage!* is *www.gsaadvantage.gov*.

Schedule Title Here
Schedule Description
Federal Supply Code (FSC) Group and FSC Class
GSA Contract # GS-00X-0000X

For more information on ordering from Federal Supply Schedules click on the FSS Schedules button at *www.fss.gsa.gov*.

Contract Period: List the start date of the contract through to five years from that date.

Company Name
Street Address
State and Zip Code

Tel: (000) 000-0000
Fax: (000) 000-0000

Website address: *www.yourWebsite.com*
Business Size: Small Business

---

1. **Table of Awarded Special Item Number (SINS):** List all SINs in your contract.
2. **SIN Maximum Order**: This is listed in the solicitation document.
3. **Minimum Order:** As stated in your contract.
4. **Geographic Coverage (Delivery Area):** As stated in your contract.
5. **Points of Production:** If necessary, put "see page **" here, and append a list.
6. **Discount From List Prices or Statement of Net Prices:** As stated in your contract.
7. **Quantity Discounts:** If Applicable. Otherwise put "N/A" here.
8. **Prompt Payment Terms:** As stated in your contract.
9a. **Notification That Government Purchase Cards Are Accepted Below the Micro-Purchase Threshold:** Government purchase cards *must* be accepted below the Micro-Purchase threshold (currently $3,000). Indicate your acceptance here.
9b. **Notification Whether Government Purchase Cards Are Accepted or Not Accepted Above the Micro-Purchase Threshold**: Will you accept payment via Government Purchase Cards of orders *above* the micro-purchase threshold?
10. **Foreign Items:** If Applicable. Otherwise put "N/A" here. Append a list if necessary.
11a. **Time of Delivery:** As stated in your contract.
11b. **Expedited Delivery:** If Applicable. Otherwise put "N/A" here.
11c. **Overnight And 2-Day Delivery:** If Applicable. Otherwise put "N/A" here.
11d. **Urgent Requirements:** If Applicable. Otherwise put "N/A" here.
12. **F.O.B Point:** As stated in your contract.
13. **Ordering Address:** Address for receipt of orders. As stated in your contract.
14. **Payment Address:** Address for payments. As stated in your contract.
15. **Warranty Provision:** As stated in your contract.
16. **Export Packaging Charges:** If Applicable. Otherwise put "N/A" here.
17. **Terms and Conditions of Government Purchase Card Acceptance:** List any conditions you have placed on the use of purchase cards.
18. **Terms and Conditions of Rental Maintenance, and Repair:** If Applicable, or N/A.
19. **Terms and Conditions of Installation:** If Applicable, or N/A.
20. **Terms and Conditions of Repair Parts:** If Applicable, or N/A.
20a. **Terms and Conditions for Any Other Services:** If Applicable, or N/A.
21. **List of Service and Distribution Points:** If Applicable, or N/A.
22. **List of Participating Dealers:** If Applicable, or N/A.
23. **Preventive Maintenance:** If Applicable, or N/A.
24. **Year 2000 (Y2K) Compliant:** If Applicable, or N/A.
25. **Environment Attributes:** If Applicable, or N/A.
26. **Data Universal Number System (DUNS) Number:** Your DUNS Number here.
27. **Notification Regarding Registration in Central Contractor Registration (CCR) Database:** Indicate that you are registered at CCR. Add your CAGE code if you wish.

Alternate Layout Example:

CUSTOMER INFORMATION	
1a.	Special Item Numbers Awarded
1b.	For Awarded Pricing see *GSA Advantage!*
2.	Maximum Order Limitation:
3.	Minimum Order:
4.	Geographic Coverage (delivery area):
5.	Point(s) of Production:
6.	Discount from List Prices or Statement of Net Price:
7.	Quantity Discounts:
8.	Prompt Payment Terms:
9a.	Government Commercial Credit Card:
9b	Are Gov't purchase cards accepted above the micro-purchase threshold?
10.	Foreign Items (list items by country of origin):
11a.	Time of Delivery:
11b.	Expedited Delivery:
11c.	Overnight and 2-day Delivery:
11d.	Urgent Requirements:
12.	F.O.B. Point(s):
13a.	Ordering Address:
13b.	Ordering Procedures:
14.	Payment Address:
15.	Warranty Provision:
16.	Export Packing Charges:
17.	Terms and Conditions of Government Commercial Credit Card Acceptance:
18.	Terms and Conditions of Rental, Maintenance and Repair:
19.	Terms and Conditions of Installation:
20.	Terms and Conditions of Repair Parts:
20a.	Terms and Conditions for Any Other Services:
21	List of Service and Distribution Points:
22	List of Participating Dealers:
23.	Preventive Maintenance:
24a.	Special Attributes:

24b.	Section 508 Compliance:
25.	Data Universal Number System (DUNS) Number:
26.	Central Contractor Registration (CCR) database:
27.	Uncompensated Overtime Policy:

~

Now that you have:

- created the spreadsheets or the text files and copied them to the SIP Import folder,
- added product photographs to the appropriate folder
- created your Terms and Conditions document and copied that to the appropriate folder

you are ready to upload the information to *Advantage!* via the SIP program.

At the SIP Home Page, under Where Do You Want to Go, click on Import Data at the bottom of the list, and follow the instructions to import the spreadsheets, text files, and photograph into the program. If there are any errors in your documents, the Import program will alert you to that, and you will have to go over them until they are correct.

Once you have successfully imported your documents, go back to the Home Page, and at the top click Communications—Create Catalog Files, and then Communications—Send Catalog Files to GSA.

The files will be sent to the contracting officer, who will review them for accuracy, and then send a Response File back. Check for the Response Files notice to appear on the Home Page, and then click Process Response Files. Once the files have been accepted, you should then be able to view your products and services on GSA *Advantage!*

Quarterly Sales Reporting (72a)

Website: *http://vsc.gsa.gov*. (185)

As we discussed earlier in the book, you must keep track of all sales made via this GSA contract. Remember! This does not just mean keeping federal government sales separate from commercial sales; you must keep track of sales separately by Special Item Number (SIN). You must also be able to keep the sales made via your GSA contract separate from any federal sales that are made outside of the contract.

Each quarter you will need to report these sales using the **72A Quarterly Reporting System**. You can find a link to the system at the Vendor Support Center (VSC) Website. Go to the Vendor Support Center site, and click on the Reporting Sales tab.

All sales, including dealer sales, for each SIN must be reported in U.S. dollars rounded to the nearest whole dollar. The reported contract sales value must include the Industrial Funding Fee (IFF).

If you have a number of dealers participating in this contract you can allow them to bill agencies and accept payment in your name, as long as you have a written agreement. The dealer(s) must agree to abide by the same terms and conditions, keep track of sales in the same way, and agree to allow an audit to confirm compliance if necessary.

Even if you had no sales under the contract for any particular quarter you must still submit the report.

Using the information from these quarterly reports, GSA will calculate the amount of Industrial Funding fee you must pay.

Paying the Industrial Funding Fee (IFF)

When you submitted pricing information with your contract, you added the Industrial Funding Fee (currently 0.75 percent) to your prices. The IFF reimburses the General Services Administration for the cost of operating the Schedules Program.

Note: the Medical Equipment Supplies and Services schedules administered by the Veterans Administration (Schedules 65, 66, and 621) currently have an equivalent Cost Recovery Fee of 0.50 percent.

There is a link from the 72A Quarterly Reporting System home page to the Online IFF Payment Website.

Modifications—Making Changes to your Contract

A Schedule contract is a long-term contract between your company and the federal government, which can be valid for up to 20 years. Of course it is inevitable that at some point you will need to make changes for reasons such as:

- Modifications may be purely administrative in nature, such as changing the point of contact name, telephone, or fax number.
- You may want to add or delete products or services from your price list.
- You may want to increase or decrease your pricing.
- You may want to alter the terms and conditions of the contract; for example, delivery times, warranties, and so on.

The Modifications clause (GSAR 552.243-72) describes the procedures for requesting contract modifications. You will submit a request to the contracting officer describing the changes you wish to make, along with a rationale for the changes. Once the modification has been approved, you will need to make appropriate changes at the *Advantage!* Website. You must also update your Schedule Price List, and send a copy of the modified document both to the contracting officer and to the Schedule Information Center in Kansas City, Missouri.

Administrative Modifications

Any administrative changes, such as changes in your company's Contract Administrator, should be made in writing to the Contracting Officer.

Increasing and Decreasing Prices: Economic Price Adjustments

The Economic Price Adjustment clause describes how your commercial prices are linked to the prices you offer GSA.

Price Decreases: GSA negotiated pricing with you based on your Most Favored Customer commercial pricing. You agreed that a certain subset of your commercial customers would constitute the Basis for Award. If your Basis of Award customer prices decrease, then your GSA prices *must also decrease* accordingly.

Price Increases: You cannot increase your prices for a period of time that is specified in the schedule documents—usually this will be for the first 12 months of the contract. After that time you may request up to three price increases in any 12-month period. There must be at least 30 days between price increases, and there will be a total ceiling percentage increase allowed. Read the appropriate section of the solicitation document to find details of your contract modification requirements. In some cases escalation rates will be negotiated before the contract is awarded; usually a series of fixed prices for the term of the contract. At other times a market indicator may be identified in the contract.

You must submit a request for price increases in writing to the contracting officer. Include a copy of your commercial price list that shows the increase.

If these proposed increases will alter any information in your Commercial Sales Practices form (CSP-1), then you will need to submit this information also. If no changes to the CSP-1 will occur, submit a statement to that effect.

After evaluating your request the contracting officer may agree that the increases are fair and reasonable; or negotiate with you for more favorable terms/prices; or decline your request. If the request is declined you may remove the products or services from your contract, in writing. The Cancellation clause (GSAR 552.238-73) allows either party to cancel the contract in whole or in part by providing written notice. The cancellation will take effect 30 calendar days after the other party receives the notice of cancellation.

Change of Company Name and Novations Agreement

If your company changes its name you will need to contact your Schedule Contracting Officer, who will guide you through the process of a Name Change Agreement. If your company is being acquired by another company, you will need to complete a Novations Agreement so that this company can be recognized as the contract holder.

eModifications

In the previous chapter we discussed the eOffer program that allows you to submit your proposal electronically. Modifications may also be submitted electronically via the eMod program.

Website: *http://eoffer.gsa.gov*. (187)

The new Central Intake Desks process all paper and e-mail modification requests. GSA is encouraging you to use the eMod program for modification requests, but you may still submit requests via e-mail or on paper if you prefer. At the Vendor Support Center home page—Central Intake Desk, you can find the address to submit your paper modification requests.

Website: *https://vsc.gsa.gov*. (185)

~Once Upon a Time~

A small company worked hard to submit its proposal, and was successfully awarded a GSA contract. Then the employee who was responsible for submitting the proposal left the company, and no one knew where any of the information was located! The complete product line with pricing and photographs had been uploaded to GSA *Advantage!*—but when they needed to make modifications they had none of the information on file…everything had to be re-created from scratch.

Keep this information safe! Remember this is a long-term contract and you will need to keep the contract current.

Receiving Orders—eBuy and the Purchase Order Portal

Website: *www.ebuy.gsa.gov*. (188)

Contracting officers may browse GSA *Advantage!* for items they wish to purchase, and then send a Request for Quote notice to vendors, via a system called **eBuy**. You will use the **Purchase Order Portal (POP)** to view, print, and download your purchase orders. You can also use the POP system to send status reports for each order. You can elect to receive an e-mail notice for each individual order, or choose a daily summary of your orders if you prefer.

You will receive an e-mail from GSA which will contain the link to the registration page, allowing you to log in to the site. Log in using your contract number, and the password you got earlier from the Vendor Support Center (the password you used to upload information to *Advantage!* via the SIP program).

At your eBuy home page you can view any messages requesting quotes. You will be able to see any Requests for Quotes for items that are covered under your schedule. You can choose a No Quote button that allows you to indicate the reason for not quoting (if you feel you do not have enough time to prepare a quote, or if you do not carry these particular items, for example). Sending a No Quote response indicates to the buyer that you are still active in the marketplace.

If you choose to do so, you will be able to submit a quote electronically via this site. The system will take you step by step through the quoting process. You can view and track the status of any submitted quotes.

Sending Invoices—FedPay®

Website: *http://fedpay.gsa.gov*. (189)

In an earlier chapter we discussed the Wide Area Workflow (WAWF) system that is used by some agencies (particularly the Department of Defense) for sending invoices to agencies. In addition, GSA has a new system called FedPay that can help you get paid in as little as 10 days! You may also use this system to track the status of purchase orders, invoices, and payments.

There are certain minimum technical requirements for your computer, and a free software program you will need to download before you can register. Using the system you will be able to submit your invoices and view your purchase orders and payments information. You will be paid by Electronic Funds Transfer (EFT) using the bank account details that you provided when you registered at the Central Contractors Registration (CCR) site.

Contractor Team Arrangements

A Contractor Team Arrangement (CTA) is an agreement between two or more GSA contract holders to work together and compete for orders as a team, when each member may not be able to qualify independently. This type of arrangement can greatly increase the potential of your contract. Each member of the team *must* be a GSA Schedule contractor.

This is *not* the same as a Prime/Subcontractor arrangement. Under a CTA each team member holds a GSA contract, unlike in a Prime/Subcontractor arrangement in which only the Prime contractor need hold a GSA contract. A Prime contractor cannot delegate responsibility for performance to a subcontractor, but in a CTA any team member may be the team leader.

The agency does not define the terms of the arrangement—this is strictly between two contract holders. This type of arrangement will need to be carefully drawn up: team leaders will need to be designated, roles and responsibilities carefully defined, and the scope and time period of the agreement must be clear. Pricing, proprietary rights, warranties, confidentiality agreements, invoicing issues, and so on will all need to be looked at carefully before an arrangement can be drawn up.

If you are proposing to submit a Request for Quote using a Contractor Team Arrangement, you should specify each of the team members and their respective contract numbers, describe clearly the tasks that each team member will perform and the associated schedule pricing, and identify team leaders. Prices must be the same or less than the prices in your respective GSA contracts. The products or services you are proposing must be part of your schedule contract. Use the information in the Schedules e-Library to find potential Schedule CTA participants.

If the agency requires it, the designated team leader may submit a single invoice for all team members, provided that the invoice includes a breakdown identifying each team member, their contract numbers, details of the products or services that were provided by each of the team members, and the pricing of each. Although you may submit a single invoice on behalf of all team members, each team member must be paid separately. The team leader cannot accept payment on behalf of the entire team. Each team member is also responsible for reporting its GSA Schedule contract sales and remitting the appropriate Industrial Funding Fee (IFF).

You may use subcontractors if your Schedule contract allows this. Subcontractors would not be considered members of the CTA, and performance responsibility would rest with the team members.

Performance Reports

Your first Report Card on compliance and performance will often take place after the first two years, when GSA can exercise its option to renew your contract (known as the Evergreen Clause). GSA will evaluate your performance and make sure that you are complying with the terms of the contract. It will also evaluate your sales tracking system to make sure that you are making accurate sales reports and Industrial Funding Fee payments. The agency will need access to your records, including your schedule price list, terms and conditions, sales records, Request for Quotes or orders you have received, invoices, and so on. You should also have copies of any contract modifications, updated price lists, warranty details, and details on any Contractor Team arrangements or Blanket Purchase Agreements, as well as an up-to-date list of any participating dealers.

Your good performance report becomes an important evaluation factor when an agency is trying to determine overall best value for a purchase. Agencies will take several factors into account—delivery times, warranties, environmental or energy-efficiency issues, technical qualifications, quantity or volume discounts, and set-aside goals. They will *also* look closely at how well you performed on any previous contracts. Agencies will use past performance as a major factor in selecting the contractor that offers the best value.

Website: *www.ppirs.gov*. (39)

A ruling in July 2009 made it mandatory for contracting officers to document the past performance of Schedule Contract holders via the Past Performance Information Retrieval System (PPIRS), a shared government-wide repository of data on contractors' work. Although the requirement to use the system has been around for a while, this ruling reinforces the importance of this system.

Veterans Reporting—VETS 100

Website: *https://vets100.vets.dol.gov*. (190)

Federal Acquisition Regulation (FAR) 52.222-35 concerns equal opportunities for veterans. FAR 52.222-37 requires a contractor to submit an annual VETS-100 report for all federal contracts above $25,000. In addition to information about your company, the one-page form requires you to report on all permanent employees (both full- and part-time), including the number of disabled veterans and Vietnam-era veterans in your company, and their job categories.

Evergreen Option

Each schedule contract is awarded for an initial two-year period, followed by an additional three years. After that time the agency may extend the contract for three successive five-year periods, for a total of 20 years in all. The option clause is found in every schedule solicitation document, and is known as the Evergreen Option. GSA will only exercise this option if it is in the agency's best interest to do so. How well you perform on the contract is one of the major factors they will consider during the evaluation.

Disagreements and Disputes

Most disagreements or disputes concern performance issues relating to the contract. If there are any disputes between you and the agency that places the order, notify the contracting officer of the problem. You and the agency will be encouraged to resolve the dispute, but if you cannot reach an agreement, the contracting officer may suggest using Alternative Dispute Resolution (ADR) procedures—basically any measures possible short of formal litigation, including assisted negotiations, mediation, fact-finding, and arbitration. The contracting officer has the authority to issue a final decision.

Marketing Your Contract

As we discussed earlier, a GSA contract is no guarantee of sales, and it is now up to you to market your company's GSA products and services to federal agencies.

Schedule Price List

You already know that you must produce your paper price list (I-FSS-600) in a specific format, and that you must distribute that list as the contracting officer requires, usually within 30 days of the contract award.

GSA *Advantage!*

You also know that you must upload your product or service information to the GSA *Advantage!* Website, usually within six months of your contract award. Of course the sooner the information is on this site the better!

GSA Logos

Now that you are a GSA contract holder, you may use one of the official GSA Starmark logos on all your company brochures, business cards, catalogs, and in any presentations, as well as on

your Website. These logos include the GSA Star Mark along with an identifier—Schedule, Contract Holder, or *Advantage!*. You may use any of these logos, but they must include both the GSA Star Mark and the identifier—you cannot use the Star Mark alone.

To download the logos, and for more information, go to *www.gsa.gov/logos*. (191)

GSA Directories

Another great source of contact information can be found at the GSA Offices of Small Business Utilization.

Website: *www.gsa.gov/sbu*. (192)

On the left side of the home page, click on GSA Publications. There are nine Regional Procurement Directories available here, with a great deal of useful contact information. For example, in the New England Directory there are lists of all the Regional Small Business Offices, Technical Assistance Offices, local Procurement Technical Assistance Centers (PTACS), Government Procurement Offices, Chambers of Commerce, Regional Federal buildings, and much more.

These directories can be a great marketing source even if you do not yet have a GSA contract award!

Conferences, Expos, and Trade Shows

Many conferences, trade shows, Industry Days, and expositions take place every year around the country, and these can be a great way to market your products and services to federal agencies. You can find them at the following Websites:

FedBizOpps:	*www.fbo.gov* (20)
GSA Events Calendar:	*www.gsa.gov/events* (193)
Excellence in Government:	*www.excelgov.com* (194)
GSA Expo:	*www.expo.gsa.gov* (195)
FOSE:	*http://fose.com/events/fose-2010/home.aspx* (196)
GovSec:	*www.govsecinfo.com* (197)
MWR Expo:	*www.ala-national.org/shows* (198)

Publications

Keep up with trends in the federal marketplace via these magazines and newsletters, at the following Websites.

Government Executive Magazine:	*www.govexec.com* (199)
Federal Computer Week:	*www.fcw.com* (200)
GSA MarkeTips:	*www.gsa.gov/marketips* (201)
Armed Forces Journal:	*www.armedforcesjournal.com* (202)
Federal Times Magazine:	*www.federaltimes.com* (203)
Military News Network:	*www.militarynewsnetwork.com* (204)
Army Times:	*www.armytimes.com* (205)
Air Force Times:	*www.airforcetimes.com* (206)
Navy Times:	*www.navytimes.com* (207)
GSA Steps Newsletter:	*http://vsc.gsa.gov* (185)

Additional Market Resources

Federal Procurement Data:	*www.fpds.gov* (181)
Federal Acquisition JumpStation:	*http://nais.nasa.gov/fedproc/home.html* (130)
Federal Govt. Agencies Directory:	*www.lib.lsu.edu/gov/fedgov.html* (131)
Military Installations:	*www.armedforces.net* (208)
Federal Yellow Book Mailing List:	*www.leadershipdirectories.com* (209)
Office of Small Business Utilization:	*www.gsa.gov/sbu* (192)
FirstGov:	*www.firstgov.gov* (210)
Federal Gateway:	*www.fedgate.org* (211)
FedWorld:	*www.fedworld.gov* (212)
GSA Steps to Success Brochure:	*http://vsc.gsa.gov* (185) (Click on Publications.)
Where in Federal Contracting:	*www.wifcon.com* (131)

Training

Center for Acquisition Excellence: *www.gsa.gov/cae* (213)
Federal Acquisition Institute: *www.fai.gov* (214)
Defense Acquisition University: *www.dau.mil* (215)

In Conclusion

We hope that this book will become your "go-to guide." Let the pages become dog-eared, as the book sits on your desk and is referred to every day!

Understand the enormous potential that is available to your small business in federal government sales. With many years of experience in this field, we feel confident that our step-by-step approach will work for you.

Although the task might seem daunting to begin with, it is definitely worth every minute of the time that you invest. Don't feel that you have to do this alone; you will have a great deal of help along the way—Contracting Officers are always willing and able to help you with any questions you might have about a specific solicitation, and your local Procurement Technical Assistance Center will work with you to gain confidence in the market.

Help!

If you have any questions about this chapter, we would be happy to try to help you. Go to our Website, *www.sell2gov.com*, and at the Contact tab you can send us an e-mail with your questions. Please put "Definitive Guide" in the subject line.

Appendix

In this appendix you will find the following:

Product Service Codes (PSC)

Product Service Codes (PSC) are used to classify services, using letters from A to Z. (For clarity, they do not use the letters O or I.) The codes are then subdivided. For example, Service Code "S" is used for Utilities and Housekeeping Services. This code is then further subdivided this way:

S201   Custodial-Janitorial

S208   Landscaping Services

S209   Laundry and Dry Cleaning Services

Here is the list of the broad PSC categories. For more detailed listings go to one of these sites:

- *www.fpds-ng.com/downloads/psc_data_10242006.xls* (17)
- *www.outreachsystems.com/resources/tables/pscs* (216)

PSC	Description
A	Research and Development
B	Special Studies and Analyses—Not R&D
C	Architect and Engineering Services—Construction

D	Automatic Data Processing and Telecommunication Services
E	Purchase of Structures and Facilities
F	Natural Resources and Conservation Services
G	Social Services
H	Quality Control, Testing, and Inspection Services
J	Maintenance, Repair, and Rebuilding of Equipment
K	Modification of Equipment
L	Technical Representative Services
M	Operation of Government-Owned Facilities
N	Installation of Equipment
P	Salvage Services
Q	Medical Services
R	Professional, Administrative, and Management Support Services
S	Utilities and Housekeeping Services
T	Photographic, Mapping, Printing, and Publication Services
U	Education and Training Services
V	Transportation, Travel, and Relocation Services
W	Lease or Rental of Equipment
X	Lease or Rental of Facilities
Y	Construction of Structures and Facilities
Z	Maintenance, Repair, or Alteration of Real Property

Federal Supply Classification (FSC) Codes

Federal Supply Classification Codes (FSC) are used to classify products, using numbers from 10 through 99. (Not all the numbers are currently in use.) These numbers are further subdivided; for example, Product Code 84 is used for Clothing. Again this is subdivided this way:

8430   Men's Footwear

8450   Children's Clothing

8475   Specialized Flight Clothing

Here is the list of the broad FSC categories. For more detailed codes, download the H2 Manual at *www.fs.fed.us/fire/partners/fepp/h2book.pdf*. (15)

10	Weapons
11	Nuclear Ordnance
12	Fire Control Equipment

13	Ammunition and Explosives
14	Guided Missiles
15	Aircraft and Airframe Structural Components
16	Aircraft Components and Accessories
17	Aircraft Launching, Landing, and Ground Handling Equipment
18	Space Vehicles
19	Ships, Small Craft, Pontoons, and Floating Docks
20	Ship and Marine Equipment
22	Railway Equipment
23	Ground Effect Vehicles, Motor Vehicles, Trailers, and Cycles
24	Tractors
25	Vehicular Equipment Components
26	Tires and Tubes
28	Engines, Turbines, and Components
29	Engine Accessories
30	Mechanical Power Transmission Equipment
31	Bearings
32	Woodworking Machinery and Equipment
34	Metalworking Machinery
35	Service and Trade Equipment
36	Special Industry Machinery
37	Agricultural Machinery and Equipment
38	Construction, Mining, Excavating, and Highway Maintenance Equipment
39	Materials Handling Equipment
40	Rope, Cable, Chain, and Fittings
41	Refrigeration, Air Conditioning, and Air Circulating Equipment
42	Fire Fighting, Rescue, and Safety Equipment
43	Pumps and Compressors
44	Furnace, Steam Plant, and Drying Equipment, and Nuclear Reactors
45	Plumbing, Heating, and Sanitation Equipment
46	Water Purification and Sewage Treatment Equipment
47	Pipe, Tubing, Hose, and Fittings

48	Valves
49	Maintenance and Repair Shop Equipment
51	Hand Tools
52	Measuring Tools
53	Hardware and Abrasives
54	Prefabricated Structures and Scaffolding
55	Lumber, Millwork, Plywood, and Veneer
56	Construction and Building Materials
58	Communication, Detection, and Coherent Radiation Equipment
59	Electrical and Electronic Equipment Components
60	Fiber Optics Materials and Components, Assemblies, and Accessories
61	Electric Wire, and Power and Distribution Equipment
62	Lighting Fixtures and Lamps
63	Alarm and Signal, and Security Detection Systems
65	Medical, Dental, and Veterinary Equipment and Supplies
66	Instruments and Laboratory Equipment
67	Photographic Equipment
68	Chemicals and Chemical Products
69	Training Aids and Devices
70	General Purpose ADP Equip. Software, Supplies, and Support Equipment
71	Furniture
72	Household and Commercial Furnishings and Appliances
73	Food Preparation and Serving Equipment
74	Office Machines, Text Processing Systems, and Visible Record Equipment
75	Office Supplies and Devices
76	Books, Maps, and Other Publications
77	Musical Instruments, Phonographs, and Home-Type Radios
78	Recreational and Athletic Equipment
79	Cleaning Equipment and Supplies
80	Brushes, Paints, Sealers, and Adhesives
81	Containers, Packaging, and Packing Supplies
83	Textiles, Leather, Furs, Apparel and Shoe Findings, Tents and Flags

84	Clothing, Individual Equipment, and Insignia
85	Toiletries
87	Agricultural Supplies
88	Live Animals
89	Subsistence (Food)
91	Fuels, Lubricants, Oils, and Waxes
93	Nonmetallic Fabricated Materials
94	Nonmetallic Crude Materials
95	Metal Bars, Sheets, and Shapes
96	Ores, Minerals, and Their Primary Products
99	Miscellaneous

Acronyms, Abbreviations, and Definitions

Federal agencies *love* to use acronyms and abbreviations! Here is an alphabetical list of the abbreviations and acronyms we have used throughout the book, for your reference.

508	**Section 508** Regulation requires federal agencies to purchase IT products that are accessible for people with disabilities.
72a	**Quarterly Sales Reports** The system used to report all sales made under your GSA contract on a quarterly basis. This amount determines the fee you will pay GSA. (*See* IFF.)
8(a)	**Disadvantaged Businesses** SBA certification for economically and socially disadvantaged small businesses.
A-76	**Competitive Sourcing Program** Used to determine whether an agency can improve efficiency and costs by using private service companies to perform non-governmental tasks. This program is currently on hold.
ABVS	**Automated Best Value System** Collects information on how well a vendor has fulfilled the terms of any previous contracts. Used as an evaluation factor when making Best Value Award decisions.
ACO	**Administrative Contracting Officer** (*See also* PCO.)
ADO	**After Date of Order** Used to stipulate delivery terms. (*See also* ARO.)

ARO	**After Receipt of Order** Used to stipulate delivery terms. (*See also* ADO.)
ARRA	**American Recovery and Reinvestment Act.** President Obama's 2009 act aims to boost the economy and create jobs.
ASFI	**Army Single Face to Industry** Website for Army sales opportunities.
BAA	**Broad Agency Announcement.** A notice from the government that requests scientific or research proposals from private firms. The proposals submitted may lead to contracts.
BEES	**Building for Environmental and Economic Sustainability** Program to encourage environmentally friendly building practices.
BOA	**Basic Ordering Agreement** A general outline of the supplies or services required.
BOD	**Bid Opening Date** The final date that a bid must be received by the appropriate government office. Particularly for IFB, sealed bidding.
BPA	**Blanket Purchase Agreement.** An agreement between a federal agency and a vendor that allows the agency to purchase goods or services on an as-needed basis.
BVP	**Best Value Purchasing** An agency may consider factors other than price (warranties, delivery dates, etc.) when making a Best Value award.
CAGE	**Commercial and Government Entity Code** A five-character code that is unique to a company. You must have a separate CAGE code for each physical location and separate division.
CCR	**Central Contractors Registration** You must be registered here in order to be awarded a contract.
CFR	**Code of Federal Regulations** A collection of publications that contains regulations for all federal departments and agencies.
CID	**Commercial Item Description** Details of a commercial item that may be purchased by a federal agency.
CLINS	**Contract Line Item Numbers** Used in solicitation documents to identity each item required.

CMR	**Contractor Manpower Reporting** Army regulation requires contractors to report on labor hours and costs for Army contracts.
CO	**Contracting Officer** Also referred to as the Procurement Contracting Officer (PCO). See also ACO.
COB	**Close of Business**
CONUS	**Continental United States** For example, when referring to delivery areas.
COTS	**Commercial Off The Shelf** Identifies an item sold in the commercial marketplace.
CPG	**Comprehensive Procurement Guidelines** Identifies environmentally friendly procurement policies.
CSP	**Commercial Sales Practices** Information on your company's commercial sales practices. Required when submitting a GSA proposal.
CTA	**Contractor Team Arrangement** Allows you to team up with other GSA contractors that complement your capabilities, and compete together for opportunities that you could not qualify for individually.
DARO	**Days After Receipt of Order** (*See also* ADO and ARO.)
DD250	**Dept. of Defense Inspection and Receiving Report** Required for shipping/acceptance of items by the DOD.
DFAR	**Defense Federal Acquisition Regulations.** Dept. of Defense supplemental procurement regulations.
DIBBS	**Department of Defense Internet Bid Board System** Dept. of Defense Website with electronic posting and awards. For products only.
DLA	**Defense Logistics Agency** Federal agency.
DoD	**Department of Defense** Federal agency.

DODAAC	**Department of Defense Activity Address Code** Identifies a specific DOD unit, activity, or organization that may purchase and/or accept ordered items.
DPAS	**Defense Priority Allocation System** DOD contracts are assigned priority ratings using this system.
DSCC/DSCP/ DSCR	**Defense Supply Centers** Located in Columbus (Ohio), Philadelphia (Penn.), and Richmond (Va.).
DUNS®	**Data Universal Numbering System** A number assigned by the Dun & Bradstreet company. Required for all companies wishing to do business with the federal government.
EDI	**Electronic Data Interchange** Computer-to-Computer system used to send and receive orders, invoices, and payments.
EFT	**Electronic Funds Transfer** Allows payment of invoices to bank account listed in your CCR registration.
EPA	**Economic Price Adjustment** Allows for modifications to pricing in your GSA contract. Price increases and decreases must reflect those offered to your Most Favored Customer (MFC) in the commercial marketplace and your Basis of Award customer identified during negotiations with GSA. The amount and timing of any price increases are stated in the terms of your contract.
EPLS	**Excluded Parties List System** Companies excluded from receiving government contracts.
FAR	**Federal Acquisition Regulations** Regulations governing federal purchasing. May be supplemented by specific agency regulations. (*See also* GSAM and DFARS.)
FAT	**First Article Testing** Agency may require FAT for some items.
FBO	**Federal Business Opportunities** Website listing federal contract opportunities estimated to be valued at $25,000 and above.
FEMP	**Federal Energy Management Program** Dept. of Energy environmental program.
FFP	**Firm Fixed Price** The awarded price is fixed for the life of the contract.

FOB Destination	**Free on Board** (Also known as Freight on Board) Destination is the shipping term used to indicate that the contractor is responsible for packing, marking, and delivery, and is responsible for any loss or damage occurring before receipt/acceptance. The contractor will pay all charges to the specified point of delivery.
FPDS	**Federal Procurement Data System** Website where you can gain a lot of information on federal procurement.
FPI	**Federal Prison Industries** (*See also* UNICOR.)
FSC	**Federal Supply Classification** Codes used to classify products.
FSS	**Federal Supply Schedules** GSA's schedules program.
FTR	**Federal Travel Regulations** Regulations governing federal travel.
GFE/GFM	**Government-Furnished Equipment or Materials** Items supplied by the agency. For example for maintenance of a government-owned item.
GSA	**General Services Administration** The agency that administers the Federal Supply Schedule Multi-Award contract program.
GSAM	**GSA Manual** General Services Administration supplemental regulations.
GWAC	**Government-Wide Acquisition Contract** For Information Technology. Established by one agency for government-wide use.
H2	**H2 Handbook** Lists all Federal Supply classification codes for products.
HSPD12	**Homeland Security Presidential Directive #12** Regulation concerning secure and reliable forms of identification for federal employees and contractors.
Hub-Zone	**Historically Underutilized Business Zone** Contracts may be set aside for this type of small business.

IAW	**In Accordance With** When referencing drawings, specifications, or standards.
IDEAS	**Interior Department Electronic Acquisition System** Dept. of the Interior procurement site.
IDIQ	**Indefinite Delivery, Indefinite Quantity** There is no guaranteed total quantity of services or products that will be acquired. There may be a guaranteed minimum quantity, or an estimated minimum/maximum quantity listed in the contract. The specific time for delivery is also not specified.
IDPO	**Indefinite Delivery Purchase Orders** See Chapter 3, on the Dept. of Defense Internet Bid Board procurement site.
IFB	**Invitation for Bid** Sealed Bidding. This type of solicitation describes exactly what the government requires and how offers will be evaluated.
IFF	**Industrial Funding Fee** Used to pay GSA for the administration of the Federal Supply Schedules program. Currently 0.75 percent is added to your GSA price. You must add the IFF to your schedule prices, and pay the IFF quarterly based on your contract sales.
J&A	**Justification & Approval** Agencies must get approval for a sole source award, and must be able to justify their decision.
JWOD	**Jarvit's Wagner O'Day** Program requires federal agencies to purchase certain products and services from the National Institutes for the Blind and Severely Handicapped. Name was recently changed to Ability One.
MAC	**Multi-Agency Contract** Established by one agency for government-wide use.
MAS	**Multiple Award Schedule** Also known as a GSA contract, or a Federal Supply Schedule (FSS) contract. Available for use by federal agencies worldwide. Administered by the General Services Administration. Federal agencies place orders directly with contractors.
MFC	**Most Favored Customer** You must offer GSA *at least* the same prices, terms, and conditions that you currently offer your Most Favored Customer.

MOL or MOT	**Maximum Order Limitation or Threshold** Each Schedule contract lists the Maximum Order Limitation or Threshold of each Special Item Number (SIN). The Maximum Order Threshold is *not* the maximum dollar amount the agency may order, but is the point at which the agency must request additional quantity/volume price reductions from the vendor.
MPIN	**Marketing Partners Identification Number** A password you create when you register your company in CCR.
MPT	**Micro-Purchase Threshold** For products or services less than the micro-purchase threshold (currently $3,000), agencies need not solicit offers from more than one vendor, but can simply place the order with the vendor that best meets their needs.
NAICS	**North American Industrial Classification System** Categorizes businesses according to broad industry type.
NAVFAC	**Naval Facilities** Navy department responsible for maintenance and management of facilities.
NECO	**Navy Electronic Commerce Online** Navy procurement Website.
NIB	**National Institute for the Blind** (*See* JWOD.)
NISH	**National Institute for the Severely Handicapped** (*See* JWOD.)
NIIN	**National Item Identification Number** The National Stock number minus the first four digits (FSC code). (*See* NSN.)
NLT	**No Later Than** When specifying delivery of an item or performance of a service.
NSN	**National Stock Number** A 13-digit number assigned to an item which is repeatedly purchased, stocked, and stored throughout the federal supply system.
O/A	**On or About** For example, used when giving an expected date for release of a solicitation document.
ORCA	**Online Representations and Certifications Application** You must complete this registration, certifying your company's business type. (See Chapter 1.)

OSDBU	**Office of Small and Disadvantaged Business Utilization** Department charged with assisting small businesses with federal contracting issues.
PACE	**Procurement Automated Contract Evaluation** A DOD automated system that evaluates bids and makes an award electronically. (See Chapter 3.)
PCO	**Procurement Contracting Officer** (*See also* ACO.)
P/N	**Part Number** Identifies a specific manufacturer's or vendor's item.
PO	**Purchase Order**
POC	**Point of Contact** You may need to identify an Electronic Business POC, a Government Business POC, and an Invoicing/Remittance POC.
POP	**Purchase Order Portal** Allows GSA contract holders to view and respond electronically to Requests for Quotes.
PPIRS	**Past Performance Information Retrieval System** Site where government agencies note how well you performed on any awarded contract. The information is shared among other government agencies.
PSC	**Product Service Code** Code used to classify services, using letters from A to Z.
PTAC	**Procurement Technical Assistance Center** Local assistance for small businesses interested in federal procurement.
PWS	**Performance Work Statement** A detailed description of the tasks required for a particular contract. (See also SOW.)
QAP	**Quality Assurance Provision** Specific requirements for Quality assurance laid out by the agency.
QML and QPL	**Qualified Manufacturer and Product Lists** Certain items must be purchased from manufacturers who have met specific quality requirements, and where the items have met strict manufacturing criteria and testing.

QSLD and QSLM	**Qualified Supplier Lists for Manufacturers and Distributors** DOD list of manufacturers and distributors who have met QML/QPL requirements.
RFI	**Request for Information** Agency is looking for capability statements from companies interested in supplying a specific item or service.
RFID	**Radio Frequency Identification** RFID tags are required on all products shipped to the DOD.
RFP	**Request for Proposal** A solicitation that describes what the government requires and how offers will be evaluated. Negotiations may be conducted. Award is based on a combination of lowest price and technical merit.
RFQ	**Request for Quotation.** A request for market information by the government, used for planning purposes. May be used to subsequently issue a solicitation.
RMAN	**Recovered Material Advisory Notices** Environmental Protection Agency notices regarding the use of products containing recovered or recycled material.
SBA	**Small Business Administration** Federal agency that aims to assist small businesses across the country.
SBSA:	**Small Business Set-Aside** A solicitation restricted to competition completed only among small businesses.
SDB	**Small Disadvantaged Business** A small business that is owned and operated by a socially or economically disadvantaged individual. (*See also* 8(a)). Solicitations may be set aside for this type of small business.
SDVOSB	**Service Disabled Veteran-Owned Small Business** Solicitations may be set aside for this type of small business.
SF	**Standard Form** Used to denote particular forms used across agencies. For example SF1449 for solicitation, contract, and award.
SIC	**Standard Industrial Classification Code** Used by the government to classify goods or services by their principal purpose.

SIN	**Special Item Number** Each GSA Schedule is subdivided by SIN in order to more closely identify products and services.
SIP	**Schedule Input Program** Software program that allows GSA contract holders to upload their contract terms and conditions, prices, product or service details, and photographs to GSA *Advantage!*
SOL	**Solicitation** A document that describes the specifications of what the government requires. May be issued as an Invitation for Bid (IFB) or a Request for Proposal (RFP).
SOW	**Statement of Work** A detailed description of the government's requirements for procuring a service. (*See also* PWS.)
SRVA	**Supplier Visibility Requirements Application** Application at the DOD procurement site containing information on the agency's future anticipated requirements.
TACOM	**Tank, Automotive, and Armaments Command** Army division.
TDP	**Technical Data Package** May contain drawings, specifications, standards, and other documents related to a particular item.
TINS	**Tax Identification Number** Either your Employer Identification Number or your Social Security number. (See Chapter 1.)
UNICOR	**Federal Prison Industries** The trade name for Federal Prison Industries, Inc.
USPO	**United States Patent Office** Federal agency.
USPS	**United States Postal Service** Federal agency.
VA	**Veterans Administration** Federal agency.

Vets100	**Veterans-100 Report** An annual report detailing the number of employees who are veterans, hired during the contract period.
VOSB	**Veteran-Owned Small Business** Solicitations may be set aside exclusively for this type of small business.
VSC	**Vendor Support Center** Support Website for all GSA contract holders.
WAWF	**Wide Area Workflow** System used for electronic invoicing and receiving.
WINS	**Web Invoicing System** System for submitting invoices electronically. (*See also* WAWF.)
WOSB	**Woman-Owned Small Business** A small business that is at least 51-percent owned and operated by a woman.

Some Common Procurement Terminology

- Cooperative Purchasing: Allows state, city, and local governments to use the GSA Schedules to acquire information technology products and services.
- Simplified Acquisition Threshold: Generally less than $100,000, although in some circumstances that amount may increase to $5 million. These purchases are governed by Part 13 of the Federal Acquisition Regulations.
- Disaster Purchasing: State and local government agencies may purchase a variety of products and services from GSA Schedule contractors in the aftermath of an emergency event.
- Schedule Price List: Your GSA contracted pricing, terms, and conditions document. Must follow a very specific format laid out in the contract, under section I-FSS-600.

Other Sites for Lookup of Acronyms, Definitions, and Terms

- Acronym Finder: *www.acronymfinder.com*. (60)
- Census Bureau Acronyms: *www.census.gov/procur/www/acronyms.html*. (61)
- Defense Supply Center Columbus: *www.dscc.dla.mil/search/acronym/default.asp*. (58)
- Dept. of Defense Dictionary of Military Terms: *www.dtic.mil/doctrine/dod_dictionary*. (62)
- EPA Glossary of Contracting-Related Terms: *www.epa.gov/oam/glossary.htm*. (63)

List of GSA Federal Supply Schedules

Source	Description
00CORP	**The Consolidated Schedule** (formerly Corporate Contracts Schedule)—The Consolidated Schedule encompasses most of the service schedules within the Multiple Awards Schedules program. This schedule provides a streamlined approach to fulfilling requirements that fall within the scope of more than one schedule for acquiring a total solution. Contractors under this schedule hold a single contract that includes two or more combined services from schedules such as: Facilities Maintenance, Office Imaging and Document Solutions, Training, Information Technology, Publications, Financial and Business Solutions, Advertising and Integrated Marketing Solutions, Language, Human Resources, Professional Engineering, MOBIS, Logworld, and Environmental.
00JWOD	**NIB/NISH products**—From the National Institutes for the Blind (NIB) and Severely Handicapped (NISH).
03FAC	**Facilities Maintenance and Management**
23 V	**Vehicular** Multiple Award Schedule
26 I	**Tires,** Pneumatic (New), for Passenger, Light Truck, Medium Truck, Bus, and Retread Services
36	The **Office, Imaging, and Document** Solution
48	**Transportation, Delivery, and Relocation** Solutions
51 V	**Hardware Superstore**—This includes Household and Office Appliances; Commercial Coatings, Adhesives, Sealants, and Lubricants; Hardware Store Catalog and Store Front; Lawn and Garden Equipment, Machinery, and Implements; Rental and Leasing (as pertains to products offered under this schedule); Tools, Tool Kits, Tool Boxes; Woodworking and Metal Working Machinery; all Parts and Accessories Related to Products Offered Under This Schedule.
520	**Financial snd Business Solutions** (FABS)—This Multiple Award Schedule provides federal agencies with direct access to commercial experts that can thoroughly address the needs of the federal financial community. FABS not only gives you access to a multitude of professional financial services, but also provides you with the ability to customize the services to meet your specific needs. The FABS schedule allows for choice, flexibility, ease of use, and access to quality firms in the financial arena.
541	**Advertising and Integrated Marketing Solutions** (AIMS)

56	**Buildings and Building Materials/Industrial Services and Supplies**—This Schedule provides a full range of commercial products and services covering such areas as buildings and building materials/industrial services and supplies. In addition, this program offers energy-saving building supplies, alternative energy solutions, and related services.
58 I	**Professional Audio/Video Telemetry/Tracking, Recording/Reproducing and Signal Data Solutions**
599	**Travel Services Solutions**
621 I	**Professional and Allied Healthcare Staffing Services**
621 II	**Medical Laboratory Testing and Analysis Services**
65 I B	**Pharmaceuticals and Drugs**—Includes Antiseptic Liquid Skin Cleansing Detergents and Soaps, Dispensers, and Accessories.
65 II A	**Medical Equipment and Supplies**
65 II C	**Dental Equipment and Supplies**
65 II F	**Patient Mobility Devices**—Including Wheelchairs, Scooters, Walkers.
65 V A	**X-Ray Equipment and Supplies**—Includes Medical and Dental X-Ray Film.
65 VII	**In-Vitro Diagnostics, Reagents, Test Kits, and Test Sets**
66	**Scientific Equipment and Services**—Test and Measurement Equipment; Unmanned Scientific Vehicles; Laboratory Instruments, Furnishings and LIMS; Geophysical and Environmental Analysis Equipment; and Mechanical, Chemical, Electrical, and Geophysical Testing Services.
66 III	**Clinical Analyzers, Laboratory, Cost-Per-Test**
67	**Photographic Equipment**—Cameras, Photographic Printers, and Related Supplies and Services (Digital And Film-Based).
69	**Training** Aids and Devices—Instructor-Led Training, Course Development, and Test Administration (Since July 2009 this has merged Into Schedule 874).
70	General Purpose Commercial **Information Technology Equipment, Software, and Services**—Cooperative Purchasing provides authorized state and local government entities access to IT offered via this schedule.
71	**Furniture**—In October 2009 several furniture schedules were merged into this single schedule.
71 I	**Office Furniture**—Merged into Schedule 71 in October 2009.
71 II	**Household and Quarters Furniture**—Merged into Schedule 71 in October 2009.
71 II H	**Packaged Furniture**—Merged into Schedule 71 in October 2009.

71 II K	Comprehensive Furniture Management Services (CFMS)
71 III	**Special Use Furniture** (Merged into Schedule 71 in October 2009)—Preschool and Classroom, Auditorium and Theater Seating; Library-Wood, Metal, or Plastic Furniture; Storage Cabinets for Forms, and Flammable Liquids Card-Size Filing Cabinets; Mail Sorting and Distribution Bins, Racks, and Carts; Light-Duty Small Parts Cabinets; Plastic Storage Bins; Hospital Patient Room Furniture; Cafeteria and Food Service; Drafting Stools, Clothing Lockers and Locker Benches; Workbenches, Worktables and High-Density Storage Cabinets and Enclosure Systems for Modular Electronic Equipment.
71 III E	**Miscellaneous Furniture** (Merged into Schedule 71 in October 2009)—Security Filing Cabinets, Safes, Vault Doors, Map and Plan Files and Accessories, Comsec Containers, and Special Access Control Containers.
72	**Furnishing and Floor Coverings**—New schedule is effective from October 2009.
72 I A	**Floor Coverings** (Merged into Schedule 72 in October 2009)—Carpet, Rugs, Carpet Tiles, and Carpet Cushions.
72 II	**Furnishings** (Merged into Schedule 72 in October 2009).
73	**Food Service, Hospitality, Cleaning Equipment, and Supplies, Chemicals, and Services**—Food Service Equipment, Supplies, and Services. This Schedule offers a variety of cleaning equipment and accessories, and cleaning products for daily cleaning—products that keep facilities clean in an environmentally friendly manner. Housing Managers and Facility Managers will enjoy the full range of Hospitality Solutions under this Schedule. In addition, all food service needs from eating utensils to an entire custom-designed food court kiosk concept that supports new branding initiatives are available. Wood, concrete, or aggregate stone waste receptacles from this Schedule can enhance the appearance of outside facilities. Also available are office recycling containers and waste receptacles, outdoor recycling containers, and industrial trash storage containers.
736	**Temporary Administrative and Professional Staffing** (TAPS)
738 II	**Language Services**—GSA's Language Services Schedule facilitates access to commercial providers of linguists who can supply an array of Language Services, including Translation Services, Interpretation Services, Sign Language and Title III work, and Training Services.
738 X	**Human Resources and Equal Employment Opportunity Services**
75	**Office Products/Supplies and Services and New Products/Technology**—Videotapes, Audiotapes, Tape Cartridges, Diskettes/Optical Disks, Disk Packs, Disk Cartridges, Anti-Glare Screens, Cleaning Equipment and Supplies, Ergonomic Devices, Next-Day Desktop Delivery of Office Supplies. Restroom Products such as Roll Toilet Tissue Dispensers, Toilet Tissue, Paper Towels, Toilet Seat Covers, Facial Tissues, and Soaps for Restroom Dispensers.

751	Leasing pf Automobiles and Light Trucks
76	Publication Media
78	Sports, Promotional, Outdoor, Recreation, Trophies, and Signs (SPORTS)— Sports equipment and supplies, fitness equipment, sounds of music, child's play, sports clothing and accessories, safety zone products, camping and hiking equipment, park and playground equipment, wheel and track vehicles, recreational watercraft, flags, awards, trophies, presentations, promotional products, briefcases and carrying cases, trade show displays and exhibit systems, and all related products and services.
81 I B	Shipping, Packaging, and Packing Supplies—Bags, Sacks, Cartons, Crates, Packaging, and Packing Bulk Material.
84	Total Solutions For Law Enforcement, Security, Facilities Management, Fire, Rescue, Clothing, Marine Craft, and Emergency/Disaster Response—The Local Preparedness Acquisition Act, signed June 26, 2008, authorizes state and local governments to purchase from GSA alarm and signal systems, facility management systems, firefighting and rescue equipment, law enforcement and security equipment, marine craft and related equipment, special purpose clothing, and related services.
871	Professional Engineering Services
874	Mission-Oriented Business Integrated Services (MOBIS)—Schedule 69, Training Aids and Devices, Instructor-Led Training, and Course Development. Test Administration has been incorporated into this schedule.
874 V	Logistics Worldwide (LOGWORLD)
899	Environmental Services

List of GSA Information Technology (IT) Contracts

Federal Supply Schedule Contracts

Schedule 70

General Purpose Commercial Information Technology Equipment, Software, And Services— Pursuant to Section 211 of the e-Gov Act of 2002, Cooperative Purchasing provides authorized State and local government entities access to information technology items offered through GSA's Schedule 70 and the Corporate contracts for associated special item numbers. Contracts with the COOP PURC icon indicate that authorized state and local government entities may procure from that contract.

Government-Wide Acquisition Contracts (GWACs)

These are task order or delivery order contracts for information technology established by one agency for government-wide use.

8(a) STARS: Streamlined Technology Acquisition Resources for Services

A small business set-aside contract that offers Multiple Award Indefinite Delivery/Indefinite Quantity Contracts for technology solutions. Some of the IT solutions offered via 8(a) STARS are: Custom Computer Programming, Computer Systems Design, Computer Facilities Mgmt, Data Processing, Internet Publishing and Broadcasting, and Wired Telecommunications Carriers. This GWAC has a 3-year base with two, 2-year option periods. Directed task orders up to $3.5 million each for federal civilian agencies are allowable pursuant to 41 U.S.C. 253(c)(5). Directed task orders up to $3.5 million each for Department of Defense activities are compliant with Section 803 of the 2002 National Defense Authorization Act 216.505-70(b)(2). Contracts have a program ceiling of $15 billion, and they are pre-competed and easy to use with a short procurement lead time. In addition, a low user fee (0.75 percent) is built into contractors' ceiling prices.

Alliant: Information Technology (IT) Services and IT Services-Based Solutions

A multiple-award, indefinite-delivery, indefinite-quantity (IDIQ) contract offering comprehensive and flexible, IT solutions worldwide. Alliant has a 5-year base period with one 5-year option and is valued at $50 billion. The scope of Alliant encompasses all components of an IT integrated solution, including new technologies that may emerge during the life cycle of the contract. The value proposition of the Alliant contract includes a robust scope aligned with the Federal Enterprise and DODEA architecture that provides access to a full range of comprehensive IT services, IT services solutions, and a highly qualified industry pool. The features of the Alliant GWAC include but are not limited to the full gamut of contract types (fixed price, cost reimbursement, labor hour, and time and materials), quick access to pre-competed easy-to-use contracts greatly reduced procurement lead times, and compliance with Section 863 of the National Defense Authorization Act (NDAA) 2009.

Alliant Small Business

A multiple award, indefinite-delivery, indefinite-quantity (MA/IDIQ) GWAC set aside exclusively for small business concerns. ASB will enable federal civilian agencies and the Department of Defense to support important socioeconomic objectives while providing Information Technology (IT) services and IT services-based solutions from the most highly qualified small businesses. The basic contract provides IT services and IT services-based solutions through the performance of a broad range of IT services which may include the integration of various technologies and support critical to the IT services being acquired. The IT services and IT services-based solutions offerings are aligned with the Federal Enterprise Architecture (FEA) and the Department of Defense Enterprise Architecture (DoD EA). The embedded support for FEA and DoD EA practices will facilitate compliance with federal policy mandates for IT investments. The range of IT services and IT services-based solutions includes existing, new and emerging technologies which will evolve over the period of performance.

ANSWER: Applications 'N' Support for Widely-diverse End User Requirements

A procurement vehicle that offers Multiple Award Indefinite Delivery/Indefinite Quantity Contracts covering all facets of Information Technology. ANSWER provides world-class contractors with unlimited subcontractor support, a 25 billion maximum ceiling value, a worldwide geographical reach, dual levels of competition, non-protestable task orders, and streamlined acquisition. Labor categories are comprehensive. Labor ceiling rates are fair and reasonable, and competition-driven discounts are available at the task order level. Task order types include fixed price incentive, fixed price award, time and materials, and labor hour.

COMMITS-NexGen: Commerce Information Technology Solutions-NexGen

A Multiple Award Indefinite Delivery/ Indefinite Quantity GWAC set-aside for small business technology firms. COMMITS NexGen is a task order contract designed to offer information technology (IT) services and IT services-based solutions to Federal customers. The COMMITS NexGen program has three main objectives. The first is to deliver top quality, performance-based IT services and solutions that meet government mission requirements. The second is to deliver IT services and solutions with a streamlined acquisition methodology. The third is to provide competitive IT solutions from a pool of exceptional small, disadvantaged, 8(a), women-owned, veteran-owned, service disabled veteran-owned, and HUBZone businesses.

Millennia Lite

A multiple award, indefinite quantity/indefinite delivery (MA IDIQ) Contract providing IT solutions under four functional areas: IT Planning, Studies, and Assessment, High-End IT Services (HITS), Mission Support Services, and Legacy Systems Migration & New Enterprise Systems Development. Millennia Lite has a base contract period of 3 years and 7 available performance-based extension years though 2010. Customers have the option of issuing fixed price, labor hour/ time and material or cost reimbursement task orders. To promote high quality contractor performance, options are based on contractor performance against the Award Term performance incentive plan. In addition, Millennia Lite has a program ceiling of $20 billion.

Millennia

An Indefinite-Delivery/Indefinite-Quantity (IDIQ) Contracts which provide the following IT services: communications, software engineering, and systems integration. This includes ancillary hardware, software and firmware. The Millennia GWAC has fixed-price and cost reimbursement task orders, and it is easy to use with assisted acquisition services and Direct Order Direct Bill (DODB) authority.

Veterans Technology Services (VETS)

A small business set-aside contract for service-disabled veteran-owned (SDVO) small technology firms. The VETS GWAC features a period of performance from February 2, 2007 to February 1, 2012 with one, five-year option. In addition, the GWAC has a $5 billion program ceiling, two functional scope areas including Systems Operations and Maintenance and Information Systems Engineering. Also, all ordering procedures are based on Fair Opportunity (FAR 16.505). The VETS GWAC assists in meeting the 3% goal for contracting with service-disabled veteran-owned firms. The VETS contracts are easy to use, pre-competed, and they have a short procurement lead time.

Network Services and Telecommunications

Everything from network services to telecommunications including purchase of hardware and software with options for self-service or assisted service (both with full customer support).

CONNECTIONS

An eight year (three base years + five one-year options) national government-wide, multiple award, and indefinite-delivery indefinite-quantity contract. It's a one-stop shop for any office building, campus, or base environment to deliver any level of demand for equipment (for example, Routers, Switches), support services (for example, Project Managers, Web Architects), or customized solutions (for example, Systems Integration, Operations Support). One third of the awardees are small business.

SATCOM-II

Multiple Award Indefinite Delivery/Indefinite Quantity Fixed Price contracts with a full range of end-to-end satellite solutions for Government Agencies.

Total GSA Schedule Sales for Fiscal Year 2009

Schedule	Total Sales	Schedule	Total Sales
CORP	$856,394,205	71 III E	$30,632,130
JWOD	$23,865,124	72 I A	$43,465,317
23 V	$191,665,807	72 II	$25,285,493
26 I	$10,215,098	73	$251,344,739
36	$848,348,490	75	$689,349,326
03FAC	$255,687,511	76	$117,810,902
48	$626,311,150	78	$378,923,443
51 V	$658,262,441	81 I B	$193,376,193
56	$559,179,346	84	$2,464,826,999
58 I	$175,590,117	520	$1,145,153,672
066	$776,376,484	541	$411,768,320
67	$41,323,819	599	$236,632,691
69	$239,135,161	736	$126,610,382
70	$15,646,895,263	738 II	$126,601,754
71 I	$1,139,502,181	738 X	$217,579,173
71 II	$104,370,708	751	$6,092,492
71 II H	$160,224,771	871	$2,946,654,659
71 II K	$50,296,180	874	$4,339,503,655
71 III	$86,248,286	874 V	$876,942,514
		899	$380,042,962
		Total Sales:	**$37,458,488,958**

(Information from GSA Schedule Sales Query Website: *http://ssq.gsa.gov*.)

GSA Commercial Sales Practices (CSP-1) Format

Name of Offeror _____

SIN(s) _____

Note: Please refer to clause 552.212-70, PREPARATION OF OFFER (MULTIPLE AWARD SCHEDULE), for additional information concerning your offer. Provide the following information **for each SIN** (or group of SINs or SubSIN for which information is the same).

(1) Provide the dollar value of sales to the general public at or based on an established catalog or market price during the previous 12-month period or the offerors last fiscal year: $_____. State beginning and ending of the 12 month period. Beginning_____ Ending_____. In the event that a dollar value is not an appropriate measure of the sales, provide and describe your own measure of the sales of the item(s). **For evaluation purposes only, provide a copy of your commercial price list that was applicable during the time period shown in this paragraph.**

(2) Show your total projected annual sales to the Government under this contract for the contract term, excluding options, for each SIN offered. If you currently hold a Federal Supply Schedule contract for the SIN the total projected annual sales should be based on your most recent 12 months of sales under that contract.

   SIN_____ $_____;
   SIN_____ $_____;
   SIN_____ $_____;

(3) Based on your written discounting policies (standard commercial sales practices in the event you do not have written discounting policies), are the discounts and any concessions which you offer the Government equal to or better than your best price (discount and concessions in any combination) offered to any customer acquiring the same items regardless of quantity or terms and conditions? YES_____ NO_____. (See definition of "concession" and "discount" in 552.212-70.)

(4a) Based on your written discounting policies (standard commercial sales practices in the event you do not have written discounting policies), provide information as requested for each SIN (or group of SINs for which the information is the same) in accordance with the instructions at Figure 515.4-2, which is provided in this solicitation for your convenience. The information should be provided in the chart below or in an equivalent format developed by the offeror. Rows should be added to accommodate as many customers as required.

Column 1 Most Favored Customer Category (MFC	Column 2 Basic Discount Granted to MFC	Column 3 Quantity/Volume Discounts	Column 4 FOB Terms	Column 5 Concessions (see 552.212-70 for examples)

(4b) Do any deviations from your written policies or standard commercial sales practices disclosed in the above chart ever result in better discounts (lower prices) or concessions than indicated? YES ____ NO____ . If YES, explain deviations in accordance with the instructions at Figure 515.4-2, which is provided in this solicitation for your convenience.

(5) If you are a dealer/reseller without significant sales to the general public, you should provide manufacturers' information required by paragraphs (1) through (4) above for each item/SIN offered, if the manufacturer's sales under any resulting contract are expected to exceed $500,000. You must also obtain written authorization from the manufacturer(s) for Government access, at any time before award or before agreeing to a modification, to the manufacturer's sales records for the purpose of verifying the information submitted by the manufacturer. The information is required in order to enable the Government to make a determination that the offered price is fair and reasonable. To expedite the review and processing of offers, you should advise the manufacturer(s) of this requirement. The contracting officer may require the information be submitted on electronic media with commercially available spreadsheet(s). The information may be provided by the manufacturer directly to the Government. If the manufacturer's item(s) is being offered by multiple dealers/resellers, only one copy of the requested information should be submitted to the Government. In addition, you must submit the following information along with a listing of contact information regarding each of the manufacturers whose products and/or services are included in the offer (include the manufacturer's name, address, the manufacturer's contact point, telephone number, and FAX number) for each model offered by SIN:

(a)   Manufacturer's Name

(b)   Manufacturer's Part Number

(c)   Dealer's/Reseller's Part Number

(d)   Product Description

(e)   Manufacturer's List Price

(f)   Dealer's/Reseller's percentage discount from List Price or net prices

Figure 515.4-2—Instructions for Commercial Sales Practices Format

If you responded "YES" to question (3), on the COMMERCIAL SALES PRACTICES FORMAT, complete the chart in question (4)(a) for the customer(s) who receive your best discount. If you responded "NO" complete the chart in question (4)(a) showing your written policies or standard sales practices for all customers or customer categories to whom you sell at a price (discounts and concessions in combination) that is equal to or better than the price(s) offered to the Government under this solicitation or with which the Offeror has a current agreement to sell at a discount which equals or exceeds the discount(s) offered under this solicitation. Such agreement shall be in effect on the date the offer is submitted or contain an effective date during the proposed multiple award schedule contract period. If your offer is lower than your price to other customers or customer categories, you will be aligned with the customer or category of customer that receives your best price for purposes of the Price Reduction clause at 552.238-75. The Government expects you to provide information required by the format in accordance with these instructions that is, to the best of your knowledge and belief, current, accurate, and complete as of 14 calendar days prior to its submission. You must also disclose any changes in your price list(s), discounts and/or discounting policies which occur after the offer is submitted, but before the close of negotiations. If your discount practices vary by model or product line, the discount information should be by model or product line as appropriate. You may limit the number of models or product lines reported to those which exceed 75% of actual historical Government sales (commercial sales may be substituted if Government sales are unavailable) value of the special item number (SIN).

Column 1—Identify the applicable customer or category of customer. A "customer" is any entity, except the Federal Government, which acquires supplies or services from the Offeror. The term customer includes, but is not limited to original equipment manufacturers, value added resellers, state and local governments, distributors, educational institutions (an elementary, junior high, or degree granting school which maintains a regular faculty and established curriculum and an organized body of students), dealers, national accounts, and end users. In any instance where the Offeror is asked to disclose information for a customer, the Offeror may disclose information by category of customer if the offeror's discount policies or practices are the same for all customers in the category. (Use a separate line for each customer or category of customer.)

Column 2—Identify the discount. The term "discount" is as defined in solicitation clause 552.212-70, Preparation of Offer (Multiple Award Schedule). Indicate the best discount (based on your written discounting policies or standard commercial discounting practices if you do not have written discounting policies) at which you sell to the customer or category of customer identified in column 1, without regard to quantity; terms and conditions of the agreements under which the discounts are given; and whether the agreements are written or oral. Net prices or discounts off of other price lists should be expressed as percentage discounts from the price list which is the basis of your offer. If the discount disclosed is a combination of various discounts (prompt payment, quantity, etc.), the percentage should be broken out for each type of discount. If the price lists which are the basis of the discounts given to the customers identified in the chart are different than the price list submitted upon which your offer is based, identify the type or title and date of each price list. The contracting officer may require submission of these price lists. To expedite evaluation, offerors may provide these price lists at the time of submission.

Column 3—Identify the quantity or volume of sales. Insert the minimum quantity or sales volume which the identified customer or category of customer must either purchase/order, per order or within a specified period, to earn the discount. When purchases/orders must be placed within a specified period to earn a discount indicate the time period.

Column 4—Indicate the FOB delivery term for each identified customer. See FAR 47.3 for an explanation of FOB delivery terms.

Column 5—Indicate concessions regardless of quantity granted to the identified customer or category of customer. Concessions are defined in solicitation clause 552.212-70, Preparation of Offers (Multiple Award Schedule). If the space provided is inadequate, the disclosure should be made on a separate sheet by reference.

If you respond "YES" to question 4 (b) in the Commercial Sales Practices Format, provide an explanation of the circumstances under which you deviate from your written policies or standard commercial sales practices disclosed in the chart on the Commercial Sales Practices Format and explain how often they occur. Your explanation should include a discussion of situations that lead to deviations from standard practice, an explanation of how often they occur, and the controls you employ to assure the integrity of your pricing. Examples of typical deviations may include, but are not limited to, one time goodwill discounts to charity organizations or to compensate an otherwise disgruntled customer; a limited sale of obsolete or damaged goods; the sale of sample goods to a new customer; or the sales of prototype goods for testing purposes.

If deviations from your written policies or standard commercial sales practices disclosed in the chart on the Commercial Sales Practices Format are so significant and/or frequent that the Contracting Officer cannot establish whether the price(s) offered is fair and reasonable, then you may be asked to provide additional information. The Contracting Officer may ask for information to demonstrate that you have made substantial sales of the item(s) in the commercial market consistent with the information reflected on the chart on the Commercial Sales Practice Format, a description of the conditions surrounding those sales deviations, or other information that may be necessary in order for the Contracting Officer to determine whether your offered price(s) is fair and reasonable. In cases where additional information is requested, the Contracting Officer will target the request in order to limit the submission of data to that needed to establish the reasonableness of the offered price.

SOLICITATION/CONTRACT/ORDER FOR COMMERCIAL ITEMS
OFFEROR TO COMPLETE BLOCKS 12, 17, 23, 24, & 30

1. REQUISITION NUMBER	**PAGE 1 OF**

2. CONTRACT NO.	3. AWARD/EFFECTIVE DATE	4. ORDER NUMBER	5. SOLICITATION NUMBER	6. SOLICITATION ISSUE DATE

7. FOR SOLICITATION INFORMATION CALL: ▶

a. NAME	b. TELEPHONE NUMBER *(No collect calls)*	8. OFFER DUE DATE/ LOCAL TIME

9. ISSUED BY   CODE

10. THIS ACQUISITON IS

☐ UNRESTRICTED OR   ☐ SET ASIDE: % FOR:

☐ SMALL BUSINESS   ☐ EMERGING SMALL BUSINESS

☐ HUBZONE SMALL BUSINESS

NAICS:

SIZE STANDARD: ☐ SERVICE-DISABLED VETERAN- OWNED SMALL BUSINESS   ☐ 8(A)

11. DELIVERY FOR FOB DESTINA- TION UNLESS BLOCK IS MARKED

☐ SEE SCHEDULE

12. DISCOUNT TERMS

☐ **13a. THIS CONTRACT IS A RATED ORDER UNDER DPAS (15 CFR 700)**

13b. RATING

14. METHOD OF SOLICITATION

☐ RFQ   ☐ IFB   ☐ RFP

15. DELIVER TO   CODE

16. ADMINISTERED BY   CODE

17a. CONTRACTOR/ OFFEROR   CODE   FACILITY CODE

18a. PAYMENT WILL BE MADE BY   CODE

TELEPHONE NO.

☐ **17b. CHECK IF REMITTANCE IS DIFFERENT AND PUT SUCH ADDRESS IN OFFER**

18b. SUBMIT INVOICES TO ADDRESS SHOWN IN BLOCK 18a UNLESS BLOCK BELOW IS CHECKED   ☐ SEE ADDENDUM

19. ITEM NO.	20. SCHEDULE OF SUPPLIES/SERVICES	21. QUANTITY	22. UNIT	23. UNIT PRICE	24. AMOUNT

(Use Reverse and/or Attach Additional Sheets as Necessary)

25. ACCOUNTING AND APPROPRIATION DATA

26. TOTAL AWARD AMOUNT *(For Govt. Use Only)*

☐ 27a. SOLICITATION INCORPORATES BY REFERENCE FAR 52.212-1, 52.212-4. FAR 52.212-3 AND 52.212-5 ARE ATTACHED. ADDENDA ☐ ARE ☐ ARE NOT ATTACHED

☐ 27b. CONTRACT/PURCHASE ORDER INCORPORATES BY REFERENCE FAR 52.212-4. FAR 52.212-5 IS ATTACHED. ADDENDA ☐ ARE ☐ ARE NOT ATTACHED

☐ **28. CONTRACTOR IS REQUIRED TO SIGN THIS DOCUMENT AND RETURN _____ COPIES TO ISSUING OFFICE. CONTRACTOR AGREES TO FURNISH AND DELIVER ALL ITEMS SET FORTH OR OTHERWISE IDENTIFIED ABOVE AND ON ANY ADDITIONAL SHEETS SUBJECT TO THE TERMS AND CONDITIONS SPECIFIED**

☐ **29. AWARD OF CONTRACT: REF. _____ OFFER DATED _____ . YOUR OFFER ON SOLICITATION (BLOCK 5), INCLUDING ANY ADDITIONS OR CHANGES WHICH ARE SET FORTH HEREIN, IS ACCEPTED AS TO ITEMS:**

30a. SIGNATURE OF OFFEROR/CONTRACTOR

31a. UNITED STATES OF AMERICA *(SIGNATURE OF CONTRACTING OFFICER)*

30b. NAME AND TITLE OF SIGNER *(Type or print)*	30c. DATE SIGNED	31b. NAME OF CONTRACTING OFFICER *(Type or print)*	31c. DATE SIGNED

AUTHORIZED FOR LOCAL REPRODUCTION
PREVIOUS EDITION IS NOT USABLE

STANDARD FORM 1449 (REV. 3/2005)
Prescribed by GSA - FAR (48 CFR) 53.212

REQUEST FOR QUOTATION (THIS IS NOT AN ORDER)		THIS RFQ ☐ IS ☐ IS NOT A SMALL BUSINESS SET-ASIDE		PAGE OF PAGES
1. REQUEST NO.	2. DATE ISSUED	3. REQUISITION/PURCHASE REQUEST NO.	4. CERT. FOR NAT. DEF. UNDER BDSA REG. 2 AND/OR DMS REG. 1 ▷	RATING
5a. ISSUED BY			6. DELIVER BY (Date)	

5b. FOR INFORMATION CALL (NO COLLECT CALLS)

NAME	TELEPHONE NUMBER	7. DELIVERY
	AREA CODE	NUMBER

7. DELIVERY ☐ FOB DESTINATION   ☐ OTHER (See Schedule)

9. DESTINATION

a. NAME OF CONSIGNEE

8. TO:

a. NAME	b. COMPANY	b. STREET ADDRESS
c. STREET ADDRESS		c. CITY
d. CITY	e. STATE f. ZIP CODE	d. STATE e. ZIP CODE

10. PLEASE FURNISH QUOTATIONS TO THE ISSUING OFICE IN BLOCK 5a ON OR BEFORE CLOSE OF BUSINESS (Date)

IMPORTANT: This is a request for information and quotations furnished are not offers. If you are unable to quote, please so indicate on this form and return it to the address in Block 5a. This request does not commit the Government to pay any costs incurred in the preparation of the submission of this quotation or to contract for supplies or service. Supplies are of domestic origin unless otherwise indicated by quoter. Any representations and/or certifications attached to this Request for Quotation must be completed by the quoter.

11. SCHEDULE   (Include applicable Federal, State and local taxes)

ITEM NO. (a)	SUPPLIES/ SERVICES (b)	QUANTITY (c)	UNIT (d)	UNIT PRICE (e)	AMOUNT (f)

12. DISCOUNT FOR PROMPT PAYMENT ▷	a. 10 CALENDAR DAYS (%)	b. 20 CALENDAR DAYS (%)	c. 30 CALENDAR DAYS (%)	d. CALENDAR DAYS NUMBER PERCENTAGE

NOTE: Additional provisions and representations ☐ are ☐ are not attached.

13. NAME AND ADDRESS OF QUOTER	14. SIGNATURE OF PERSON AUTHORIZED TO SIGN QUOTATION	15. DATE OF QUOTATION
a. NAME OF QUOTER		
b. STREET ADDRESS	16. SIGNER	
c. COUNTY	a. NAME (Type or print)	b. TELEPHONE AREA CODE
d. CITY e. STATE f. ZIP CODE	c. TITLE (Type or print)	NUMBER

AUTHORIZED FOR LOCAL REPRODUCTION
Previous edition not usable

STANDARD FORM 18   (REV. 6-95)
Prescribed by GSA-FAR (48 CFR) 53.215-1(a)

SOLICITATION, OFFER AND AWARD		1. This Contract Is A Rated Order Under DPAS (15 CFR 700) ▶	Rating DOA5	Page 1	of	Pages 37

2. Contract Number	3. Solicitation Number W52H09-09-R-0229	4. Type of Solicitation ☐ Sealed Bid (IFB) ☒ Negotiated (RFP)	5. Date Issued 2009OCT19	6. Requisition/Purchase Number SEE SCHEDULE

7. Issued By Code W52H09	8. Address Offer To (If Other Than Item 7)
TACOM-ROCK ISLAND CCTA-AR-C ROCK ISLAND IL 61299-7630	

NOTE: In sealed bid solicitations 'offer' and 'offeror' mean 'bid' and 'bidder'.

SOLICITATION

9. Sealed offers in original and ___1 signed___ copies for furnishing the supplies or services in the Schedule will be received at the place specified in item 8, or if handcarried, in the depository located in _____ until _____ (hour) local time ___2009NOV19___ (Date).

Caution - Late Submissions, Modifications, and Withdrawals: See Section L, Provision No. 52.214-7 or 52.215-1. All offers are subject to all terms and conditions contained in this solicitation.

10. For Information Call: ▶	A. Name MARY SEAHOLM	B. Telephone (No Collect Calls)			C. E-mail Address MARY.SEAHOLM@US.ARMY.MIL
		Area Code (309)	Number 782-8601	Ext.	

11. Table Of Contents

(X)	Sec.	Description	Page(s)	(X)	Sec.	Description	Page(s)
		Part I - The Schedule				**Part II - Contract Clauses**	
X	A	Solicitation/Contract Form	1	X	I	Contract Clauses	20
X	B	Supplies or Services and Prices/Costs	7			**Part III - List Of Documents, Exhibits, And Other Attach.**	
X	C	Description/Specs./Work Statement	10	X	J	List of Attachments	29
X	D	Packaging and Marking	12			**Part IV - Representations And Instructions**	
X	E	Inspection and Acceptance	14	X	K	Representations, Certifications, and Other Statements of Offerors	30
X	F	Deliveries or Performance	17				
X	G	Contract Administration Data	18	X	L	Instrs., Conds., and Notices to Offerors	34
X	H	Special Contract Requirements	19	X	M	Evaluation Factors for Award	37

OFFER (Must be fully completed by offeror)

NOTE: Item 12 does not apply if the solicitation includes the provisions at 52.214-16, Minimum Bid Acceptance Period.

12. In compliance with the above, the undersigned agrees, if this offer is accepted within _____ calendar days (60 calendar days unless a different period is inserted by the offeror) from the date for receipt of offers specified above, to furnish any or all items upon which prices are offered at the price set opposite each item, delivered at the designated point(s), within the time specified in the schedule.

13. Discount For Prompt Payment (See Section I, Clause No. 52.232-8) ▶	10 Calendar Days (%)	20 Calendar Days (%)	30 Calendar Days (%)	Calendar Days (%)

14. Acknowledgment of Amendments (The offeror acknowledges receipt of amendments to the SOLICITATION for offerors and related documents numbered and dated):	Amendment No.	Date	Amendment No.	Date

15A. Name and Address of Offeror	Code	Facility	16. Name and Title of Person Authorized to Sign Offer (Type or Print)

15B. Telephone Number			15C. Check if Remittance Address is ☐ Different From Above – Enter such Address In Schedule	17. Signature	18. Offer Date
Area Code	Number	Ext.			

AWARD (To be completed by Government)

19. Accepted As To Items Numbered	20. Amount	21. Accounting And Appropriation

22. Authority For Using Other Than Full And Open Competition: ☐ 10 U.S.C. 2304(c)( ) ☐ 41 U.S.C. 253(c)( )	23. Submit Invoices To Address Shown In (4 copies unless otherwise specified) ▶	Item

24. Administered By (If other than Item 7) Code	25. Payment Will Be Made By Code

SCD   PAS   ADP PT

26. Name of Contracting Officer (Type or Print)	27. United States Of America (Signature of Contracting Officer)	28. Award Date

IMPORTANT - Award will be made on this Form, or on Standard Form 26, or by other authorized official written notice.

AUTHORIZED FOR LOCAL REPRODUCTION
Previous edition is unusable

Standard Form 33 (Rev. 9-97)
Prescribed By GSA-FAR (48 CFR) 53.214(c)

Index

About the Authors

As an independent sales and marketing professional for more than 30 years, MALCOLM PARVEY assists small businesses in securing federal government contracts. Mr. Parvey works exclusively with small businesses, and assists them in every aspect of the government marketplace, from finding appropriate opportunities, through locating drawings or specifications, to completing the paperwork and following up on the awards.

Mr. Parvey also specializes in working with small businesses from any industry to submit their General Services Administration's "GSA Schedule" proposal, as well as the Department of Defense's "E-Mall" program, and offers his expertise in all aspects of the federal government marketplace.

"I started looking into this market in 1977," he says. "I read everything I could find, went to seminars, visited agencies, and spoke to anyone that would talk to me. At a time when computers weren't on everyone's desk, much of the work had to be done through the mail. Written requests for information about a pending bid opportunity could take as long as 10 days to receive! While holding down a full-time job and maintaining a wife and two kids, it took me more than two years to submit my first offer. After a few false starts, I put in an offer on behalf of a food broker to supply dairy products to five Veterans Administration hospitals, and we were awarded the contract! One reason for the success of this bid was that I was able to find out the current price of the contract through the Freedom of Information Act *before* we submitted our bid. A year later I had six clients, and I quit my job."

Since then, Mal has worked with many different small businesses, in many diverse markets, so that his experience is not limited to just one type of business, but rather spans a wide range of companies in the commercial marketplace.

In 2008 Mal coauthored the successful book *Winning Government Contracts* (Career Press, 2008). The book showed small businesses how to get involved in selling to the federal government, taking a step-by-step approach, and assuming no previous knowledge of this marketplace.

"Many small businesses wish to get involved in this market," Mal points out, "but have no one to help them get started. This book shows someone with no experience in this marketplace exactly where to begin."

Mr. Parvey lives and works in Lancaster, Massachusetts.

DEBORAH ALSTON was born in Great Britain, and attended the University of Wales in Swansea, where she obtained her Bachelor of Arts Honors Degree in English Literature. She has lived in the United States for more than 20 years. She previously worked in the information department of a large biotechnology company, and has worked closely with Mr. Parvey for the last eight years.

In 2008 she coauthored the successful book *Winning Government Contracts* (Career Press, 2008). The book showed small businesses how to get involved in selling to the federal government, taking a step-by-step approach, and assuming no previous knowledge of this marketplace.

Deborah currently lives in Louisville, Kentucky.

59052157R10162